Y0-ASO-228

Project Lending

Project Lending

Edited by T H Donaldson, FCIB
Managing Director and Chairman
European Credit Policy Committee
J P Morgan

Butterworths
London, Boston, Brussels, Dublin, Edinburgh, Hato Rey,
Kuala Lumpur, Singapore, Sydney, Toronto, Wellington
1992

United Kingdom	Butterworth & Co (Publishers) Ltd, 88 Kingsway, LONDON WC2B 6AB and 61A North Castle Street, EDINBURGH EH2 3LJ
Belgium	Butterworth & Co (Publishers) Ltd, BRUSSELS
Australia	Butterworths Pty Ltd, SYDNEY, MELBOURNE, BRISBANE, ADELAIDE, PERTH, CANBERRA and HOBART
Canada	Butterworth & Co (Canada) Ltd, TORONTO and VANCOUVER
Ireland	Butterworth (Ireland) Ltd, DUBLIN
Malaysia	Malayan Law Journal Sdn Bhd, KUALA LUMPUR
New Zealand	Butterworths of New Zealand Ltd, WELLINGTON and AUCKLAND
Puerto Rico	Equity de Puerto Rico, Inc, HATO REY
Singapore	Malayan Law Journal Pte Ltd, SINGAPORE
USA	Butterworth Legal Publishers, AUSTIN, Texas; BOSTON, Massachusetts; CLEARWATER, Florida (D & S Publishers); ORFORD, New Hampshire (Equity Publishing); ST PAUL, Minnesota; and SEATTLE, Washington

All rights reserved. No part of this publication may be reproduced in any material form (including photocopying and storing it in any medium by electronic means and whether or not transiently or incidentally to some other use of this publication) without the written permission of the copyright owner except in accordance with the provisions of the Copyright, Designs and Patents Act 1988 or under the terms of a licence issued by the Copyright Licensing Agency Ltd, 90 Tottenham Court Road, London, England W1P 9HE. Applications for the copyright owner's written permission to reproduce any part of this publication should be addressed to the publisher.

Warning: The doing of an unauthorised act in relation to a copyright work may result in both a civil claim for damages and criminal prosecution.

© The contributors 1992.

A CIP Catalogue record for this book is available from the British Library.

ISBN 0 406 16518 1

Photoset by Phoenix Photosetting, Chatham, Kent
Printed and bound in Great Britain by Billings Bookplan, Worcester

Preface

Project finance has a long history; in some senses it goes back several centuries.

In its modern sense, however, it largely developed in the post-war period. It was used to develop a wide range of raw materials – including all types of metals, oil and gas – to finance the building of plants, roads, bridges, etc; sometimes alone, sometimes as part of a wider project.

There were a number of reasons for choosing project finance, which are discussed in the book. During the 1970s and early 1980s what had been an exciting new form of finance became relatively mature and routine. This is not to say it was easy; it required detailed knowledge and skill at all times. But there were few new types of project being financed, and the theory of project finance had been exhaustively analysed and written about. It would not have been hard at this stage to write a sound book on project finance, but it would have been hard to write one with any claim to originality.

During the mid to late 1980s this began to change. The trend to privatising previously government-owned companies, particularly utilities; the growing tendency for governments to allow or even require the private sector to finance infrastructure projects instead of doing it themselves (the Channel Tunnel is the most spectacular but by no means only example); the need of lesser developed countries in Latin America and Africa and more recently Eastern Europe for finance they could not support on their own; private sector projects of new types such as Euro Disneyland; and the willingness of banks to consider longer periods and even equity finance – all of these began to change the face of project finance. Not all of them have yet turned into actual financings, but all are causing banks and others furiously to think.

At the same time, the older forms of project finance remain valid and continue to provide business for those with the necessary expertise. They also provide the basic principles which lenders must apply to new types of project, however much they may need to adapt the precise details.

This book then tries to provide both a description of the proven approaches and a view of how the principles apply to the new. In some cases these are already being applied; in others they perhaps will be. In yet others, government or the market will need to develop further to make the most of project finance.

The book focuses on project lending, and is written mainly by bankers. However, there are some chapter authors whose experience has been in other aspects, or who were asked to represent different viewpoints. Brief details about the contributing authors appear at the end of each chapter.

T H Donaldson

Contents

Preface v

PART 1 INTRODUCTION: THE OLD AND THE NEW 1

1 The traditional approach *(T H Donaldson)* 3
   Introduction 3
   Project lending defined 3
   Risks in project lending 6
   Lenders' attitudes to risk 9
   Protections available 12
   Why borrowers choose project finance 16
   Special features 17
   New influences 20

2 New influences *(Brian H Weight)* 21
   The historical perspective 21
   New influences emerge 24
   Project financing today 31

PART 2 TRIED AND TRUE, AND STILL VALID 33

3 Ship finance *(Taco Th van der Mast)* 35
   1 Introduction 35
   2 Summary 36
   3 History 36
   4 Industry characteristics 37
   5 Types of shipping 37
   6 Types of vessel employment 39
   7 Types of ship finance 41
   8 Credit analysis: ship finance is cash-flow based 44
   9 Credit structuring 48
   10 Newbuilding financing 49
   11 Security structure 50
   12 Covenants 52
   13 Lender liability 55
   14 Risks associated with country of flag and of corporate residence 55
   15 Other roles of the banks 58
   16 Insurance 58
   17 Newly emerging risks 59

18 Work-outs   60
19 Conclusion   63

4 Mining: extractive and processing *(Keith Palmer)*   65
Introduction   65
Country or political risk   66
Project finance in developed countries   74
Structuring the project finance vehicle   76
Processing industries   78
New approaches to financing mining projects   78
Conclusion   79

5 Aircraft and other mobile assets *(Ian Hosier)*   80
1 Introduction   80
2 The commercial aviation market   81
3 The suitability of the aircraft asset for an asset-financier   84
4 Key issues/principles of aircraft asset-based finance   89
5 Examples of aircraft asset-based finance   93
6 Summary and conclusions   99

6 Leasing and tax-based project finance *(Peter J Whitney)*   101
Leasing   101
Power project   106
Other tax considerations   114
Appendix   119

PART 3 PROJECTS UNDER THE NEW INFLUENCES   135

7 Transportation infrastructure: recent experience and lessons for the future *(Chris Elliott)*   137
Introduction   137
Government policy   137
Experience to date   138
Risk profile of infrastructure finance   139
Characteristics of infrastructure finance   142
Role of the sponsor   143
Lessons to be learned   144

8 Project finance in the utility industries *(Michael R Smith)*   146
1 Introduction   146
2 Utilities – an ideal area for project finance?   146
3 Sources of finance for projects   147
4 Project finance in the UK   149
5 Financing of utility projects   151
6 Conclusion   158

9 Project finance in the developing markets of Central and Eastern Europe *(Douglas Helfer)*   160
Financial position of countries in the region   160
Structuring a project in the present market   161
Sources of financing   162
Official export credit guarantee agencies   163
Multi-lateral lending agencies   166
Other sources of finance   166

Contents ix

Insurance 166
Examples of project finance in the region 168
Conclusion 169

10 Project finance – legal aspects *(Roger McCormick)* 171
1 Introduction 171
2 Choice of structure: legal considerations 174
3 Importing 'foreign' legal concepts 185
4 Role of security 188
5 Host government support 190
6 Comfort letters 191
7 Re-characterisation 193
8 Recurrent elements in negotiations 196

11 A borrower's view of project lending *(Tony Lighterness)* 200
Project finance vs corporate debt 202
Project finance – a form of risk management 203
The project holding structure 206
Appointment of financial adviser 207
The range of lenders 208
The negotiating stage 210
The security package 212
The way forward 213

Index 217

Part 1
Introduction: the old and the new

1 The traditional approach

T H Donaldson, J P Morgan

Introduction

There is a long history of project finance. In the form discussed in this book, however, it really began in the late 1960s and reached its peak in the early 1980s. During that period the techniques were honed to a high level and the theory refined in the light of practical experience. If that were the whole story, there would be little new to say.

However, there have been a number of new areas opening up to which project finance, in the classic sense or with modifications, can contribute; and some new forms of project finance are developing.

These developments are recognised in this book, and so is the fact that to understand the new project opportunities we have to understand the classic forms. They remain both valid and the basis of all forms of project finance, new or old.

The form of the book fits this division. The rest of this chapter defines project finance, and describes the general features which apply to all types. Chapter 2 outlines the new influences and the new types of project finance developing. Part 2 describes four main types of traditional project finance. Part 3 covers some projects under the new influences, with the last two chapters containing comments from two interested sources: the specific legal view of issues in documentation and the borrower's viewpoint. Most writings on the subject, inevitably, focus on the lender's viewpoint.

Project lending defined

The essence of project lending is its focus on the project being financed. The lender looks, wholly or mainly, to the project as the source of repayment; its cash flows, and assets where appropriate, are dedicated to service the project loan. The project cannot even begin to provide for repayment until it is operational, and then depends on continued sound operation, so that its analysis is critical. If any major aspect fails, lenders probably lose money, perhaps the whole loan. Moreover, most projects lack the variety of products or established markets open to most companies. And again, any assets surviving the failure are often highly specialised, of little value outside the project, and sometimes geographically remote. They rarely provide the strong second way out which banks like to see.

Project lending's narrow focus makes it inherently high risk and demands a high reward, although lenders can reduce the risk by skilful analysis and structuring. The other side of the coin is that the project's cash flow is dedicated to repaying the debt; most borrowers have other demands on their cash flow which may compete with debt service. Nevertheless, the borrower must expect to pay for the skill needed to reduce the risk, and for the remaining risk.

The owner's risk is confined to whatever equity or guarantee is needed to make the project viable; where the owner plays another role – for instance, operator or contractor – he bears the normal risks of these roles. (For the purposes of this book, the owner is any person, company or grouping which owns equity in the project and benefits from its success, with a limited loss if it fails. The contractor is responsible for bringing the project to a state where it can operate – building the plant, drilling the well or installing the rigs, etc. The operator runs the project once it is complete. Anybody can play more than one of these roles, but they are separate and are often played by different bodies.) In return for the limited risk, and because the lenders usually risk larger amounts, the owner will often not take anything out of the project before the debt has been repaid; only the strongest projects allow earlier withdrawal. Once the project is debt-free everything that remains is his.

There are broadly speaking three degrees of project dependence, which are as follows.

Pure project lending

A pure project loan requires some sort of equity contribution, but apart from that is the sole source of finance for the project and is repaid only from it. In some cases, another party covers a specific element of risk, such as completion risk (see below). We can argue that it becomes pure project finance only when such cover falls away; or that these protections are an inherent part of the package.

Pure project lending is possible in all types of project, but is best suited where the risks of the project are well understood. Projects at the frontier of technology, or in geographical frontiers such as the North Sea or Alaska, tend to require more support, and may be more likely to come into the second category.

The best-known current project is probably the Channel Tunnel. Apart from equity from the public markets, the sole finance is various types of bank or bank-guaranteed debt. The sole source of repayment is the revenue the Tunnel expects to earn when it opens. A failure to complete the Tunnel; delays in completion, or increases in the cost of completion (perhaps due to the delays); higher operating costs than expected when it opens; or lower revenues than forecast: any of these or any combination of them could reduce or wipe out the project's ability to service the debt or pay a return to shareholders. (At the time of writing the project looks certain to be completed; all the other risks either remain or have already occurred to some degree, as discussed later in the chapter, and in other chapters.)

One of the classic risks of project finance is already apparent in the Tunnel. The original funding has proved insufficient; to complete the project and protect funds already advanced, lenders and shareholders had to provide more before they could be certain that the project would succeed; even that may turn out to be insufficient. The decision to lend more to improve the recovery of what you have already lent, rather than cut your losses, is hard in many types of lending; it is perhaps hardest of all in project finance.

Until recently most projects as large as the Tunnel were seen as government responsibility, although lesser-developed countries too weak to borrow on their own credit, still allowed project finance. Now, however, the privatisation of risk is one of the new aspects discussed in chapter 2.

Project finance, pure or partial, is common in a wide range of mining and extraction projects, ranging from the North Sea to copper mines in Pacific islands. It may cover just the mine or drilling rig, or a range of ancilliary projects, such as ports, roads or railroads and rolling stock – sometimes even housing and schools for the workforce.

Conventional power stations have been built with project finance, as have a wide range of schools, hospitals and similar products.

Qualified or partial project lending

Qualified or partial project finance is similar to pure project finance, but with limited additional support; a major risk remains on the project, although repayment in full no longer depends solely on it.

The support can take several forms. One, a completion guarantee, has already been mentioned; where the guarantee is absolute, and given by a party whose credit is undoubted, the lender comes fully on risk only when the project is in full operating order. Even here, however, a delay or bad publicity about the cause of the pre-completion problem may have adverse repercussions on the viability of the project after it is complete; these may not be covered by the guarantee.

Even a complete project can still fail to operate to full potential after an initial success. Sometimes there will be a guarantee covering this.

Some projects are built in countries where there is political risk. Even developed countries may have licensing or tax rules which can be enforced, or changed, in ways which weaken the economics of the project. Sometimes project lenders will require protection against these risks.

A more common case is of a partial guarantee by a corporate owner or beneficiary of the project. This may cover cost overruns, either totally or up to a stated level; or it may cover some specific part of the operation for which the company is responsible. Or users of the end product of the project may commit to buy, in ways which are discussed more fully post (pp 12ff), as are the various forms of take or pay.

Unless a corporate or government commitment assures payment regardless, a major element of project risk remains. This may be true even with a full corporate guarantee, if the project is so important that its failure would undermine the credit of the guarantor.

Corporate or country lending with a project element

Sometimes borrowers raise money in their own name, to fund a major project. Where the borrower's credit is so strong that it can stand the complete failure of

6 Introduction: the old and the new

the project without any significant weakening, this is not project risk for the lenders, although it may be for the borrower.

Countries or companies may overestimate their own credit-worthiness, or underestimate the risks of the project. In these cases, failure of the project may weaken the borrower even where it does not alone destroy it. If there is any chance of this, the lender's analysis, and perhaps the conditions on which they lend, become more project-oriented. The weaker the underlying credit of the borrower, and the larger and riskier the project, the more important it is for the lenders to understand and monitor its risks.

This is particularly true where the project is vulnerable to events which also threaten the borrower's general health, as with a copper mine in a country which already relies heavily on copper for exports.

Risks in project lending

In broad terms there are three areas of risk in project lending: pre-completion risk, operating risk and market risk. Not all projects carry all three, but all types are capable of doing so. Each project will have a different mixture, and lenders must understand the key risks they are taking. There are types of risk which spread across these three areas; for instance, force majeure can undermine a project at any stage, and is one of the key aspects in the analysis of any project; technology risk can be part of any one or of all three, as can political risk. But the division of the risk into three sections helps to bring into focus not just the cause, but also the result if the project fails. Lenders need to understand both.

Pre-completion risk

Pre-completion risk covers a project before it is complete and able to produce its end product.

Pre-completion risk in its starkest form is thus the risk that the project is never finished, never generates any revenue and repays none of the debt.

Less extreme risks are delays which threaten the viability of the project, or cost overruns, sometimes caused in part by delays. These increase the finance, and usually debt, needed to complete the project, making it less likely that the revenues can service the debt in full. Finally, there is the risk of a partial failure of other parts of the project due to weaknesses before completion. This partial failure may be operational: the project never produces as much, or as high quality, as expected, or costs more to run; or operating or market failures after completion may be made worse by the pre-completion delays, or by the failure of the project to live up to specification.

The Channel Tunnel is a good example of both levels of completion risk. It was, in mid-1990, not yet certain that the Tunnel would be completed; cost overruns threatened its financing, and could have become so serious that it was never finished; or there could still have been unexpected geological problems in tunnelling under the Channel. While neither disaster scenario ever happened, the substantial cost overruns needed financing; this has been provided by a mixture of equity and debt, increasing the cost of debt service and diluting the equity.

Even now the Tunnel is struggling to avoid major delays; and some of its adjuncts, such as the rail link to London, will certainly be late on stream, and perhaps worse than that since the route is a political football. This will delay the receipt of the full revenues; at worst it might give ferries, airlines and other transport the chance to compete so strongly that revenues never reach their projected levels.

Operating risk

Where the lenders accept the whole of pre-completion risk, the gap between it and operating risk may be less important. Otherwise it is critical to understand and define the difference beyond doubt.

Project finance agreements define a project as complete once it has reached, and usually maintained for a minimum period, a certain level of operating efficiency. The exact test varies, but must be valid for the particular project, and provide objective evidence that the contractors have done their work, so that the responsibility for the project can rightly pass to the operator. The test may well be the same for the contractors, who need to prove their right to payment, and for lenders who take the operating risk but not the completion risk. A turnkey project is one method of isolating all the completion risks in one package, so that the owner only has to accept marketing and operating risk; the contractor takes all the prior risks – or his banks, if that is the arrangement.

Operating risk starts when the project can operate to specification. It reflects the fact that 'can operate' and 'operates' are not necessarily the same. Again the precise form operating risk takes depends on the nature of the project. A ship might break down more frequently than expected; or it might use more fuel, or have a lower cruising speed. A processing plant might have more breakdowns, prove difficult to run at full capacity, fail to meet quality standards, etc; a road might prove to be too small for the volume of traffic, so that it is always jammed, or of the wrong quality surface, so that it breaks up too fast.

Operating failures of these sorts can come from three main sources:

- firstly, weaknesses in the contractors' work, so that the quality is not what was expected. This may be recoverable from the contractors; more often, once the operator has accepted the project he has no comeback;
- secondly, from inadequate specifications, so that the contractor is blameless; or
- thirdly, from poor operating management.

Operating costs can also vary for reasons related to markets. For instance the price of raw materials can vary, or wage rates in the economy generally. This becomes a market rather than an operating risk only if the impact is the same on all competitors. Where a product depends heavily on the price of energy, an increase should hit all producers equally hard; the project should not then lose market share, even though the market may shrink. Where, however, management fails to control the amount of energy used, its higher cost hurts the project disproportionately, and the lenders' risk rises.

The costs of raw materials and labour are both affected by management. A producer with a high wastage rate cannot avoid responsibility for the extra

8 Introduction: the old and the new

harm suffered when the price rises. The same is true of a manager who pays higher wages for lower productivity than his competitors.

Indeed, operating risk usually includes management failure in some form. Some risks are at one level inherent, as with the extremes of climate in the North Sea or Alaska; they are then also foreseeable, and competent management should be prepared to deal with a foreseeable even if extreme difficulty.

This is also true of technological risk. This can take two main forms: either the technology does not work – or works late, inadequately or at too high a cost; *or* it is made uncompetitive by newer technology.

The first type is at least as often a pre-completion risk as an operating risk. Introducing new technology into a major project is always high risk, and has come close to bankrupting major companies, as well as projects, more than once. In the worst case, which is clearly pre-completion risk, the technology simply does not work. In less serious but still pre-completion cases, it takes dangerously long to make it work, perhaps involving major design changes. These add to costs and, if the lenders are bearing the risk, to the debt service when the project starts to perform.

Technology as operating risk means the technology is difficult to operate or unreliable. It may need more technical skill than the operator can provide; or the technology may be suspect, or cause unexpected side effects. Perhaps the process is too corrosive, requiring frequent stoppages to replace parts; perhaps it generates pollutive wastes which need expensive storage or control; and so on.

Whatever its precise nature, management should foresee that new technology carries these types of risk. It should ensure that there are some financial reserves to fund them, as well as some fat in the profit and cash flow projections. It should also of course be sure that it understands the technology, the type of risk most likely to strike and the best way of protecting against it.

The risk for the lender is that management weakness in this risk assessment prevents the project earning enough to repay the debt. Generally speaking banks and other lenders do not make the detailed assessment of technology themselves, but rather assess an outline of the risks. They need to understand these to judge two things: what sort of reserve financial strength is needed to ensure that the project can deal with problems and still repay the loans; and how competent the management is. If management cannot deal with severe problems, financial resources become irrelevant.

Market risk

A project which is completed successfully, and operates to specifications, may still fail if a change in the market makes its product uncompetitive or unwanted.

The change may be absolute, so that the product is not saleable at any price; more often the project limps along generating some sales and cash, but not enough to service the debt.

The aspects of market risk break down into demand, supply, and cost. In outline, they are the same risk that any product runs; demand may decline because of fashion, obsolescence, environmental concerns or cost, to mention only a few reasons; new technology can be a reason on its own or a supporting factor to one of the other reasons; equally, supply can be excessive for a range of reasons which apply to non-project business, such as new producers entering the market or greater supply of a competing product. Projects are perhaps more vulnerable than most to what might be called 'lumpiness of supply'. Certain products (aluminium is one) have a cyclical supply pattern, because the minimum economic size, and therefore break-even level, of a plant is high. New plants are only built when supply is short, so that the new plant can obtain high volume from the start. Meanwhile, the shortage pushes prices up sharply and encourages over-ordering. Several suppliers may, unknown to each other, start to build new plants which all come on stream at about the same time, causing heavy over-supply and a costly failure to achieve break-even. These big plants are often just the sort to attract project finance.

Again, as with any other product, the supply and demand affect volume and selling price. Either you can only sell the planned volume at a lower price, or a lower volume at the planned price or, most probably, a lower volume at a lower price. Either way margins, earnings and cash flow are lower than planned and threaten the repayment of the debt. How serious a threat depends on the margin for error built into the financing, which in turn depends on the rigour of the risk assessment.

Cost can cause loss of market share, margin, or both when it arises from reasons outside management's control, but still affects the project more than competing supplies.

Thus these market risks are not unique to project finance. They are, however, greater because of the need to judge demand so far into the future. For some projects lenders take a view of market conditions for as much as five years until the project starts to produce, and throughout the payback period which may be as long as another five to ten years.

Lenders' attitudes to risk

The nature of the risks affects lenders' willingness to accept them. This section looks at lenders' attitudes and the next at protections they can build or buy against some of the risks.

Pre-completion risk

In the early days of project lending bank lenders refused pre-completion risk. They required another strong source of repayment, which they would allow to drop away at completion. The various forms this source could take still apply to those pre-completion risks which banks will not take even today, and are covered post, pp 12ff.

With greater sophistication and experience, as well as the pressure of competition, banks now take a higher level of pre-completion risk than in the past. Indeed, sometimes, as with the Channel Tunnel and Euro Disneyland, they will take the bulk of it. One danger is that under either political or 'relationship' pressure, they may take risks for reasons unrelated to the project. Another is that they may underestimate the force majeure risk.

Bank lenders do not own the project and obtain no extra benefit from a greater than expected success. Since pre-completion risk is arguably equity risk, banks insist that owners put in some equity even when the banks take most of the pre-completion risk. How much equity, and on what terms are discussed post, pp 12 and 13ff.

An equity cushion is not a panacea for pre-completion risk. Banks must analyse the remaining risk carefully, not only to decide whether to accept it, but also to judge how best to protect themselves.

It is hard to generalise in a changing market how great a risk banks will accept. Whatever their definition of 'too great', however, banks still need criteria to decide which projects meet it. In some types of project, the risk – or at least some parts of it – can only be assessed with specific technical knowledge. For instance, outside consultants report on geological and other data before any bank will finance a North Sea oil well. Even then the bankers making the decision need to understand and assess the consultant's report, which will be an important input to the decision.

Banks may well refuse pre-completion risk where the project involves unproven technology. There are too many factors which are difficult to assess, and too many cases of projects (however financed) going wrong because new technology did not live up to expectations. There are three levels of the risk. One is that the technology is so unproven that in fact the project never reaches completion at all. This is the least likely, since the project's sponsors will be convinced of its viability before they commit themselves. Nevertheless, whenever companies introduce complex technology, something unforeseen always may prevent it working. Even successful pilot projects sometimes fail to identify problems that cripple full-scale plants. Generally speaking therefore banks will not finance the first project to incorporate major and complex new technology, and often not the second or third.

The second level of technological risk is that a crucial but independent part of the process will not work; this part may then need to be replaced with older technology or significantly changed. Either remedy can be very expensive and cause major delays, whether in correcting the technology which fails or, if it is necessary to replace it, adjusting the rest of the project to the replacement technology. An example was the attempt to incorporate carbon fibre blades in the Rolls Royce RB211 jet engine. When the blades failed and had to be replaced with more conventional, but still advanced, material the cost and delays played an important part in bankrupting Rolls Royce, even though in the end the engine was successful.

The third level of technological risk is that the technology is too complex for the contractor installing it. A contractor trying to break into a new field for the first time may take on more than he can handle, even though the technology is proven. This risk may be acceptable if the contractor can throw resources at the problem until he solves it, and pay compensation for the costs caused by the delay; since most contractors cannot do this, the banks may look for protection (see post, pp 12–14).

Other factors which can increase pre-completion risk to an unacceptable level include:

- **Environmental factors of three types.** Even proven techniques may fail if they are exposed to new conditions, as with the early oil wells in the North Sea and Alaska. Even proven companies may fail if they are operating outside their normal boundaries; something as simple as a road or a school may prove unexpectedly difficult to complete on time and budget if a contractor is unfamilar with local labour practices,

government regulations or red tape. And thirdly, with growing concerns about the damage to the environment from various projects, the danger of extra costs imposed by local government, or of protests which delay and perhaps prevent completion, is a concern.
- Managerial competence or lack of it. However inherently sound a project, it requires a competent and experienced management to see it through; competent not just in general terms but in the specific skills required for the particular project; and competent not only when things are going smoothly, but able to react quickly to unexpected difficulties.
- The labour environment. Depending on the nature of the project, a fair amount of skilled labour may be needed. Some of this can be imported if it is not immediately available at the site of the project, but most, and often much larger numbers of unskilled labour, must be recruited locally. Most projects are planned against tight deadlines, which labour can disrupt. A history of poor labour relations and damaging strikes in an area can make pre-completion risk unattractive.

Operating risk

Banks active in project finance have always been willing to take operating risk. Provided the project meets certain criteria, which banks analyse carefully before committing themselves, the risks should be manageable. Operating a plant of whatever nature, once built, carries less uncertainty than building it.

One proviso of course is that the banks are satisfied with the market risk, since even the best operated plant will not cover its costs if there is no market for the product.

Most of the subjects already mentioned under pre-completion risk arise in a slightly different form under operating risk. If the technology is new or known to be difficult to operate, the risk of complete or partial failure rises and may become unacceptable. Particularly in this case but also more generally management competence is critical; labour, the environment, actual or potential government interference can all have damaging or favourable implications depending on the nature of the project. And, of course, force majeure remains a possibility.

Given that the project does not usually become 'operational' until it has operated to specification for a minimum period, complete failure is unlikely. The concern is more that it should produce to specification, and within budget, and where appropriate be flexible enough to meet changes in markets which were foreseen and built into the assumptions about the project. Failures in any of these areas may reduce cash flow below what is needed to service the debt in full; they are less likely to eliminate it altogether.

Market risk

As with operating risk, banks have always regarded market risk as something that they can accept. However, the lead time between taking the decision and the first product becoming available is sometimes so long that banks feel they need some protection against the worst that can happen. This is most important if the price of the product is known to be volatile, or if competitive products threaten market share, or a permanent loss of demand for the product occurs. The same factors apply in reverse in terms of cost; if the principle raw material used in the project fluctuates in cost, or if there is any chance of a competing raw material or process coming into prominence and undermining the project's product, the lenders will look for extra protection.

Protections available

Equity

Equity is the key protection against all three types of risk. However well-judged the project, however well managed, carefully researched and predictable, even however good the protection against other risks, something always goes wrong. Since the owner will reap all the extra profit from success, projects need equity to absorb the uncharted risk.

How much equity, and on what terms, is more variable. Sometimes all the equity must be used to start the project before any debt; sometimes debt and equity go in together in agreed proportions; sometimes the amount of equity is fixed from the start, sometimes there is an up-front injection, with more on call to meet cost overruns.

Market conditions and bargaining strength will affect both the level of equity and the terms. (The word 'equity' in this section includes preference shares and even subordinated debt with terms acceptable to the senior lenders.) With that proviso, the nature of the project, and of any pre-completion risk the banks take will be the main factor. Broadly speaking, there are three types of situation.

Where the banks take little or no pre-completion risk, equity is needed purely as a cushion against operating and market risk. The amount of equity will then be more important than its timing. All the finance, except perhaps for working capital, will be committed before completion puts the banks on project risk, so that it matters less which component goes in first.

Where banks take all or most of the pre-completion risk, they will want all the equity in the project at the point where they could first known that something is wrong. With some projects the critical point comes right at the end of the construction period, when most of the funds have been disbursed; the timing of the equity injection is again less important than its amount. With others the success or failure of either the whole project or a key part of it is known fairly early. In this case the lenders will want equity to go in first. Then, if the project fails the major loss will be born by equity; and debt is not disbursed until at least some of the uncertainty has passed.

From a different viewpoint, the equity contribution will depend on the nature of the risk. With untested technology for all or part of the risk, banks will want to see a high equity content. Where the problem is less of complete failure, and more of delay, cost overruns, or a project which produces below specification, they may be content with a smaller initial contribution, but the ability to call for more equity if necessary. This may be achieved by a phasing of the equity and debt, so that 25% or 50% of the equity is in place before any of the debt; or by putting them in pro rata, say £1 of equity for every £4 of debt. Or the initial equity and debt contribution may be set to cover the total expected cost; if this cost is exceeded, at least a minimum amount of equity will be injected before any further debt; sometimes equity will cover the whole overrun.

This fits with the general principle that equity is to provide for uncertainties. In cases where cost overruns or delays causing them are a major aspect of the risk, it is right that equity should deal with them. This principle applies in deciding how much equity banks require as well as its timing. The more predictable and controllable the various risks are, or the more secure the various forms of protection, the less equity is needed; and vice versa. In cases where the uncertainty comes late in the process, the final decision as to how much equity is needed can do likewise.

Pre-completion protection

Except for working capital, project finance is spent during the pre-completion period. However, equity also protects against operating or market risk leaving too little cash flow to service the debt. Nor is equity the only protection before completion.

The first and most critical form is the standing of the contractor, a key aspect in the analysis of pre-completion risk. Does he have:

- the general management strengths to carry through a project of this size and complexity?
- the specific skills necessary to handle the technical and other difficulties of this project? and
- the financial strength and other resources in reserve to handle unexpected difficulties?

If the answer to all three questions is an unqualified 'yes', then this and a reasonable equity cushion may be the only protection needed.

Where the answers, while positive, are less resounding, the most common extra protection is some form of guarantee or insurance. Broadly these come in three forms: the owner(s) may be major corporates or governments who guarantee completion, or specific aspects of it, reducing or eliminating the project risk. Weaker owners may also guarantee, but can only reduce the reliance on the project, not eliminate it.

The second type of guarantee comes from a bank or insurance company close to the contractor, or occasionally from a contractor's strong parent. A typical example is the refundment guarantee given by Japanese banks to cover the obligation of a shipyard to deliver a vessel on time and to specification; if it fails to do so the Japanese bank repays the loan, and looks to its client.

The third type is a performance guarantee from a bank or insurance company, or a group of them. The owners of the project may well require this even when it is not being project-financed; their interest, after all, is more than purely financial. A good example of this was the Conoco requirement for performance bonds on the construction of a refinery in England. The English contractor, experienced in a number of other types of construction but not refineries, heavily overran its budget. Conoco persuaded the guarantors that it was cheaper to complete the refinery than to repay all the finance so far sunk into it. In brief, the performance guarantors take the pre-completion risk and should go through the same analysis as a lending bank.

Banks also use a controlled drawdown to reduce pre-completion risk. Each advance is conditional on an engineer's or architect's certificate, or other independent evidence, that the work has been properly done and has reached a certain stage. In a straightforward project, such as a road or port, progress reduces risk of non-completion or cost overrun roughly pro rata. In a more complex or doubtful project, the staged drawdown gives the banks the chance to check the technology before advancing more funds. If the technology fails, they may not recover the money already advanced, but at least they can limit their losses.

To judge whether technology has failed may require a level of scientific knowledge which most bankers do not claim. Thus a further protection is the use of consultants.

Operating protection

The critical protection against operating risk is the completion test. This must be well designed and rigorously carried out; otherwise part of completion risk may be wrongly designated as operating risk. Even where the project finance carries both risks, both lenders and owners need to be sure that the project will operate properly before releasing the contractors from liability.

Confidence in the operator's managerial and technical skills is also crucial. In some cases this may be relatively easy to establish. A ship operator builds up a record by operating a number of ships, for instance. A bank can check this and relate it to the requirements of the charter it is financing.

It may not be so easy to judge a company's ability to operate the first plant of its type, with technology which has never been used for this purpose before, or perhaps at all. Nor is it easy to judge whether a company with a sound record in one field necessarily can adapt to a field which is new to it.

It is, however, critical. A weak management can easily drag down a sound project; even a routinely competent management can lose control of a complex project. New technology is almost bound to throw up some unexpected strains to which only capable and flexible managements can be sure – well, fairly sure – of reacting fast and correctly.

Management is almost the sole protection against operating risk since there is not much in the way of tailored protection. A strong parent may provide support, even guarantees, but this is not so much a protection as a move away from the project risk. Some projects are relatively straightforward to operate, so that the level of management needed is lower. But where a project taxes the skills of the best management, there are unlikely to be specific protections against management failure, since the cause is not identifiable in advance in a way which allows protection.

Protection against market risk

The above is not true of market risk. Banks can protect against lower prices or lack of demand by some variant of forward sales. At one extreme is the 'take or pay', under which the buyer is bound to pay for a product even if he does not want it – sometimes even if the project cannot deliver – and to do so at a price which covers both operating costs and debt service.

In a sense such a take or pay is the same as a corporate guarantee; the legal technicalities are different, but the economic effect is similar, and the corporate backer takes responsibility for the eventual payment of the project loan. The lender then only loses money if both the project and its corporate backer fail.

The take or pay can take various slightly different forms depending on the nature of the project; for instance a pipeline may have a throughput agreement or a processing plant a tolling agreement, but the underlying point is the same.

In this extreme form a take or pay agreement protects against operating risk as well as market risk; it may, depending on when it triggers, even protect against pre-completion risk. It would be unreasonable to expect a third party to take such a risk; this extreme form is therefore rare unless the provider is heavily committed to the project, with an economic interest in its success. Usually he also controls, and therefore takes responsibility for, the operation of the project.

In a less extreme form, the obligation to take arises only if product is actually available, and meets defined quality standards. It is therefore more clearly protecting against market risk, leaving most or all of the operating risk with the lenders. In effect, this form of take or pay says that 'if you produce in the right volume and at the right quality, we will take care of price.'

Where a take or pay is not available from a strong enough owner or customer, the bank may seek firm contracts from independent third parties. Again the form will vary according to the nature of the project, but the underlying idea is the same. Here, however, the protection is narrower and clearly confined to market risk. The independent third party will pay only for value received. If an operating failure prevents value being given, or allows it only at a cost which puts debt service at risk, that is of no concern to the third party.

This form of pre-sale can protect against price changes, volume changes or both. Thus for instance a property may be pre-let at a level which covers financing needs, even where there is no fear that it might prove unlettable. Equally, a ship may be chartered while it is still being built either because the bank and owner are unwilling to risk the availability of long-term charters later, or because they expect a fall in the charter rate. Or a copper mine may pre-sell at a price linked to that on the London Metal Exchange. This protects against failure to sell at all but accepts a price risk.

Pre-selling, whatever the form, carries a cost, which can be regarded as an insurance premium. The pre-buyers will expect a favourable price in return for their commitment, and the seller loses the opportunity to take advantage of later price increases. The lenders may therefore not require pre-sale of the whole output of the project, particularly where a higher price is seen as protection against cost increases. Then only part of a major building need be pre-let, or only enough copper presold to provide a base load for the mine, smelter, etc. It can be quite a delicate judgement, balancing the need for certainty of revenue against the cost of missing a higher price later. As a rule, lenders will take a more conservative view than owners, who benefit from the leverage effect if the price rises. It is likely after all that the owner expects the price to rise; often this was a major justification for the project in the first place.

Pre-selling requires the lender to analyse the buyers, particularly where one or two account for the whole pre-sale. A pre-charter to pay out a $50–$100 million ship loan requires a charterer with a strong financial condition, or one who can be relied on to generate revenue by his use of the ship, or some combination of the two. A copper mine whose output is pre-sold to 100 different companies may be less dependent on any one of them. Nevertheless, the lender needs to look at the average strength of the pre-buyers; if it is too low, it may fail to reduce the value of the pre-sale. Or too heavy a concentration of buyers may carry the same risk. If they come from the same country or region, they can be hit by the same set of adverse economic, political or even military mishaps; as they can if they in turn sell to the same end users.

Pre-selling also requires a watertight contract. A pre-sale contract which lets the buyer off liability just when reliance on it is most wanted, has little value. Too onerous a contract may in practice be unenforceable whatever the lawyers say, so lenders need to review this aspect too.

Why borrowers choose project finance

The original and still frequent reason for choosing project finance is to isolate the risk, taking it off balance sheet so that failure does not damage the owner's financial condition. This may be a genuine economic reason, where the owner(s) do(es) not want to mix the risk of the project and the normal risks of their business. At one stage, however, it became as much a matter of accounting as of economic or business logic. Even where the owner retained some real risk in the project, if he could get if off balance sheet this risk would not show to his creditors or investment analysts, or would be outside the coverage of covenants on his bank loans; or so he hopes. More sophisticated analysis has reduced the incidence of purely accounting motives.

The desire to isolate risk may combine with the desire to spread it. Most project financings cover major projects; only the largest companies and sometimes not even those can absorb the whole risk alone. By isolating the risk in a project, it can be easier to bring in partners who can share it. And of course project finance in itself is a means of getting the banks to share the risk.

There can be other reasons for wanting to isolate the risk. For instance a strong partner in a project may be unwilling to carry a weaker partner, even though it is able and willing to finance its own share of the whole project. By arranging project finance, with a limited equity or other contribution from the owners which the weak partner can meet, it avoids the risk of having to choose between carrying its partner and seeing a sound project fail. Or the owners may be forced to agree to one of their number acting as operator for the project and lack the confidence they would have if they were operating it themselves. Finally, there may be a pollution or other risk attached to the project, which they are reluctant to accept in their own name. By setting up a separate company, in which no one owns a majority of the shares, and the banks provide most of the finance, they can hope to avoid the worst of these risks. Equally, however, the banks do not want to end up absorbing the risks without having recognised that they were doing so, and expect to be paid for this element of risk if they take it willingly.

Tax is often an important benefit to project finance. The tax benefits vary widely from country to country and project to project. In some project financings, such as tax-based leasing, the tax benefits are a main reason for choosing this form of finance. In others they are merely a secondary but welcome benefit for using the best method of finance. Even where tax is not even a secondary reason, there may still be some tax benefits.

Finally, the projects covered by project finance are often highly visible politically. In some cases a large project in a less developed country may influence the prospects of the economy for years ahead. Naturally governments are interested in the project, sometimes corruptly; equally naturally, the owners do not want to pay too high a price for political support, or to be subject to interference or even expropriation. Project finance spreads this risk to the banks; it sometimes allows the owners to hide behind the banks when they do not want to meet a particular government demand. And at least at one stage governments were thought to be less likely to expropriate a project where the banks had a large stake, or to refuse to allow funds to go abroad to service the finance. Whether this last point has much remaining validity is open to serious doubt.

Special features

Many features of project finance are the same as in any other type of finance, only more intensive. There are a few areas, however, where the difference warrants mention.

Insurance

Because repayment of the loan depends solely on the project, it is more than usually important to insure against anything that could interfere with repayment. In lending to a company, even one which depends heavily on one or two plants, banks often rely on the company to maintain a normal level of insurance. With project finance they need to be certain that the correct insurance is available in the right amounts from a sound insurance company. Moreover, with a corporate borrower banks can accept that insurance against some risks is either not available or too expensive; the company's overall balance sheet strength can absorb the risk. This option is rarely acceptable in project finance. Since the project is the sole source of repayment, anything which threatens its viability is critical. If the cost of the premium is so great as to threaten repayment of the loan, or if a risk is simply not insurable, this may kill the project. This applies particularly to any type of force majeure risk.

Where the uninsurable risk covers a part of the project which can be replaced, the answer may be to build up other protections to a higher level. For instance, a particular part of the process might be so prone to fire or explosion as to be uninsurable. However, proper precautions might ensure that the fire could not spread to the rest of the project; the part destroyed might be replaceable at a manageable cost. The project lenders might then accept tight precautions against the fire spreading and an injection of extra equity to cover the replacement cost.

To ensure that a project is fully insured against all risks requires knowledge of the project, and also of the insurance available. A ship, for instance, can have as many as four different types of insurance. Lenders must also understand something about insurance law. In some countries at least it is rather different from normal contract law. The difference can shift the onus of proof onto the insured, or make what seems to be a trivial oversight critical to the duty to pay. Above all the insurance motto 'utmost good faith' applies solely in favour of the insurer.

The lender also needs to know the calibre of the various insurers. Some are more sophisticated in their assessment of risk than others. Some will accept and meet the obligations to pay faster than others. And some are of doubtful solvency, at least when the cycle is moving against them. Since the project owner pays the insurance premia, he may be tempted to insure with the cheapest rather than the best. At one time, for instance, some Greek shipowners had this reputation, and there were certainly cases when banks had to wait a long time to recover insurance claims on sunk or damaged ships from mid-Western American insurers; there may even have been cases when the bank never recovered.

Confidence in management must extend to its meeting the conditions of any insurance policy at all times; if it does not, the lender may find the project is uninsured at the critical moment. This confidence can be purely a matter of managerial competence; there may be strict technical requirements, to meet which require tight management controls. Or it may be a matter of management integrity; some ship insurance requires that a ship does not enter a war zone without prior notification to the insurer. In at least one case a ship with such insurance entered a war zone without notification; when it was damaged it tried to conceal the fact by sending a retrospective notice and falsifying the date of the damage.

Finally, the bank must have the insurance assigned to it and its interest noted; and it must have controls to ensure that the premiums are paid on time. If necessary, it must be able to pay them itself to avoid losing the insurance.

Security and documentation

As with insurance, the narrow source of payment in a project loan must be closely tied into the original borrowing and its repayment. This often means that the assets generated by the project, and revenues they generate, as well as the land occupied, must be pledged to secure the debt. The nature of the assets subject to project financing often makes this unusually complicated. For instance mineral rights may be owned differently to the land rights; sometimes they may remain the property of a government or other party and the project may merely have a licence to extract and sell; to pledge the proceeds of the sale without having a pledge on the underlying asset can be complex, and may require co-operation from a government or third party. In some cases the government may even have to legislate to allow the lenders the sort of security they need to finance the development of a national asset such as North Sea oil.

Where the project is covered by a single purpose company, with no other assets or borrowing and only wages and suppliers as creditors apart from the project debt, a pledge of assets in the formal sense may not be necessary. Whether it is or not, however, the documentation of the loan will nearly always be complex, and ensuring that it covers every eventuality critical.

The various protections described earlier all need careful documentation. Whether it is the terms of the equity injection or of a take or pay; of the certificates against which the bank must advance funds or the terms of the completion test; of the government licence or of the pre-sale, or any of the other myriad of items, the wording must be precise, the legal effect must be clear, and the people who have to operate the loan from both the borrower's and lender's side must be able to understand what they are supposed to do and why.

An additional complication may be the need for the documentation to work under special types of law. Shipping loans for instance (whether classified as project loans or not) must comply with marine law as well as with the law of whatever country the agreement is drawn under. The need to meet special laws regarding mineral rights has also been mentioned and there may be others in some countries. Even where there are no special types of law which are relevant to a project, it may still be subject to the laws of two or more countries. It is all very well to draw up an English law agreement covering a loan to develop a nickel mine in Ruritania. Because the project is physically in Ruritania, its law will apply to most of what the project does, and will be particularly important if the project ends up in bankruptcy. Certainly, if the banks want to take a specific pledge over the assets making up the project, its validity will depend on Ruritanian law.

In brief, with or without the need for a specific pledge, documentation on project loans is more complex and more critical to recovery of debt than in most other loans.

Governments

Because of the size of most projects which justify project finance, governments tend to take an interest in them, deriving from one or more of several bases:

(a) as owner/operator of the project, and thus as borrower or guarantor;
(b) as owner of the land on which the project stands or from under which the project hopes to extract minerals, ie as landlord or economic licensor;
(c) as regulator in advance or in arrears, ie as regulatory licensor;
(d) as taxing authority and general beneficiary of any wealth, particularly in the form of employment, the project generates, directly or by creating local opportunities. This may, but need not, include corrupt benefits.

While not mutually exclusive, these roles can conflict and may be held by different, and sometimes competing, government departments. The energy department may seek the most generous financial terms and minimum regulation for an offshore oil rig, for instance. The finance department may focus on extracting revenue, and the environment department may seek tight guarantees against pollution. At least in this situation the project has one government department on its side; in other situations it may have them all seeking their pound of flesh.

This is not the place to explore all the ramifications of government involvement; that can better be done in the following chapters on each major type of project. The point here is that government, in various different forms, is likely to be heavily involved even in countries which favour free enterprise. The managers of the project must be able to handle the problems government can cause. Project lenders must be able to protect their own specific interests, and ensure that management has received a reasonable deal from government, and can live up to it. One of the risks for all parties to the project is of a change in government attitude after the project is under way. While it may sometimes be possible to insure against this, the experience of those few banks that have claimed under political risk insurance is not encouraging.

New influences

In one sense this chapter is incomplete, in that it has not covered the new influences; that has been deliberately left to the next chapter. However, the basic principals outlined in this chapter apply to all projects. The means of implementing the main points may vary, but the points themselves remain valid.

T H Donaldson, FCIB, joined Morgan Guaranty in New York in November 1963, after working for the Empire Trust Company and W E Hutton. He returned to London in June 1964.

During his early days as an account officer, he passed out first in all England in the Bankers' Institute exams, and began to be interested in writing and lecturing. Always fascinated by credit, he has been Morgan's senior specialist in London since 1974 and Europe since 1980. In that capacity he was heavily involved in the rescues of Union Explosivos Rio Tinto in Spain and Johnson Matthey plc in England; he was also involved in the restructurings of the debt of WPP and IBC. He is now a Managing Director, and Chairman of the European Credit Policy Committee.

He helped to draft the evidence of the American Bankers Association in London (ABAL) to the Wilson Committee.

He writes and lectures on various aspects of credit, and is the author of *Lending in International Commercial Banking*; *The Medium Term Loan Market* (with J A Donaldson); *Understanding Corporate Credit*; *How to Handle Problem Loans*; *Thinking About Credit*; and *Credit Risk and Exposure in Securitisation and Transactions*, all published by Macmillan.

2 New influences

Brian H Weight, J P Morgan

The historical perspective

By the early 1980s, project finance in its many and diverse forms had become a booming and highly visible line of business for commercial bank lenders. Demand for debt funding of new projects was now truly global. From copper projects in Brazil to oil and gas fields in the Cameroon to petrochemical facilities in Singapore, banks were lending billions of (predominantly) US dollars to finance major natural resource developments all over the world.

During the period from the mid-1970s onwards, banks had dedicated more and more professionals to the business of project finance, building teams and then whole departments to provide the necessary specialist expertise to evaluate project lending risks and, increasingly, to provide advice to project sponsors on how best to structure the legal, tax and accounting aspects and the funding arrangements for their projects. The American commercial banks had been in the vanguard of this growth but were soon joined by British, French and other Western European banks and then many others. By 1980, one Australian bank had built a team of around twenty project financiers working on projects in Australia itself but also in Papua New Guinea, Indonesia and other countries located on the western Pacific rim.

There were two key factors fuelling the substantial increase in the use of project financing techniques over a decade and a half – the strong growth in worldwide demand for energy and mineral resources and the satisfaction of such demand only by exploitation of primary resource deposits located in increasingly diverse and, often, remote geographical areas.

Firstly, it will have been noticed that the majority of specific types of projects mentioned in chapter 1 were natural-resource related – installation of drilling rigs, development of oil and gas fields, mining and extraction of mineral ores, processing of primary natural resources into refined derivatives (bauxite – alumina – aluminium, crude oil – petrochemicals, timber – forest products). Natural resource development is amongst the most capital intensive of enterprises and, as a result, sponsors of these types of projects concentrate more than most on the possibilities for segregating the financial burden and risks inherent in their projects from other mainstream activities. To the extent that lenders are prepared to lend a substantial portion of the capital required and that they will substantially limit their recourse for repayment of loans only to the project and its cash flows, the project sponsor (or sponsors) can take on the development of the specific project while maintaining greater flexibility than would otherwise have been the case in using its capital to support other (perhaps less capital intensive but riskier) businesses.

Furthermore, during the period in question, the world economy was broadly on something of a roll and demand for natural resource commodities strong. As a result of the two 'oil-shocks' in the 1970s, the price of Saudi Light crude oil had risen from $1.80 per barrel in 1970 to $32.00 per barrel in 1980. There was talk about and some action in attempting to develop alternative energy sources (shale oil, synthetics) as well as greater efforts to discover and develop non-OPEC, non-Communist bloc oil reserves. Mineral ore commodities (copper, lead, zinc, bauxite, coal) were also on the upside of their variously cyclical demand curves, as indicated by the following table.

Selected historic US producer metals commodities prices 1970 and 1980 (yearly averages)

Prices in cents per pound except for Platinum (dollars/ounce)

	Copper	Lead	Zinc	Tin	Aluminium	Platinum
1970	57.7	15.6	15.3	174.2	28.7	130.0
1980	101.4	42.5	37.4	846.0	69.5	439.4

Source: American Bureau of Metal Statistics Inc

Bank lenders, increasingly confident in the economic risks of projects able to sell their output at high and rising prices, provided more and more project funding. And this funding was made available to projects throughout the developed and lesser-developed world. For many of the major natural resource deposits were located in the poorer, younger countries of Africa, Asia and Latin America.

So we come to the second key factor in considering the phenomenal growth in project finance in the 1970s. This decade was, of course, the period of massive transfer of capital, predominantly debt capital, to the lesser-developed countries (LDCs). While much of this debt was made available to governments which in turn allocated funds (with greater or lesser efficiency) to priority end-users, development of indigenous natural resources was an integral part of the individual LDCs' pursuit of increased net revenue to aid overall economic growth.

Commercial banks had extended their international networks generally and particularly in the LDCs. They had become more and more comfortable with the broad political risks of lending to these countries or specific ventures within these countries. This comfort was equally applicable to project finance. Thus, bank lenders were increasingly willing to provide funding for projects where both substantial economic and political risks were assumed. While expropriation is perhaps the obvious but extreme form of political risk, what the banks were more likely to be exposing themselves to was the risk of changes in a particular government's fiscal or foreign exchange policies. If the country experienced economic difficulties, increased taxes and constraints on the transfer of funds out of the country were primary measures open to the government of the day. Both the risk that commodity prices can fall beyond expectations and the risk that governments can and will interfere with cost structures and cash flow availability had to be faced squarely by project lenders in the 1980s.

The early 1980s were a period of major structural change in the natural resources industries. Chronic overcapacity in metals commodities resulted in price collapse. Lead fell from a peak average price of 53 cents per pound in 1979 to 19 cents per pound in 1985. Copper fell from an average of 132 cents per pound to 69 cents per pound in the same period. Other key mining commodities such as coal suffered a similar fate. Many projects financed in the late 1970s and early 1980s failed to produce sufficient cash to service scheduled debt repayments and restructuring of credit packages became necessary. In the main, banks did not actually lose money from their project lending but they did have to accept slower repayment and, crucially for the buoyancy of the business of project finance, uncertainty as to future repayment. Mining-related project lending dried up.

As noted earlier, after the second Middle Eastern 'oil shock' of 1979, the price of benchmark Saudi Light crude oil averaged $32 per barrel in 1980. During the latter part of 1985, downward pressure on the price of oil as a result of substantial over-production by OPEC led to a gradual withdrawal of banks from new oil and gas field financing. The crash of 1986, when the oil price dropped to single figures ($9 per barrel in July) for the first time since 1973, was traumatic for lenders. Financings for oil projects located anywhere from the North Sea to the South China Sea became 'doubtful debts' on banks' balance sheets and in some cases capital reserves were made against them.

In fact, no losses were ultimately incurred by banks against their oil production and development lending. Major losses were to be made in oil rig lending – massive overcapacity resulting in the 'stacking' of redundant rigs for years. In 1986, however, the future looked decidedly uncertain for any kind of oil-related project lending. As was made clear in chapter 1, there is always uncertainty in project lending. As in all business ventures, but particularly in financing a single specific project, a bet is being taken on future economic and political conditions. There are times, however, when the dice appear to be unacceptably loaded and a bank's project finance department was often only a few stops on the lift away from the Latin American department.

In the early 1980s, the problems of the over-borrowed Latin American economies came home to roost with their bank lenders. Much of the money provided by lenders to the countries of South America had been lent to government agencies for the development of specific infrastructure projects – roads, railways, dams, electrical plant and transmission lines. But the obligor on the debt was the government, not the specific project enterprise, and the government faced a very obviously negative balance of payments position. Bank lenders could not be repaid.

For a time, the combination of seizure in traditional specific project finance business and the inability of lenders to obtain repayment of loans made to governments to finance projects created inertia. On the one hand, the natural resource industries which had been the prime recipient of project lending for more than a decade had become unbankable. On the other hand, lending to the developing countries of the world was now proving to be the source of substantial losses for banks, irrespective of the fact that, in many cases, the original borrowed money had been used to finance eminently viable projects, particularly infrastructure projects.

New influences emerge

1 Governmental deregulation and privatisation – new types of project finance opportunity

In the US, project lenders found a new use for their expertise and understanding of the energy production/consumption chain in financing the plethora of US domestic independent energy projects being developed as a result of the 1978 Public Utilities Regional Policies Act ('PURPA'). The purpose of this legislation was to encourage the development of alternative energy sources to stem the increasing American reliance on imported crude oil as domestic output fell. The Federal Energy Regulatory Commission ('FERC') established new regulations which allowed PURPA's goals to be translated into practice and a whole new industry was born. By far the most common type of independent power project ('IPP') was based on so-called 'cogeneration' technology. Cogeneration essentially involves the use of a single fuel (oil, coal or gas) to power a turbine which generates both electricity and steam. Gas has been the most popular feedstock because of price, technical and environmental advantages. But unconventional fuels such as waste and peat have also been used. By using both electricity and steam in their own process plant, companies have a clear advantage over traditional power plant which vents off the steam. Alternatively, the company owning the cogeneration plant can sell one or other of the products not used in its own operation to a third party; for example steam can be sold to food processors or district heating companies.

This business dominated the activity of project finance departments in the US until the late 1980s. Importantly, it demonstrates the transferability of project financing techniques from old industries to new industries. In the early years of the IPP industry, lenders were having to understand the risks inherent in a new power-generation technology. Increasingly, they became comfortable with taking the pre-completion risk that cogeneration plants would work – and work efficiently. In fact, some did not and, in a few cases, lenders lost money. But the enormous response from banks to share risk on this new industry illustrates the momentum which project finance techniques had achieved within lending institutions as a viable and flexible business. Partly, this was the 'law of the gaps' at work – traditional project lending with its higher-than-average earnings returns to lenders had dried up and new opportunities were scarce. However, what lenders were prepared to do for IPPs was a signpost for the remainder of the decade.

We have already seen that there was significant pre-completion risk underwritten by the banks. The second important development was the length or term of these IPP financings. Power projects, whether conventional or cogeneration, are by their nature slow, if steady, cash flow generators. After the construction period (often less than 2 years for IPPs, much longer on a conventional coal or oil-fired plant), the market price of power to the consumer characteristically earns a low but long-term annuity return on initial capital invested. So long as a particular plant is servicing a core market demand (and, of course, is operating efficiently) cash will continue to flow many years into the future based on a more-or-less inflation-adjusted margin. As a result, the term of the finance raised to build the plant must be long. In the early 1980s, it was unusual for limited or non-recourse lenders to provide a loan for more than 10 years. These lenders were exclusively banks and banks did not expect to fill the long-term lending role traditionally provided by insurance companies and pension funds. Suffice to say that, since these latter financial institutions were not limited or non-recourse project lenders, the banks gradually extended term to meet the market. A 15-year term became not uncommon and some 18-year transactions were arranged.

How did lenders become comfortable with locking up such long-term risk assets? Firstly, they had determined that so long as the plant was contracted to an end-user(s) of power representing core market demand, the loan would eventually be repaid; that is, they could accept a long-term market risk, perceiving a stable underlying consumer demand. Secondly, the assumption was also made that, once an efficient and therefore profitable operating track-record had been established, the original project financing would be re-financed by eager investors from the long-term bond or other capital markets. The project would by then have achieved the status of a mini-utility. This increased flexibility in assessing pre-and post-completion risks is a vital ingredient when we consider what project lenders turned their attention to in other parts of the world.

In Europe, during 1985, the joint British–French initiative towards the building of a 'fixed' link across the English Channel was reaching a crescendo. The two governments had called for bids from private sponsors to produce detailed designs, cost estimates and funding packages to create the link, all against a fierce timetable for selection of the most attractive proposition, the passing of enabling legislation and commencement of work in 1987. Many schemes were proposed encompassing the gamut of tunnels, bridges, tunnels and bridges in combination; railways, roadways, railways and roadways in combination.

The English Channel at its narrowest point is still 23 miles wide. There were few precedents for the engineering technology required for this feat and the history of those which came close was a dismal record of unforeseen technological problems and resultant massive cost overruns. For example, in Japan, the Seikan underwater tunnel between Hokkaido and Honshu was finally completed 10 years late and at a cost three times original budget. Yet here we find a *government* impetus to build and finance the most complex bi-national infrastructure project yet attempted based on private investment. If the momentum for proceeding with this project on an entirely private sector basis derived primarily from the tenets of Prime Minister Thatcher and her advisers in the UK, the Mitterand administration in France was content to endorse this approach as the optimum method of achieving intra-European economic progress. It could be seen as a major step forward in the consolidation of efficient EEC trade flows at no expense to the EEC taxpayer. Also, there was apparently no lack of private sponsorship to take on this task.

The scheme finally selected, 'Eurotunnel', was in fact the cheapest of the four practical proposals short-listed. Yet, at the time funding was put in place in 1987, the cost estimate including contingencies was £5 billion. It was determined by the British and French financial advisers that, of this amount, £1 billion in equity could be raised from domestic and international markets with the balance to be debt-funded. This massive loan (in fact, £2.6 billion, FFr 21 billion and US$ 450 million in loans and letter of credit facilities were raised) would not be guaranteed by sponsors or governments. As discussed in chapter 1, this would be a pure project loan – the biggest ever.

In considering the risks they were being asked to assume, bank lenders found themselves poring over data regarding numbers of cars per day, rail freight volumes and rates, average travel times, comparison of the tunnel with current ferry links and much more statistical information. While some lenders may have looked at traffic studies of this kind before in considering, say, a shipping loan to a ferry operator, many had not. Nor had any financed a hole in the ground on a non-recourse basis out of which came not coal or iron ore but a railway train. Yet the financing was put together, with a little difficulty and without the participation of almost any North American banks (the original leaders in project lending). The tunnel is not scheduled to be completed until 1993/4, while the tunnel concession runs for 50 years. The original 1987 loan, since then much repackaged, had a base term of 18 years, to 2005. Here again, as in the US experience with IPPs, we find project lenders prepared to take substantial pre- and post-completion risk for an entirely new kind of venture.

It is in fact probable that some lenders to the Channel Tunnel undertook less than the most rigorous analysis of its technology, costs and economics and put emphasis rather on the intangibles of the political will of the two governments to see the tunnel finished – i e to step in and provide financial support if major problems arose during construction. There was probably also again something of 'the law of the gaps' involved – a dearth of interesting alternatives. However, the deal was done and construction of the Channel Tunnel, financed as a pure project, commenced.

The most important outcome of this bellwether project financing was the focus now placed on the opportunities for other infrastructure projects where the combination of private equity ownership and project-based borrowing could relieve a government of its (and ultimately its taxpayers') traditional responsibility to fund heavy capital expenditures.

Britain has led the way in Europe in the privatisation of historically nationalised industries. While many of the privatised enterprises are fully fledged corporations in their own right, the privatisation of infrastructural projects – roads, railways, bridges and tunnels, even airports – is a decidedly different exercise. It is not, as is often suggested, new. The origins of the railways and many of the roads in Europe and the US lie in nineteenth century private enterprise. Prompted by the competitive urge to obtain the high profits inherent in a local, then more widespread, monopoly, private entrepreneurs were mainly responsible for building our major road and rail arteries, earning back a return on their capital through the charges made for the carriage of passengers or freight and the tolls levied for use of the highway. Banking houses played a part in financing this development in Europe but the archetypal – and most extreme – form of bank involvement was perhaps J P Morgan's virtual takeover of large parts of the US railroad system in the late nineteenth century. Roads and railways can make money. They can also, as whole networks, soak it up like a sponge.

Most of the infrastructure projects considered for project lending in the UK have therefore been on a significantly smaller scale than the Channel Tunnel. The optimum approach in terms of raising project finance is to parcel up a discrete transportation link with an expected high and continuous user demand and avoid taking on responsibility for as much of the peripheral but linked infrastructure as possible. For example, either side of a bridge connects to a road. Make that somebody else's responsibility and avoid the construction and maintenance costs of owning the feeder roads unless those costs can be reflected in a level of toll charges that the user (the motorist) will accept. The Dartford Crossing is the best example of what has already been achieved in project financing privately owned infrastructure in the UK. Any second Severn Bridge is expected to be similarly financed. Future opportunities may include the much discussed private toll motorways.

Similar projects are also under consideration across Western Europe. The Orly-Val Mass Transit line in Paris has already been project financed and a number of other light-transit urban systems are viewed as candidates for private ownership – and project finance. Again, the thrust is to find a discrete, manageable transportation link avoiding the uncertainties inherent in broad networks. For the larger scale, high cost ventures – for example, the long high-speed rail links being built or under consideration between the major European cities – there is the distinct possibility that some combination of government funding and private investment (and funding) can achieve a similar goal of greater efficiency and profitability while reducing the burden on government spending.

This trend towards private ownership of infrastructure spreads beyond Western Europe. Privatisation is an element of government policy in Malaysia, the Philippines, Singapore, Thailand, Turkey and certain African and Latin American countries. Turkey in particular should be mentioned because it has been perhaps the most visible and regular proponent of an approach to developing national priority infrastructural and other projects known as BOOT or BOT. The acronyms stand for 'build, own, operate and transfer' or 'build, operate and transfer' but are essentially synonymous.

It will be remembered that, in discussing the Channel Tunnel project, reference was made to a 50-year concession. The Channel Tunnel is not owned by private investors in perpetuity. At the end of 50 years, the governments of Britain and France can choose to take the link back into government control. This is the basis on which BOOT or BOT projects, projects of national importance, are given up to private ownership. Turkey has encouraged the use of this structure for a broad range of infrastructural projects as well as electric power facilities and certain other kinds of processing plant (eg fertilisers) considered to be of national, social and economic importance – and hitherto funded directly by government.

Reflecting the overall BOOT/BOT concept, project finance structures have been developed which range from pure non-recourse lending through all of the variants of partially credit-supported limited-recourse finance. There is a difference between the Channel Tunnel project (based in the highly stable political environment of Western Europe) and projects based in the developing or less-developed countries. In the latter case, where laws and regulations are not long-established and governments tend to be more volatile and interventionist, there may be a requirement for the government to guarantee certain arrangements reducing the risks to which the project and its lenders are exposed. For example, given that infrastructural projects by their nature generate local currency revenues, it is often required that foreign exchange convertibility guarantees must be provided by the central bank of the country in question to ensure that local revenues can be used to repay foreign currency debt. In some cases, the government is required to undertake that no competing project will be developed until debt has been repaid on the current project. If project cash flows are to be generated from a politically sensitive market (for example, road tolls in a poor country), the government may be required to guarantee a minimum level of revenue. Often the government is one of the sponsors investing in the project, providing equity and other undertakings necessary to make the project economic.

Private ownership participation in infrastructure and other national priority projects, partial or outright, is an enormous stride forward in relieving governments of a significant proportion of their traditional budget spending requirements. Importantly also, private ownership generally leads to more cost-effective construction and efficient operation. There is an accountability so often lost in large government works. Project finance plays its (large) part in this.

2 Developed countries and a new world order – new places for project finance opportunity

Much of what has been said in this chapter so far deals with the new *types* of projects being financed and the flexibility with which the techniques of project finance have been used to meet new opportunities. We will now focus on the *location* where these opportunities have arisen and where they are likely to be found in the future.

Perhaps the most striking feature of recent years has been the number of projects and project financings undertaken in the developed countries – of North America and Europe, in particular. The economic difficulties of Latin America and the resultant constraints on bank lenders' appetite to provide new credit have already been mentioned. Similar problems, exacerbated by unstable political conditions (economic and political instability often go hand in hand), have affected the amount of lending, including project finance, made available to the countries of Africa. Bureaucratic hurdles have often been at the root of lenders' ambivalence to hot pursuit of opportunities in the Indian sub-continent.

The prime reason for the revival of project lending in the developed countries has been the trend towards privatisation discussed in this chapter. In Europe, this is likely to be fuelled by the growth and increasing integration of the European Economic Community. The Channel Tunnel is the most visible example of inter-governmental co-operation. More can be expected for infrastructural development such as high-speed rail links, electrical power grids and cross-border gas pipelines.

The dismantling of Communist power in Eastern Europe and the redefinition of the social, economic and political characteristics of Eastern European countries will provide many opportunities for project finance. Already, the massive cost of infrastructural improvements in what was East Germany have become clear. Government budgets will be stretched to extremes and there will certainly be a place for co-operation between governments and private enterprise sharing the financial burden. Where a viable project can be wholly or partially developed by private sponsors, project lenders will be sought to provide funding and share in the risks. The biggest challenge will be to develop project finance structures which deal effectively with the political risks inherent in lending to countries where constitutional, civil and legal procedures are new and unstable. Business law, taxation, import/export regulations, currency convertibility – these all have an impact on the viability of a given project and project lenders require a level of certainty that the rules are clear, established and unlikely to change. The experience of Latin America's problems and the losses incurred from writing off bad debts is too recent for lenders to consider the political risks lightly.

Having said this, there is an argument to be made that lending to a specific project is, all other things being equal, a better risk than general purpose lending to a government obligor when economic and political disturbances occur. Of course, there is the risk of governmental interference or even expropriation if a particular project is a vital and successful earning asset and the government of the day sees a 'quick fix' to its problems by diverting cash flows by whatever means. However, there is a substantial history of project lenders in a given country continuing to receive debt repayments from a successful project while sovereign lenders accepted a delay or moratorium on payments.

Since project finance generally offers greater earnings returns to lenders than general corporate or government lending, and in recognition of the argument that specific project lending can have the advantage of being insulated to some extent from the broader political environment, project lenders have revived their interest in lending to Latin American and African projects. Albeit selectively, they can again be found lending to, for example, oil and gas projects in Venezuela or Nigeria.

However, project lenders have learnt some lessons from previous experience. Today, a key structural component will often be the ability to collect the payments made by a foreign buyer of the project's output into an escrow account outside the country where the project is located. This enables the lender to avoid the risk that cash generated from product sales made by the project may be frozen as a result of government-imposed restrictions on outward flows. If the buyer is paying in hard currencies, the lender has no risk through the local currency except to the extent that some of the funds held in the escrow account must be made available to pay the project's operating and other costs. To the extent that these costs are local-currency denominated, there is still, of course, the foreign exchange risk of how much local currency the hard currency will buy.

In many cases, outward flows have already been frozen although the sovereign obligor has made repayments which the lenders concerned must leave on deposit with the local central bank or otherwise within the domestic financial system. This has given rise to consideration of so-called debt-for-debt swaps. Rather than leave the money stranded in a low-earning deposit, bank lenders would re-lend to specific projects which generate a higher return. The interest can be paid to the lender and, in time, the principal as well. Alternatively, an offshore escrow account structure would allow for payment of principal on a current basis. A further variant on this approach is the debt-for-equity swap where lenders would replace a debt instrument with an investment in a local project. Of course, these techniques are only worth the time and effort where it is considered that the local national economy is on an improving trend and free flow of funds will eventually be reinstated, or where the offshore escrow account structure is permitted by the government of the country where the project is located. While only a few projects (in Latin America) have been financed utilising the swap concept, there is clearly potential in pursuing the approach.

3 Mega-projects, capital market capacity and the banks' response – increased scope for project financiers' involvement

The reference to bank equity investments brings us to the third major influence on the direction of project finance today – the *scale* of bank involvement in structuring and participating in the capital structure required for a given project. As this chapter has indicated, the last 20 years have seen massive growth in project lending, predominantly from banks. In tandem with the increase in the number of projects which have been financed on a limited – or non-recourse basis, the sheer size, in terms of capital cost, of a typical project has also grown substantially. When BP's Forties Field in the North Sea was financed in 1971 with almost $1 billion equivalent in borrowings, it was by far the largest funding ever raised. It remained so for many years. Today, we can look back on the Channel Tunnel (£5 billion equivalent in facilities), Woodside Petroleum's North West Shelf gas project in Australia (US$1.7 billion), Euro Disney's Theme Park in France (FFr 7 billion) and many more where borrowings are raised in billions, not millions.

Where possible, and appropriate, the funding package for these mega-projects is provided not only by banks (who nevertheless provide the lion's share) but also by other government and multinational agencies and institutions such as export credit agencies, the World Bank, the International Finance Corporation (IFC), the European Investment Bank (EIB) and so on. Until recently, the banks were the sole lenders of limited – or non-recourse credit but some of the above-mentioned sources of debt are developing programmes under which they too will consider taking project risk.

As the size and diversity of projects increases, project lending banks are often appointed to advise the project sponsors on optimum capital structure and, as a result, optimum sources of funding to be tapped. Increasingly, this advice (and the arrangement role which follows) encompasses both debt and equity. Broadly speaking, the advisers and arrangers of the debt and equity components were traditionally separate – commercial banks took care of the debt, merchant or investment banks specialised in the equity. In the US, this distinction was, until recently, a legal requirement arising from the provisions of the Glass-Steagall Act. The separation of commercial and investment banking activity imposed by this Act is rapidly being dismantled. In Europe and Asia no such firm legal divide ever existed and, particularly in Continental Europe, banks have never been prohibited from lending to and, at the same time, investing in the equity of a given enterprise. The traditional separation was therefore more the result of specialisation, a perception of 'horses for courses' which was self-perpetuating. For projects, the blurring of these historical roles can lead to the appointment of a sole adviser/arranger who can provide the benefits of 'one-stop shopping'. The project sponsor and adviser work together from start to finish in developing and implementing project structure. Furthermore, there are often cost savings to be made for the sponsor in avoiding the route of multiple advisers and, therefore, multiple fees.

Perhaps the most exciting outcome of the broadening of banks' involvement in project capital structure is the trend towards banks actually taking a piece of the equity themselves. Although the roots of this interest are the 'equity kicker' – the issue to lenders of an equity-like instrument in a relatively small nominal amount and with little or no cash component designed to provide some potential enhancement to the basic return generated from lending – there are signs that banks will more actively consider investing hard cash equity in projects. Banks have already done this in financing leveraged buy-outs (LBOs) and, in many cases, made substantial profits as a result. Most projects will not provide the same level of equity return potential as an LBO but as banks look to improve returns achieved on traditional lines of business (like project finance) the opportunities will not be ignored. Banks have taken equity in the Channel Tunnel and the Dartford Crossing. They have also made (admittedly limited) investments in oil and gas developments in the United States and elsewhere. Mega-projects require a large amount of debt and equity. Consortia of project sponsors – industrial corporations, contractors, banks and other financial institutions – spreading the equity risk and solving the problems of market capacity, are increasingly common.

Project financing today

In considering the new influences on project financing we have looked at the *type*, *location* and *scale* of projects today. We have seen the importance of the trend towards private sponsorship of projects which had hitherto been viewed as part of the public, governmental domain and the major role which project financiers are playing as a result.

In addition, traditional project lending – for hydrocarbons, minerals, ships, aircraft, property – continues. But it is in the adaptation of project finance techniques, on a limited or non-recourse basis, to new industries and technologies, new business parameters and to new demands for imaginative solutions to problems of sheer scale, that project finance has demonstrated its maturity and its important place in enabling successful new economic developments in a rapidly changing world.

Brian Weight was a graduate of Trinity College, Cambridge University in 1972, gaining his MA in 1976. He joined J P Morgan in London and worked for the bank in Singapore, Australia and New York before returning to London in 1984. He was an energy and project finance specialist between 1977 and 1989, most recently Head of European Project Finance. He has been closely involved in or responsible for over 60 project advisory and finance mandates. He featured as team leader for a complex Indonesian project financing in the chapter on J P Morgan in *Behind Closed Doors*, a book on banking innovation. He is currently Head of European Credit Portfolio with a continuing consultative role in project finance.

Part 2
Tried and true, and still valid

3 Ship finance

Taco Th van der Mast, J P Morgan

1 Introduction

Shipping is one of world's oldest, best known but least understood industries. Yet it was and is vital to the development of the world economy. Transportation by sea still provides the cheapest method of mass transportation of goods over long distances. Financing this industry, which is surrounded by romantic connotations of wealthy tycoons, high profits and distant shores, is a specialist business. Where it concerns secured lending for one or more vessels, it presents the lender with a multitude of generic risks and is project financing in its purest form.

Shipping is one of the last industries where the principles of free competition and open markets still reign to a great extent. It is an industry which therefore attracts both individual and corporate entrepreneurs. The members of the international shipping community tend to know exactly what happens elsewhere, who is buying or selling ships and what freight rates are obtained. Shipping is very much a people business, a business with very special people.

When wondering what influences the state of the health of the international shipping business, one should realise that the development of the availability of transportable cargo itself has historically not been the factor most important to the industry's well-being. Although they of course were of influence, the fluctuations in the world economy have not held back the total volume of cargo shipped by sea from virtually continuous growth. The supply of tonnage is probably the main factor deciding the state of health of the industry at any one time. Because of this, and because of the fact that newbuilding activity tends to happen in sudden spurts, shipping is a highly cyclical industry. Capital is its main entry barrier.

Building a new, or even buying a used ship involves large sums of money. Although shipping is often associated with personal wealth, traditionally the asset-financed part of the shipping industry has been highly leveraged. Financing rates of 75–80% of acquisition value are no exception. Banks have therefore always played an important role in the business life of a ship owner. When realising that this high leverage is combined with an industry with a high volatility in its income streams, one can understand that the financing of shipping should be practised with great care and firm credit principles.

Ship financing can be practised on an unsecured basis, relying on the corporate balance sheet of a major, often listed, corporation, with the added comfort of covenants and negative pledges. Most ships, however, are financed on the traditional basis of a loan secured by a mortgage on the vessel, often with additional security from the ultimate owning company. As only this last type of ship financing is genuine project finance, this is what will be concentrated on in the context of this chapter.

2 Summary

In this chapter the subject of ship finance will be treated in such a way as to give an overview of the issues arising when structuring the financing of shipping projects. All issues which play a role in general project financing are also applicable in the case of shipping projects but here the more specific shipping related issues will be concentrated on.

Based upon historical development, the characteristics of the industry and an explanation of the economics of shipping and the way vessel employment generates income, the case is made for a *cash flow* rather than asset-based structuring and risk assessment. After an overview of structuring items for cash flow-based ship financing and a discussion of the various ways of providing security for shipping loans, a number of recent developments are mentioned which increase the risk profile of ship finance. Finally, alternatives are discussed relating to problem solving and the various ways open to the lender in the case of failure of the project.

3 History

Shipping was one of the first industries to attract outside investor funding. When for example the first East India companies were set up in the Netherlands to fit out their ships setting sail for the Indies at the end of the sixteenth-century, their founders looked for investors to provide the means. The object of financing, however, was not the vessel but rather the expedition to the Far East to find and bring back the cargo. The investors took an equity position or 'part' in the financial return on the cargo brought back. If the ship was lost, so was their money. They were equity providers, not debt financiers.

Most of the earlier companies were each in principle set up with respect to one project, a particular expedition. When the earlier companies merged into one and the United Dutch East India Company was formally incorporated in 1602, it became one of the world's first corporations with liability limited by shares and an open-ended life. At a later stage, when merchant bankers and traders all over Europe financed the acquisition and fitting out of vessels through taking one or more of 64 'parts' in a vessel, what they really financed was still an equity stake in the cargo.

The business in which the owners of ships were active was trading, not ship owning. The vessel was merely a tool to carry out the project of finding, importing or exporting the cargo and making a profit thereon. This situation lasted for a long time and, to a degree, still persists, for example in the case of oil companies, grain houses and car makers. Only in the last century ship owners per se emerged, providing a pure transportation service to third parties, but often still engaged in trading themselves. The taking a of a 'part' in a vessel also still persists and is used in Norway, Germany, France and the Netherlands, although it is today partially driven by tax-based motivations and often takes the form of a limited partnership.

Concepts similar to ship mortgages were known in the days of the expeditions to the East. Although not used to provide security to the financiers of the vessel or the expedition (as they were really equity holders), the contract of 'bottomry', which dates back to the days of the ancient Greeks ('nautikon danaion') and Romans ('foenis nauticum'), was used to finance working capital for the vessel, especially in a foreign port, to enable it to complete the voyage. Under bottomry, the owner or the captain of a ship could pledge the vessel or its keel as security for an advance. After safe completion of the voyage, the principal had to be paid back together with a high rate of interest. Rates of 30% or more were common. A specific difference with today's ship mortgage, however, is that the loan or advance under bottomry was not repaid in the case of loss of a vessel. Again, there was an element of equity risk in this financing.

Secured ship financing as we know it today in particular developed during this century. One great difference between the current situation and that before the Second World War, is that leverage generally was much lower. The equity content of projects was higher, while on the other hand the shipping markets' volatility was lower.

4 Industry characteristics

As mentioned in the introduction to this chapter, ship finance and its structuring should be specifically geared to the characteristics of the shipping industry. These characteristics revolve around the following features: the cyclicality of shipping markets, a persistent lack of equity, continuous over-leveraging, all of which often result in the occurrence of liquidity squeezes with many ship-owning companies. For the lender it is therefore important to base both his credit decision and the transaction structure on cash flow analysis as opposed to purely asset-based lending criteria.

There is a direct relationship between the industry particularities mentioned above and the fact that there are not many publicly listed pure shipping companies and that, with a small number of exceptions, the credit rating of most shipping companies does not reach investment grade levels.

5 Types of shipping

In order to understand the business of shipping and the impact of the risks involved for the financier, it is important to distinguish between the various ways in which shipping is practised and to note the commercial and financial consequences of these differences. The way in which cash flow is generated under various scenarios is particularly important from both a repayment and a security point of view.

A Liner shipping

Liner vessels are operated in a scheduled service on a fixed route between two ports or series of ports. The cost of carriage of cargo is subject to a fixed tariff. Operators of liner services will usually accept any quantity of cargo above a certain minimum size or weight. Although liner vessels would historically be suited for general cargo or breakbulk, these days many liner routes are partly or fully containerised. Passenger and freight ferry shipping is also a form of liner shipping.

Liner companies operating on the same route often organise into *freight conferences* to regulate competitive practices and to stabilise and set freight rates. The conferences will normally also regulate how much cargo each conference member is allowed to carry on a specific route. Although the operator loses some of his independence, he gains the advantage of avoiding competitive rate wars. The conferences re-set their rates regularly in conjunction with the market situation. Liner companies participating in the trade on the same route as the conference members without becoming members themselves are generally referred to as *outsiders*.

Operationally, each liner vessel usually forms part of the liner operator's total service network, which may include stevedoring, warehousing, distribution, road transportation and an integrated data control system. The cargo-carrying contract is normally entered into by the line, regardless of which of the line's vessels will actually be carrying the goods. This is why financing a liner vessel cannot be seen separate from the operator's total business operation, since it is the cash flow from that business, not from any ship in particular, which services the debt. As a result of this practice, it is difficult to perfect efficiently an assignment of a particular liner vessel's earnings to a financial institution.

B Tramp shipping

In tramp shipping, the vessel is chartered as a whole, on a voyage charter or time charter basis and is in principle prepared to take anything anywhere, as directed by the charterer, who himself takes the risk of being able to obtain a full or part cargo. The cost of hire is determined by conditions on the open market. Dry bulk carriers and tankers tend to be operated in this way. The cash flow generated from a tramp shipping operation is identifiable and can be allocated to a particular ship. An assignment to a lender can therefore easily be perfected.

C Special purpose shipping

Certain vessels are built for a particular purpose and are operated in particular trades, often on a contract basis by the party controlling the cargo. Examples are: car carriers, liquefied natural gas carriers, refrigerated cargo carriers, forest products carriers and offshore supply vessels. The cash flow from the operation of special purpose vessels is often independent from open shipping market conditions and more directly related to the particular industry in which the vessel is employed. Financing risk is in such cases not necessarily a shipping industry risk, but rather a risk associated with the employer's industry. This kind of shipping is also referred to as *industrial shipping*.

D Cruise shipping

Cruise shipping is in itself a form of special purpose or industrial shipping. Its earnings are not associated with the shipping markets but much more with the hotel, tourism and leisure industries. Although certain risk factors are the same as for ship financing transactions, particularly those relating to a newbuilding, the cash flow risks of cruise shipping are not related to the transportation markets and financing should therefore be dealt with on an individual project financing basis, much like the financing of a hotel or leisure project. Cruise shipping will therefore be ignored in this chapter.

6 Types of vessel employment

A ship owner has various alternative ways to employ his vessel. Some of these are dictated by the custom of the particular trade, some are dictated by the type of vessel he seeks to employ. The risk and cash flow characteristics of the various ways to employ a vessel are crucial to the structure of a financing arrangement. It is therefore important to understand which types of typical contractual relationships exist between ship owner and shipper. The most commonly used types of employment are the following:

- Voyage charter
- Time charter
- Bareboat charter
- Contract of affreightment

The main differences between these types of employment are to be found in the determination of which party takes on which risks and who pays for which costs, as well as the typical duration of the employment. The differences between these various forms of contract are important for the financier to understand as they form the basis for his debt service cash flow and determine its volatility and risk pattern.

A Voyage charter

In the case of a voyage charter, the ship owner contracts to transport a certain quantity of cargo, usually taking up the entire carrying capacity of the vessel, during a single voyage or an agreed number of voyages, from one port to one or more other ports. The charterer pays the freight at a certain rate per ton of cargo carried and is responsible for loading and discharging costs. The owner pays for all vessel running costs and for voyage costs such as fuel and the remaining port expenses.

Voyage charter parties are commonly used for general dry cargoes as well as for oil tanker chartering. As voyage charters usually only last for a relatively short period of time, for the financier the only security provided by this kind of charter is to be found in an assignment of the freight payment. Since the earnings of one voyage will only pay off a small portion of debt and as there is no certainty of a follow-up cargo, an assignment of the freight resulting from this kind of employment should never be the sole basis for a financing decision by a lender.

B Time charter

A time charter is a contract whereby the charterer contracts for his use of the vessel for a certain period of time. Within this period, the charterer is responsible for the voyage costs, fuel, port charges, canal dues and pays a hire based on a fixed sum per day. The ship owner remains responsible for the daily running cost such as crew's wages and victualling, maintenance and insurance. It is the charterer who provides the master of the vessel with voyage instructions. He arranges for the cargo and the hire is independent of what quantity of cargo is actually carried.

Time charters are used in the dry bulk and tanker trades, but also by liner companies who charter in additional tonnage to sail in their scheduled services. The typical period for time charters ranges from six months or one year (with options to extend by similar periods) to a number of years. An exception is the spot or trip time charter, which is a single voyage carried out on a time charter basis. Because of their longer-term nature, time charters to financially solid charterers can form the basis of a financing. Particularly long-term time charters to major oil importers or exporters, as a result of the stable and predictable cash flows they generate, can be a useful means of providing the owners with a higher level of financing than would otherwise be acceptable to a lender.

An assignment of the earnings from a relatively long time charter can provide substantial comfort to a lender. For example, it may provide assurance that the first portion of a repayment schedule will be met and that the debt is reduced to a level where it is more acceptable for the lender to be exposed to market risk.

C Bareboat charter

A bareboat charter is best compared to a net lease arrangement. The ship owner lets his ship to the charterer for a long period and the charterer arranges and is responsible for all costs, including insurance, crewing, maintenance, fuel and voyage costs. The owner retains no operational responsibility whatsoever and the master of the vessel is employed by the charterer.

As a bareboat charter is basically a financial arrangement, it is an ideal tool for structuring a financing. With added purchase options or obligations, it can be made to suit virtually any financing structure.

For tankers, its future as a financing tool has been put into doubt as a result of the Oil Pollution Act of 1990 ('OPA 90') in the US, which makes the lessor of a vessel liable for pollution claims. This will render it unattractive for financial institutions or investors to act as a lessor, even more so if they are US-based.

D Contract of affreightment

This is a contract for a series of voyage charters, normally on a consecutive basis, against a certain, pre-determined freight which may be open for re-negotiation after a certain period of time. It can relate to a specific vessel but it can also leave the ship owner free to provide a vessel of a certain size or quality.

Contracts of affreightment are used for the tanker and dry bulk trades but also for certain specialist trades. For example, owners of refrigerated cargo vessels, car carriers or chemical tankers often enter into a contract with a shipper to transport his goods at a fixed rate during a particular period of time, whereby the shipper guarantees a certain minimum amount of cargo. As such contracts may not cover full employment for the vessel during the period, they only guarantee a minimal cash flow level. From the viewpoint of the lender, they still expose the shipowner to the volatility of the open market.

E 'Hell-or-high water' charters

Certain long-term time charters or bareboat charters are written with the intention that they should be unbreakable. Often such charters relate to projects where an assured flow of cargo exists in conjunction with a supply contract, such as oil, coal or ore exports and imports or liquefied natural gas projects.

These so-called 'hell-or-high water' charters can provide an ideal basis for long-term ship financing. If structured as a time charter, they usually provide the owner with a fixed profit, while certain maximum increases in cost can be put through to the charterer by an increase in the hire. Although normally these contracts will run for their full period, it is by no means unusual that the charterer under such contracts attempts to renegotiate the charter in case of a change in the situation of the underlying project. It is therefore important for the potential lender to ascertain the contractual situation through legal opinions from specialist lawyers, ideally during the stage before the contract is entered into by the shipowner.

Types of ship finance

A Financing the acquisition of second-hand tonnage

Most project-related shipping financing transactions relate to acquisition of second-hand tonnage. It is a peculiarity of the shipping industry that ship owners often ultimately make the required return on their capital only through the sale of the asset at the right time rather than through operating profits generated. Sale and purchase decisions are therefore often driven by asset values at certain moments in time. As a result, it is not unusual for a vessel to change hands several times during its lifetime. Even newbuildings are sometimes resold before their delivery from the yard.

The amounts involved in the acquisition of a used vessel are usually lower than those of newbuildings which means that the amounts to be financed are also lower. As prices of newbuildings and second-hand vessels are driven by the same dynamics of supply and demand, their prices fluctuate in the same way. Thus historically it has happened that a newbuilding, upon its delivery, could only command a resale price which was a fraction of the original building cost.

In itself, the financing of a second-hand vessel does not have to involve more risk than that of a newbuilding. The pre-delivery risk which differentiates newbuilding financing and which is discussed below, is non-existent.

Obviously, the age of a vessel comes into play for a financing decision as the debt service has to be met from future earnings. The net present value of a vessel's perceived future earnings also has a direct relationship with its current market value. These future earnings in turn depend on the acceptability of the vessel in chartering markets. For a ship of up to 15 years old there is normally no problem as long as it is fully in compliance with the requirements of its *classification society* (an independent organisation issuing certificates confirming a vessel's seaworthiness and its general compliance with the society's regulations, inspecting the vessel regularly.) After such age, and particularly after an age of 20 years, charterers may have to pay additional premiums for the insurance of their cargo.

The remaining economic life of a vessel is therefore important to the financier. The quality of a vessel's construction and particularly of its maintenance determine its remaining economical life and potential future earnings much more than purely its age. The assessment of these factors is as important to the financier as it is to a potential charterer. Many charterers, particularly oil companies, carry out rigorous inspection programmes, whereby they will accept a certain ship for a certain period of time. Financiers can also engage an independent surveyor to carry out an inspection and assess the condition of a vessel they have financed or will finance.

B Financing newbuildings

The risks involved in newbuilding financing are similar to those for financing existing ships with the main exception in the pre-delivery phase, as will be explained below. One difference which normally manifests itself, however, is the amount to be financed. This is the direct result of the high building costs. Because they provide the necessary credit enhancement in an industry so devoid of equity, it is particularly in the financing of newbuildings that long-term charter commitments from first class charterers are valuable.

It is difficult for a potential lender to assume that the average required time charter equivalent needed to service a substantial debt on a newbuilding will be available throughout the life of the loan. Careful and conservative projecting of cash flows is therefore necessary to determine the maximum level of financing. It is unlikely that a lender would assume that, for a 280,000 dwt very large crude carrier, which costs US$ 100 million to build, there would be available on the open spot market over a full period of eight years the average time charter equivalent of over US$ 45,000 per day (which is the level required to service and repay a financing of 50%) if he knows that these rates have over the last ten years fluctuated between US$ 10,000 per day and US$ 40,000 per day. A medium or long-term contract from a credit-worthy oil major would therefore be a useful incentive for a financier to accept a level of financing which would otherwise not be achievable without a substantial equity contribution.

C Leasing

Leasing is mainly used for the financing of vessels which have long-term fixed employment and where the lessor is willing to take some of the residual value risk. It has however never been as popular for vessel financing as it is in the financing of aircraft. This was partly the result of the lack of sufficient long-term contracts to back up the lease structure, partly it was a matter of most lessors not being able to cope with the residual value risk as a result of the sometimes wildly fluctuating second-hand values of vessels. Pure operating leases, where the residual value risk remains with the lessor, and particularly tax-based international leasing structures which pass on the tax-saving to the ship owners, are an exception and can provide benefits for ship owners. With complex put and call options structured into the lease, some of the residual value risk can often be dealt with.

Given the present structure of the shipping industry and its volatility, the number of ship owners who would qualify for leasing transactions is limited. With the advent of OPA 90, which makes the lessor of any type of vessel liable for pollution damages under this new legislation, the appetite for financial institutions to act as lessors is also diminishing. In theory, and in particular if the OPA 90 problem can be solved, lease-structured ship financing should still have a future. There certainly is a requirement for off balance sheet financing by many of the major ship operators and it is one of the few ways in which the lack of equity, which is so prevalent in the shipping industry, can be dealt with.

D Subsidised financing

A number of countries subsidise the acquisition or, more particularly, the construction of ships. Subsidised newbuilding financing is generally geared to support the local shipbuilding industry and is provided through a local development bank or import-export bank and normally takes place along the lines of the model agreed by the OECD-countries to avoid excessive competition among the ship-exporting nations over the terms of ship export credits.

Typical OECD financing provides funds of up to 80% of the building cost, with a term of eight and a half years from delivery, repayable in equal six-monthly or annual instalments and at an interest rate of 8%, net of all charges. The export-import bank may make the financing available directly to the purchaser or through a supplier credit to the shipbuilder. It usually requires as security either a mortgage on the vessel, or, more frequently as it does not want to concern itself with the credit risk of the purchaser, a letter of credit or bank guarantee from a first class recognised bank, which bank can then secure itself through a mortgage.

Shipyard subsidies can also take the form of the yard obtaining a subsidy directly in order to be able to match pricing offered by countries with cheaper labour. Other forms of subsidised financing are also available with country-specific restrictions. In Belgium for example, other than soft loans or direct subsidies made available to the shipyards, it is possible for ship owners building a vessel at a Belgian yard to obtain soft loan financing at a very low interest rate, but the financing is made available in Belgian francs and the vessel must use a Belgian crew for a certain period of time. In such cases, owners are well-advised to calculate thoroughly the effects of such financings on their business, especially in the light of their cost structure under their usual flag and taking into account the cost of hedging currency risks. As country-specific programmes are usually politically driven, they are subject to continuous change and their availability should be monitored from time to time.

8 Credit analysis: ship finance is cash flow-based

Ship finance structures are mainly based around term loans. When structuring these loans, the most important factor to be kept in mind is that of the cash flow of the project. A loan should be structured in such a way that the projected cash flow from the vessel over the term of the loan can reasonably be expected to service the debt and provide the source for its repayment. Below, the most salient elements of a typical shipping term loan will be discussed. Before coming to this, the all-important subject of shipping cash flow must be explained.

A Cash flow lending versus asset-based financing

Historically, it has often been assumed, by both ship owners and bankers, that when a financier advanced funds for the financing of a vessel and obtained a mortgage in return, the value of the asset was the main comfort he looked to as security. Policies for levels of financing were therefore often expressed as a percentage of the acquisition price or the value of a vessel. In certain cases today this is still the view of some owners and even of some bankers and their credit committees. It is the wrong approach.

A loan is repaid from the *cash flow* which the asset, in this case, the vessel, can generate to service interest and repayment of principal. It is not repaid from the value of the asset. The value of the asset serves as a back-up in case a problem develops with the cash flow of the loan. A lending decision should be based on the economics of the project, on the projections made by owner and lender as to the revenues and cost during the period of the financing, and on the level of financing which can be supported by the resulting cash flows, while building up and maintaining a comfortable level of liquidity to provide a buffer during periods of poor shipping markets.

As revenue levels in most shipping transactions are highly cyclical (the exceptions will be discussed later), the projections made should include a realistic downside case based upon historical information for the particular trades in which the vessel operates. The use of computer-based cash flow projection modelling has made these projections manageable for both owner and lender.

Promoting cash flows as the basis for ship finance does not mean that the asset value and the maintenance thereof is wholly unimportant. As second-hand market values of vessels fluctuate, it is usual for the lender to require a *minimum value clause*, which allows the lender to be able to ask for top-up of security or a partial prepayment if the market value of the vessel falls below a certain pre-determined percentage of principal outstanding. This does not, however, make up for financing on the basis of a conservatively projected cash flow element, as often the value of the vessel drops when the cash flow reduces and the owner may not have the means to provide the top-up or make the prepayment.

Scrap values (the value of the vessel's steel weight at a given time) are also often used to provide comfort to the lender. This may be acceptable when determining the level of a final balloon payment for a term loan. In such case the cautious lender will use conservative assumptions of scrap metal prices, which historically have tended to show a high volatility, linked to both the level of activity in the steel industry and the tonnage on offer for scrapping. As the two are economically inter-related (low steel production can cause poor shipping markets and therefore may encourage owners to scrap), it has not been uncommon for the first to be low while the latter was high.

B Cash flow projections

The income and cost structure of a shipping project is distinguished by the elements of cyclicality and unpredictability. A lender must therefore run his own projections and make his own assumptions for future market fluctuations and cost increases. This requires an understanding of the particular shipping market in which the subject vessel will operate and the reasons for its historical fluctuations. It also requires an understanding of the composition of the running cost for the particular type of vessel, in combination with an assessment of the way in which the prospective ship owner manages his fleet and controls his costs. This understanding is required to deal with the *operating risk* of the shipping project.

Assessing the income stream is made easier if the project concerned is supported by long-term charters, either on a time charter or bareboat charter basis. If the charterer and his business has a higher credit rating than the ship owner, and if the charter party (the charter contract) has a reasonable level of 'unbreakability', this obviously makes projecting the income cash stream easier. An example of such contracts are the 'take or pay' shipping contracts relating to certain liquefied natural gas ('LNG') export projects. Such LNG contracts typically have a life of 15 to 20 years, are usually covered by the credit risk of the exporters, usually major oil companies, and provide that hire is payable whether gas is available for shipment or not.

C Cash flow modelling

Computers greatly facilitate the credit assessment of a shipping project. They allow the prospective lender or the arranger to create projections of income streams and cost developments under various scenarios, which then results in the *cash flow available for debt service* or 'CFADS'. From this CFADS, the projected debt service and repayment structure can then be deducted in order to assess its influence on the working capital liquidity of the project. Using different assumptions of income, cost, interest rates, repayment schedules, balloon payments, term and starting liquidity, the most ideal financing structure can be created or, as the case may be, it can be concluded that the project carries too much cash flow risk.

D Cash flow modelling – the income side of a shipping project

A certain degree of conservatism should be considered by a lender when modelling cash flows. Time charter hire is paid in a certain amount (usually in US dollars) per day. The charter will allow the charterer to put the vessel *off-hire* for the period it is not available to him, generally for technical reasons, for example as a result of maintenance or drydocking. A downside case should always assume a reasonable number of days off-hire. This number will vary with the kind of vessel and employment but the historical performance of the ship owner in this respect should provide a reasonable starting point.

In the case of no certain hire pattern as a result of a charter commitment, the income assumptions should be based upon (a) the expectation of market developments, supply and demand assumptions and the development of tonnage supply and transportation patterns and (b) historical fluctuations. There is a wide-ranging availability of general and specific statistics, studies and other information which can be used on the input side of a cash flow model and using these, scenarios can be developed to test the ability of the project to service the debt and in particular its ability to provide and maintain that most important of items in shipping cash flow: *liquidity*.

E Cash flow modelling – the cost side of a shipping project

No cash flow can be modelled from the income side only and due consideration should be given to the cost side of the shipping project. The cost side can probably be more accurately assessed than the income side, as most of its component parts, with some exceptions, have shown an historically logical development.

The direct costs of operating a vessel are generally referred to as *daily running costs*. These costs can be expressed in a fixed budgeted amount per day and are not conditional upon the quantity of cargo carried, the speed of the vessel or the costs of the ports visited. They consist of the following items:

- Costs of crew wages
- Victualling and provisions
- Stores and lubricating oils
- Cost of technical maintenance
- Accrual for drydocking expenses (depending on the owner's method of budgeting)
- Ship management/overhead charges
- Insurance

The *crew cost* will depend on the flag of the vessel (further discussed below) and the nationality of the crew. It increases as a result of developments in industrial relations and general inflation and certain assumptions can be made as to the development of crew cost. *Victualling and provisions* are directly related to the composition of the crew and to the efficiency of the ship owner's ship management operation. For the cost of technical *maintenance* and of *stores and lubricating oils* the owner's operational track record should provide a basis for acceptance of his budgeting.

The cost of drydocking is sometimes accrued for in the running costs but in some cases is budgeted for fully in the year in which it occurs. In recent years, these costs have risen substantially. While the world fleet ages, a number of owners have faced drydocking bills which were substantially higher than expected and have therefore run into cash flow problems. Although many of the extra costs are recoverable from insurance, many others are not, and the ship owner himself always has to deal with the deductible of his insurance coverage. When modelling a cash flow, drydocking costs should be handled with a healthy dose of conservatism.

Ship management and overhead charges are an important factor in the assessment of the cash flow of a shipping project and they are sometimes *the* factor which makes or breaks the success of a project or of a shipping company. Many ship owners control these costs as efficiently as they control the more direct operating costs of the vessel but in a number of cases the overheads have been allowed to surge, either as a result of lack of efficient control or simply as the result of an unchanged organisation managing a shrinking fleet.

In a ship financing on a project basis it is therefore prudent to restrict in the loan documentation the ship management cost and overheads which the owner's ship management organisation can allocate to the particular vessel, with a fixed increment per year. The level of such costs can always be compared with the cost which reputable independent ship managers quote for managing vessels of the same type for third parties.

F Asset quality and cash flow

Asset quality is not just determined by the actual technical condition of a vessel but also by the quality of its technical management. A prospective lender should satisfy himself as to both before, as well as during, the life of a project. The evolving environmental protection legislation has added to the importance of this aspect as a high standard of maintenance and safety policies have a major impact on the reduction of the environmental risk.

A vessel's condition is continuously assessed by its classification society for purposes of insurance and marine safety. Records can be inspected and an independent surveyor can make a detailed report on technical condition at a relatively low cost. It is wise for any shipping lender to assess regularly the condition of its fleet in this way, not solely with respect to the maintenance of the collateral value of the asset financed, but more particularly in relation to the maintenance of a vessel's cash flow generating capacity.

The assessment of the quality of ship management is more difficult for the lender. Although major oil companies now frequently carry out 'ship management audits' with owners whose vessels they charter, a financial institution is less geared to carry out such an audit. The lender must therefore obtain a thorough understanding of the owner's ship management policies and practices, his general instructions to the masters of his vessels, standing policies with respect to safety and pollution prevention and the frequency with which crews are changed. Apart from being directly linked to the operating risk of the project, the quality and efficiency of ship management has a great influence over the cash flow generated available to service debt.

9 Credit structuring

Whether financing is required for newbuildings or for second-hand vessel acquisition, the term loan is still the most commonly used tool. Although occasionally syndicated revolving credits are used to finance entire fleets of vessels for corporate-type ship owners, the cyclicality and risk pattern of shipping and its cash flows in most cases dictate the use of an amortising term loan.

A Term of the loan

Usually, the term of the loan is not sufficient to match the full economic life of the vessel. Assuming that a vessel has a useful life of around 20 years, then high levels of financing are only justified in the first 8 to 15 years. The quality of construction and the use and maintenance of the vessel will be important when determining the length of a loan for a second-hand ship.

Generally, shipping term loans will not extend beyond 8 to 10 years. The risks of the industry, combined with the fluctuations of vessel values which are directly linked to its earning power in the current and generally expected shipping market make it imprudent for the term of a loan to cover more than such a period. Projection of earning patterns is already difficult for the shorter-term: for periods beyond 5 years they are virtually impossible. A re-financing at the end of the first loan period will then take account of the earning power of the ship's remaining economic (and technical) life.

The fact that a vessel is the subject of a long-term charter contract from a major industrial corporation or an oil company may provide some comfort to the lenders to extend the term beyond the usual period, but in such a case a credit judgement will be required as to the charterer. Also, as already mentioned before, it should be realised that genuinely 'unbreakable' charter commitments are rare.

B Repayment

Vessel loans should have a repayment schedule with roughly equal periodic repayments, sometimes with a balloon payment at the end. In project-type financings, it is not unusual for the repayments to be higher in the first years, simply as a result of being able to project more accurately what cash flow can be generated in the first few years of a loan, either as a result of an existing charter or, more generally, because market developments in the near-term are more predictable. This then reduces the risk for later years.

Grace periods for instalments are sometimes granted in the case of newbuilding financing, particularly where the vessel has a long-term charter arrangement securing the cash flow. Bullet loans are less suitable in shipping, simply because of the volatility and unpredictability of the shipping markets.

C Balloon payments

The final *balloon payment* should relate to an estimated minimum value of the vessel at the end of the loan period. This can be based upon the net present value of the cash flows the vessel should conservatively be able to generate during its remaining economic life after final maturity, the so-called *refinancing balloon*. For older vessels, with a shorter remaining economic life, it is more prudently based upon the vessel's scrap value. Lenders should in that instance be wary of assuming that scrap levels are stable. In the first place, steel prices fluctuate, in the second place, when many vessels are offered for scrap as a result of extremely bad charter markets, scrap rates plunge. To illustrate, during the 1980s scrap price levels fluctuated between US$ 280 per ton and US$ 60 per ton. Conservatively, scrap levels at the lower end of the range should be assumed for a *scrap balloon*.

10 Newbuilding financing

Financing the construction of a ship entails a totally different set of risks to be considered by a lender than when financing the acquisition of an existing vessel. In particular, the period between the signing of the newbuilding contract and the delivery to and, importantly, acceptance by, the owner can be testing even for the most experienced banker.

In the first place, there is no cash flow during this period. Although the lender is providing funds to the owner for the progress payments to the shipyard, his interest and, eventually, service of principal, needs to come from other sources. Secondly, the security he relies upon, such as refund guarantees and a lien on an unfinished vessel, are subject to the contractual relationship between the owner and the yard and will in most cases be far less valuable than the mortgage security available to the lender once the vessel is accepted by the owner. Finally, he runs the risk of the technical competence of the builder and the *political risk* of upheavals in the builder's country or strikes at the shipyard. The remedies and security open to the lender are different and the main characteristics of this type of project financing are set out below.

A Pre-delivery risk

Once a ship owner signs a building contract, he will be obliged to make progress payments during construction and to take delivery of the vessel and make the final payment if the vessel is delivered to specifications and on time. In this simple statement are hidden some of the most gruesome risks a ship financier can face.

Normally, newbuilding financing will involve the lender in paying a certain percentage of the progress payments which are made at certain fixed moments, such as signing, steel plate cutting, keel laying and launching. With the progress payments, the owner pays his equity portion. Security is provided through an assignment of the building contract, an assignment of any interest the owner has in insurances during construction, and the assignment of any refund guarantee provided by the yard. If the lender does not obtain further security from the borrower (or possibly the borrower's parent or another affiliate), he may end up facing an equity risk.

B Completion risk

If for any reason the vessel is never finished, if it does not meet its specifications, or if there is a dispute regarding any of these issues between the owner and the yard, the lender is out-of-pocket and has only a limited set of options to recover his outlay, other than unrelated security or comfort provided by the borrower, which he would be wise to obtain as, in particular, disputes between owners and yards have sometimes taken years rather than months to be resolved.

C Refund guarantees

The terms of the shipbuilding contract, specifically those regarding disputes, are therefore of great importance to the lender. As the refund guarantees will be his main security, he should investigate under exactly which circumstances these guarantees can be called upon and he should support the owner when negotiating these issues with the yard. The owner normally has the right to approve the bank issuing the guarantee and, in turn, the lender should obtain this same right of approval of the guaranteeing bank from the borrower.

D Contractual risks

A particular item to be closely looked for is any incongruence between a default under the loan agreement and a default under the building contract. It might be that the owner is in default under the loan documentation without the yard being in default under the (assigned) building contract, which will mean that the lender has no option but to continue to build the ship in order possibly to sell it after completion. This is an unenviable position for a bank to be in.

If possible, the financier should be involved in discussion with the owner in the earliest stages of the negotiations between the yard and the owner. In that way, he can ensure that the owner negotiates a building contract which leaves maximum flexibility for the financing contract and limits dangerous incongruences between the two contractual relationships to a minimum.

11 Security structure

Security is of course a typical characteristic of project financing and in the case of ship financing, a long history of secured lending has provided a well-proven and internationally recognised set of security items.

A Mortgages

The mortgage is probably the best known security device in ship financing. In the current thinking of cash flow-based lending the mortgage, however, is the security of last resort. Only if all else has failed and no other reasonable avenues are open to salvage the project or to exercise security does the lender use his rights as a mortgagee to sell the vessel. There are two reasons for the mortgage being the security of last resort. Firstly, selling through the courts (which in many cases will be the only way in which the mortgagee can exercise his foreclosure rights) will always produce the lower yield of an obviously distressed sale, not the true market value and therefore can lead to a loss for the financier. Secondly, it involves many ancillary costs such as the keeping of the vessel until the date of the foreclosure sale. This waiting time is required in order to give third party creditors the time to come forward and present their claims. One benefit of selling a vessel through the courts is that the buyer acquires a vessel which is absolutely free and clear of any previous claims or maritime liens, which might otherwise follow the vessel, even under new ownership. The options which are open to a mortgagee who finds himself in possession of a vessel are discussed post, p 63.

B Assignment of earnings

An assignment of earnings can be a substantial part of the security provided by a borrower in a shipping-based project financing. In cases where the vessel is the subject of a long-term charter arrangement with a creditworthy charterer, the assignment can provide credit comfort to the lender. The legal status of the assignment remains in doubt, however, unless it is perfected. The way in which this perfection is achieved will depend on the jurisdiction involved, but it generally means a notification of the assignment to the charterer and his confirmation to the assignee of the acceptance of this notice. The charterer will then normally pay his charter hire directly into a designated security account, from which the lender has the right to take his debt service and will release the remainder for operating costs to the assignor, if so agreed. Ship owners are sometimes sensitive to notification to the charterer and will object, it being feared that the notification from the lender to the charterer would create an unfavourable impression of the ship owner. Professional charterers do, however, understand that a ship owner requires financing and that the cash flow from his charter helps provide the means to secure this.

An even stronger form of assignment is the *assignment of the charter* itself. Acceptance of this assignment by the charterer will mean that the assignee has the right and ability to take the charter over himself and perform the assignor's obligations under such charter. It is obvious that a charterer will generally only accept such assignment under special circumstances, for example where the transaction is long-term and where the continued performance under the charter is of prime importance to him. This could for example be the case with long-term transportation contracts where the vessels involved were purpose-built for the contract.

Although an assignment of earnings is a generally accepted and fairly standard form of security, there are a number of instances where its perfection is difficult. This is mainly the case where the vessel in question is operated in a liner operation or in a *pool* together with other ships. The charterer there has the obligation to pay to the pool-operator and not the real owner of the vessel. The owner of the vessel can only assign his rights in his pool-share. As a result, the lender may find his security in the owner's assignment to be worthless in circumstances where the group to which the owner and the pool-operator belong finds itself in financial difficulty.

C Assignment of insurances

An assignment of insurances is also a typical standard feature of any vessel financing transaction. It is notified to the underwriters through the insurance brokers and is confirmed by the underwriters who agree only to pay out any insurance proceeds to the mortgagees in the so-called *loss payable clause* which is attached to the policy. A lender should always as a matter of due diligence check the insurance policies directly and he can obtain an opinion on the effectiveness of the insurances placed from one of several independent insurance advisers. The various kinds of insurances important to the lender are described in more detail post, pp 58ff.

D Pledge of shares

A pledge over the shares of a single vessel-owning company can provide the mortgagee with an alternative to taking the ship through a court sale. The pledge agreement will authorise the mortgagee, in the case of a default, to exercise the shareholders' rights attaching to the shares. In many cases such a pledge is accompanied by signed but undated letters of resignation from the directors, so that the mortgagee can promptly elect his own directors. Taking over the shares can provide flexibility, particularly when a court sale is to be avoided or a vessel contract is to be fulfilled in order to safeguard the cash flow it generates. If the party taking over the shares of the single ship company is a bank, it should be aware of the risks involved in becoming, be it indirectly, responsible for the vessel. Especially in connection with oil pollution liability, the dangers of the exercise of such rights should be carefully weighed against the apparent advantages. See post, pp 62ff for more detail.

E Guarantees

If the cash flow of a specific shipping project is either too low or too unpredictable, or the risks of the single vessel project are too high, it is common practice that guarantees are required by the lender from either parent or sister companies, providing the added comfort of access to the cash flow from other vessels or activities. Personal guarantees are used in the case of single ship companies without a common group holding company structure with a substantial cash flow, where the common supporting factor is an individual ultimately controlling the asset being financed.

12 Covenants

In addition to the specific items of security, covenants form an important part of making the security structure more effective.

A Financial covenants

Financial covenants imposed in the financing of shipping projects should mostly relate to those of the company's figures which are most important to its success: cash flow, leverage and liquidity. Commonly used covenants are as follows:

Interest cover

$$\frac{\text{profit before tax and interest expense}}{\text{interest expense}}$$

In the case of an interest cover covenant, the numerator must be greater than the denominator by a certain agreed factor. The exact ratio will depend upon the nature of the project and the analysis of the projections.

Cash flow coverage

$$\frac{\text{operating cash flow}[1]}{\text{total interest bearing debt}}$$

Operating cash flow should here be required to bear an agreed ratio to total interest bearing debt, which ratio again depends on the nature of the specific project.

Debt to net worth

$$\frac{\text{total interest bearing debt}}{\text{(shareholders' equity + reserves)}}$$

In this covenant, interest-bearing debt must bear no more than an agreed ratio to net worth.

Other examples of important covenants used for ship financing are *minimum liquidity* or *minimum working capital reserves* which are discussed below.

B Minimum value clause

The minimum value clause has already been referred to above. It is one of the oldest and most simple forms of protecting a lender against the risk of the strongly fluctuating market value of vessels. A borrower covenants that the value of the vessel in question, as determined by a panel of independent ship brokers, will always remain at least, say, 125% of the outstanding loan. Should the value of the vessel drop below this level, then the borrower must either prepay the loan to a level at which the covenant is complied with or provide top-up security which brings the security package to the required level. Minimum value clauses provide an 'alarm-bell' which forces the lender and the borrower around the negotiating table when values are dropping, in order to discuss a solution.

---

1 Operating cash flow is defined as profit after tax plus depreciation and adjusted for other non-cash items in the profit and loss account.

C Minimum working capital and liquidity

The requirement of a minimum working capital level or a minimum liquidity level is crucial to the security structure of a project-based ship financing. By using the cash flow modelling described above, the financier can determine the level of working capital or liquidity which the project requires to survive sudden changes in its income stream or unexpected developments on the cost side. He can therefore prescribe a minimum amount of starting working capital or an amount to be retained from a certain fixed income stream in order to build up such a reserve.

Historically, and particularly during the shipping crisis of the mid-1980s, most problems with shipping projects have been caused by lack of liquidity at a point approximately midway through the project. Since the occurrence of such a cash crisis in most cases could have been avoided had sufficient working capital been available from the start, it is only prudent for the borrower to accept the discipline which a minimum liquidity level imposes.

D Information covenants

As shipping is such a fluctuating and volatile industry, the financier wants to be abreast of all developments with the project or company financed, whether it concerns the business or the financial state of the client. In addition to maintaining a close contact with his client, not just during the period of structuring and negotiations but in particular during the life of the project, it is important to provide for covenants which require the regular and timely provision of adequate information. In order to set such covenants, the financier must at the outset obtain a proper understanding of the dynamics of the project or company and its business, as he will want only the right information, where quality is more important than sheer quantity. He should not bother the client's administrative department with unnecessary work but on the other hand always be comfortable with his level of awareness.

E Negative pledges and prohibition on dividends

Other ways of securing that no influence from the outside can damage the project being financed is a negative pledge of the other assets of the owning company or of the guarantor of the transaction, and a prohibition on dividends unless certain profit or cash flow levels have been reached or the loan has been paid down to a certain pre-determined level.

F Obligatory interest rate hedging

A financier can be of the opinion that the risk package he is requested to manage through the structure of a project-based ship financing has sufficient industry related risks which cannot be hedged. However, any other risks which actually can be provided for, such as the exposure to interest rates or foreign exchange risks, should be taken care of. It is therefore becoming a frequent requirement to impose an interest rate hedging strategy upon the project through the requirement in the loan documentation for an interest rate cap or other derivative hedging product.

13 Lender liability

The issue of lender liability is hotly debated, although in some countries more so than in others. It involves risks which for large financial institutions with perceived 'deep pockets' can have far-reaching consequences. Particularly in the US, lender liability is topical, especially so since the introduction of OPA 90 and after certain court decisions relating to lender liability with respect to on-shore pollution.

The main rule with respect to ship financing remains that a financier should avoid becoming a 'mortgagee in possession', ie once a financing institution has exercised its mortgagee rights to take possession of the vessel it will be regarded as its owner and with this attracts the liability of a vessel owner. Even in the case of a foreclosure and a subsequent sale, the bank cannot avoid responsibility if at the moment of foreclosure, but before the sale, an event causing liability happened.

The same risk pattern is involved with the less easily definable issue of 'control'. In many jurisdictions, a lender may attract liability if he is too closely involved in the operational decision-making process of a project. This is something to keep in mind when structuring documentation with extremely strict approval clauses. It is wise to always take proper legal advice on issues of lender liability. However, lenders should bear in mind that the area of lender liability is an evolving one and that advice in this area may be necessary on a continuing basis during the life of a loan.

14 Risks associated with country of flag and of corporate residence

Since in ship finance the security element for the lender is one of the reasons for being able to enter into the transaction, it requires utmost care in its preservation. This includes ensuring that the lender will at all times be able to exercise his rights as a mortgagee. The choice of the country and legal system governing the rights of the lender under the mortgage, which for most purposes is the country of registration of the vessel and of its flag, is of great importance to the lender-mortgagee. The country of incorporation of the ship-owning company, which is not necessarily the same as that of the flag, is also important.

A Jurisdiction of registration

The country of registration of the vessel will provide it with the right to fly its flag. The choice of this jurisdiction is essential for the secured lender as his rights as a mortgagee and the enforceability of the mortgage will in large part be determined by the legal system prevailing in this jurisdiction. It will therefore often be advisable for the lender to preserve a veto right over the choice of flag, which right must of course be executed within reason.

(a) The lender as mortgagee

As mentioned above, the main concern for the lender remains the effect the choice of registry has on the mortgage and its enforceability. The lender should be, and continue to be, aware of the differences between the various registers as they, and their jurisdictions, develop. He should be aware of *political and legal risks* from time to time associated with the country of the flag. He should determine whether the country is party to principal United Nations and other conventions applying to shipping, and whether financing a vessel under the country's flag causes any problems with his own bank regulators.

Related to political stability and risk is the ability to de-register a vessel. Most jurisdictions into which a vessel is moved after the exercise of a mortgagee's rights or otherwise, will want to see a Certificate of Deletion from the previous register. A lender should judge whether the jurisdiction of the flag may at any time object or refuse, for political or other reasons, to de-register a vessel should the owner or the mortgagee decide to exercise his rights. Normally, the only condition for release would be the payment of overdue taxes and fees, but it has happened that certain countries refused to delete the registration of vessels (and aircraft, for that matter) for purely political reasons.

The lender should also ascertain that the flag country actually maintains a physical register where his mortgage will be entered, so that third parties inspecting this register may be aware of his preferential rights. The legal system, which determines many of the mortgagee's rights, must be acceptable to the lender. Legal opinions may provide a certain level of comfort when entering into a transaction. A number of 'flag of convenience' jurisdictions have simply adopted a system based on a well-established foreign system. Liberia, Vanuatu and the Marshall Islands use a system principally based on New York law. Bermuda and the Bahamas base themselves on the British registration system. This certainly facilitates obtaining and understanding legal opinions which are essential for proper ship finance documentation. However, in certain circumstances, such as the current situation in Liberia, a legal opinion cannot substitute for what is really a political analysis of the existing legal and political regime and the prognosis for its future composition and stability.

(b) Operational considerations for choice of flag

Vessels financed on a project basis can either be all owned by one or more corporate entities resident in the country of the operator-owner and flying its home flag, or by single ship-owning subsidiaries, while registered in a 'flag of convenience' jurisdiction. Reasons for this last structure, which is commonly used, are manifold.

In the first place there is the issue of manning costs. Flag of convenience countries usually allow more flexibility in the constitution of the crew by nationality. This offers the owner scope for cost-savings when compared to, for example, regulations under a European national flag, while not necessarily affecting the quality of operations. Secondly, the cost of registration and tonnage taxes varies from register to register. Thirdly, and this is most important to the lender, certain registers are more lenient than others when it comes to safety regulations and maintenance requirements. Finally, an important reason for owning a ship through a single ship-owning company is the limitation of liability and the possible avoidance of sister ship arrest in case a third party attempts to enforce a lien upon a sister ship.

Generally a cost saving for the owner is positive for the lender as it enhances the net cash flow from the operation of the vessel. However, where it comes to safety and technical maintenance requirements, the lender's main security asset is at stake. Hence it is important for the lender to keep himself informed regarding the safety and technical requirements and implementation thereof by the various registers.

(c) Single ship-owning companies
The use of single ship-owning companies and the limitation of liability issue has been much debated recently after the OPA 90 came into force in the US. Although in many countries (with the exception of, for example, South Africa) the use of a single ship-owning company will indeed avoid sister ship arrest, there is an increasing tendency to impose liability upon others than the owner and OPA 90 looks to owners as well as to operators and even lessors.

For the secured lender against a single ship, the single ship-owning company structure may offer some protection. It avoids confusion with claims which third parties may have against other vessels owned by the same parent or ship owner and it enables the lender to isolate the project cash flow from the vessel, to take an assignment of the earnings, insurance monies and possibly a pledge of the shares of the owning company in addition to the mortgage. However, given the possibility that courts may disregard the corporate form and 'pierce the corporate veil', particularly where the single ship-owning company is inadequately capitalised and does not observe corporate formalities, lenders must not assume that use of a single ship-owning company will provide complete protection.

B   Jurisdiction of incorporation

Although most of the lender's concerns with jurisdiction are related to the registry as the basis for his security, he will also need to exercise due diligence when it comes to the country of incorporation. Normally this is the same as the jurisdiction of registry and flag, but certain structures will separate the two. A vessel can for example be owned by one company and registered in one jurisdiction, and then be bareboat chartered out to another company in a different jurisdiction, where the vessel will be registered in the name of the bareboat charterer. The vessel will then fly the flag of the bareboat charterer's registry. Reasons for such structures can be operational (bareboat charter to a genuine third party) or related to financing (leasing), or to tax considerations.

For the lender, it is important to know that he can convince himself from time to time of his borrower's corporate existence. It is normally easier to move a vessel to a different flag than to a different owning company without doing damage to a lender's position.

15 Other roles of the banks

A Syndication versus 'club deals'

Shipping loans are only rarely syndicated among large groups of banks. This is the correct approach, as the specialism of the industry requires banks and bankers who are committed to an understanding of the industry and its problems. The technical requirements of obtaining security in vessels can also result in voluminous and complex documentation if a large number of lenders are involved. The 'club deal' with a group of three to four specialist banks generally provides a more professional and reliable forum for the borrower, particularly when the weather turns against him. Wide syndications become appropriate where the risks involved have less of a special 'shipping' character and are for example related to charters to oil majors or other energy-related companies with a solid credit rating of their own. It is the role of the banker to the shipping company to advise him on the best syndication strategy.

B Hedging strategies

The financier can play a further role by advising the originator of the project on the possibilities of hedging those risks to which the project is exposed and that may actually be dealt with. Interest rate hedging strategies, foreign exchange risk cover and fuel price hedging are examples of a financier's product skills which can help the borrower reduce the range and extent of risks to which a project is exposed.

16 Insurance

Insurance is one of the important protections for the financier of a vessel. When structuring a vessel financing, the documentation should set out clearly which insurances the financier expects the owner to take out and maintain and which level of insurance cover is required. Normally, for *hull and machinery insurance* and *war risks insurance*, a certain percentage, often 130%, of the outstandings under the financing at any time will be required. The level of insurance from *protection and indemnity associations*, which are mutual insurance institutions mainly covering the ship owner's third party liability, is normally the maximum available under the associations' rules. This insurance is not just important to and required by the financier, but will often also be a requirement from charterers. Another insurance which can be taken out by the owner and insisted upon by the financier in the case where he is financing the vessel partly on the basis of a certain time charter contract, is *loss of hire insurance*, which protects against the income from a certain time charter falling away as a result of the vessel going off-hire for vessel-specific operational reasons.

The lender should be careful to avoid being too specific with respect to the types and amounts of required insurance cover. The insurance industry is in a state of upheaval and the prudent lender will require the borrower to obtain such cover as the lender shall require, including without limitation those mentioned above. In addition, in an environment in which the creditworthiness of insurers is increasingly being called into question, the identity of the insurers should be subject to the lender's approval.

The financier as the mortgagee can also take out certain insurances. *Mortgagee's interest insurance* ('MII') covers the risk of the vessel's own insurance not paying out where the owner had not fulfilled his side of the contract, for example if the vessel was not seaworthy or fraud was suspected. As there is this connotation of dishonesty, many ship owners have long considered it an affront if the mortgagee took out such insurance and refused to reimburse the mortgagee with the cost. This is now changing, particularly as mortgagee's interest insurance is now being used to cover some of the newly emerged risks which relate to the pollution legislation in the US.

An example of this is the *MII-additional perils (pollution)* cover, which was developed specifically to cover the risk that a financier would run if a vessel he finances causes an oil spill which gives rise to a claim under the OPA 1990 legislation in the US. Such a claim could create a situation where the vessel is arrested and the claimant's right would take precedence over the mortgage. The financier could therefore lose the value of his mortgage and it is this risk that is covered by this new insurance. It is standard practice that the premium for this insurance, which is taken out by the mortgagee, is reimbursed to him by the ship owner. Another enhancement to the basic MII policy covers the risk to the lender if the owner fails to carry out his required quarterly reporting to the protection and indemnity association on calls made by his vessel to the US. Such failure or negligence can result in calls to the US not being covered by the policy, which in turn puts the mortgagee at risk. Financiers and the insurance industry are in this way constantly adapting the insurance packages available to the rapidly changing risk profile of ship finance.

As mentioned earlier, the financier should insist upon a loss payable clause mentioning him as the loss payee of the insurance. He should also insist upon the policy being written in such a way that the broker or underwriter warns him well in advance that his insurance will lapse as a result of unpaid premiums. The financier should have a good understanding of the mechanics of the marine insurance industry. He can also call upon the assistance of one of the brokerage and consultancy firms which specialise in services to the banking industry, whether by placing insurances, reviewing policies or advising on the structuring of insurances.

17 Newly emerging risks

A Pollution

At several points in this chapter, the risk which the financier runs as a result of, in particular, the new oil pollution legislation in the US (OPA 90) has been mentioned. It is important to note that the problem does not just relate to tankers, as in theory liability for a spill can arise with respect to a liner vessel, bulk carrier, a trawler or any other kind of vessel if it causes an accident with a tanker, or simply causes pollution itself. The risk arising from oil pollution liability is a typical example of a new and additional risk which has emerged and to which the financier should react swiftly in order to protect not just his position in new transactions but also his existing portfolio.

The risk to the financier caused by OPA 90 primarily relates to his security in the vessel, which is potentially at risk if the vessel causes a spill in the US and a claim is made against it which cannot be met by its insurance or its owning company. In such a case the danger exists that the vessel is arrested to satisfy such claim, which might be construed as arising out of the concept of tort and therefore take priority over the rights of the mortgagee. The result can then be that the mortgagee loses the value of his security. It has to be understood that a remedy for this risk can be found in the additional perils (pollution) insurance described elsewhere in this chapter ante, p 59. The creation of this policy was a swift reaction from the banking and insurance broking industries following the identification of this new risk and shows how financiers need to be constantly aware of the changing risk pattern in the industry.

B Concentration risk

Financiers often do a great number of transactions in one particular segment of the shipping industry, without realising that at some stage in the future, a multitude of the vessels he finances are on charter to the same charterer. In such a case his exposure is no longer spread over the industry segment as a whole but is very much related to the credit of the particular charterer. As an example, the chartering market for very large and ultra large tankers is currently dominated by a handful of charterers. In itself, this should not present a problem to the financier, but he should be aware of the possibility of such concentration of risk.

18 Work-outs

No matter what preventive measures may have been taken, unexpected circumstances can always force a company in any industry, including a shipping company, into trouble. A number of banks discovered this during the shipping crisis of the mid-1980s and some of today's work-out specialists had their training in dealing with shipping industry-related problem cases. Because of its asset-intensiveness and cash flow-driven character, working out a shipping problem is complicated and time consuming but, and this an important difference with non-asset based industries and a number of other industries, in many cases successful.

What the banker needs in the first place is patience. He also needs a good contact with, and confidence in, the ship owner or the management of the shipping company, in the case of a more corporate entity. Since in most cases the problem was created by external circumstances, the company must adapt itself quickly to the new situation, in an attempt to repay the financier, but also for the company to survive, be it often in a smaller or different form.

The financier should be prepared for developing problem situations and his best defence consists of spotting the problem at its earliest stages. Apart from the alarm-bells mentioned below, a continuous awareness of the financial and business situation of the client is imperative. The financier should have the client regularly provide information which enables him to check on the borrower's credit standing, he should confirm maintenance and value of the assets and follow developments in the industry to avoid surprises. Ship finance is an attention-intensive business, not simply when structuring a financing but also after making the loan, all the way to the completion of the project. Avoiding surprises leaves the financier with the widest choice of action and best chance to avoid or minimise losses.

A Documentation

In some cases, the problem is created by the company's own structure, particularly its financial structure. As mentioned before in this chapter, a liquidity crisis is probably the most frequent reason for a company's downfall. This phenomenon is directly linked to lack of equity and excessive gearing. Those responsible for structuring a company financially would do well to realise this at an early stage.

Building into the documentation of a financing arrangement alarm-bells relating to liquidity and cash flow generation, which will sound before the situation becomes untenable, will help the financier and his client to take action in time. Generally, the structure of the documentation is of the utmost importance for the financier of a shipping transaction. If properly set up, it will provide him with alarm-bells, triggers, remedies and a host of different actions he can take to safeguard his own exposure and minimise his loss under various different circumstances. Not least, it will also provide him with the tools to help his client, if a chance for ultimate survival exists and if the client has shown commitment to his financiers and is willing and able to go through an often painful process of restructuring, led by the financier.

B Managing the work-out

If the financier decides on the route of a work-out as opposed to an immediate foreclosure, this implies he is prepared to work with his client on a co-operative basis. He has confidence in the willingness of the client to co-operate and has decided to dedicate much time and effort to recover his money or provide himself with a better chance to do so in the future and his client with a chance to survive. The essence of a work-out is to devise a plan of action which will lead to the required result. This may involve selling vessels, placing vessels on long-term charters, forging joint-ventures with other ship owners and looking at the overhead charges of the company and ways to reduce these.

During a work-out the financier may find himself involved with a great number of the tasks normally handled by the ship owner alone. Before deciding on the work-out route, he will have sent in a team to assess the financial situation of the company and he will constantly monitor this during the work-out. He will be involved in the making of payments, freight and hire will be collected by him and he will monitor the chartering efforts of the owner. He must be close to developments in the freight markets and the sale and purchase market for vessels. This is why it is important for bankers to maintain a relationship with a number of first class shipbrokers.

The financier will make sure the vessels remain covered by insurance and that the vessel's classification is kept up to date. All this may involve cost which, ideally, the owner can still pay for. Should this not be the case and the financier is asked to provide further advances, he should only do so if he has a certain take-out in the form of assigned hire payments coming in or possibly the proceeds from asset sales.

One of the most important ingredients for a successful work-out is the continued confidence of the shipping and chartering community in the ship owner and in his chances to survive. Matters become complicated if such confidence partially or totally disappears. Third party creditors, whether they have maritime liens or not, and particularly smaller ones, can seriously harm a company's continued existence by arresting vessels in the expectation of being paid out by the mortgagees who are perceived to have much more to lose. This then has a domino-like effect on suppliers to the vessels of essential goods such as bunker fuel and other stores and provisions. Having the benefit of at least one or two months' credit normally provides the owner with working capital, as he often collects his freight or part of his time charter hire at the beginning of the voyage and can therefore pay for his bunkers and stores after receipt of his freight or hire. The lack of such credit worsens the liquidity crisis which the owner faces. A bank can precipitate such events by taking the wrong kind of action and making the financial difficulties of the shipping company a self-fulfilling prophecy.

C Alternatives to foreclosure

There are a number of ways in which the lender can realise a better value for the asset and provide himself with a better chance to recover his money than by the ultimate means of exercising his rights as a mortgagee and proceeding to a foreclosure sale of the vessel.

If he has negotiated a *pledge of the shares* of the single vessel-owning company, he can exercise his right under this pledge and take the shares. This makes him the owner of the vessel and he has the choice of continuing to operate it or to on-sell the shares privately. If he continues to operate it he may do so with the help of an independent ship management company, who provide the crew and take care of the vessel's commercial employment, or he can place the ship in management with another ship owner, until either the market has improved and the vessel can be sold at a better price, or the vessel has provided sufficient cash flow to repay the loan.

If the vessel or its owning company is on-sold privately, the lender must be careful to obtain the highest price available in the open market, as he may expose himself to claims from the original owner or his liquidators. He also must understand that taking over the shares in the ship-owning company is not without risk. In the first place, the vessel is not cleansed of the claims from its trade (and other) creditors who have claims relating to its trading under the original owners. Many of such claims (depending upon the jurisdiction they can relate to items as crew wages, taxes, port dues, bunker deliveries, repair costs) give rise to maritime liens and therefore follow the vessel regardless of a sale, unless it is sold at a public auction. Before going this route, the financier must assess whether, and how many, old claims could surface and might need to be taken care of. Secondly, the financier who owns the shares of the single vessel company could be at risk from claims arising from pollution liability, particularly as claimants will consider a financial institution a 'deep pocket' and a potential target for a claim based on a 'piercing the corporate veil' theory. Furthermore, the financier could incur such, and other liabilities, if he were perceived to be exercising 'control' of the client's company. Notwithstanding that financial institutions do not generally have the intention to be or remain a ship owner and that they will only want to be this for the shortest of periods, the flexibility offered by the pledge of shares makes it an important tool.

An alternative to be considered is placing a vessel with another ship owner without changing its ownership. This alternative requires the full co-operation from the owner but offers the advantage of the ship being able to trade independently from the problems of the owner under reputable management and unaffected by the potential crisis of confidence in the markets from which the owner may suffer. Its cash flow is then protected and can be used to pay the financier directly.

D Foreclosure

The simplest action a financier can take when the ship owner is in default and generally the action of last resort is to arrest the vessel as the mortgagee and to sell it at a public auction. Such pre-emptive action is not always the best way to proceed. Given that prices obtained at auctions tend to include a discount from the open market value, that there will be a cost to keep the vessel prior the auction and that other creditors with preferred liens will need to be paid off first, this is certainly not the most efficient way to deal with the asset's value. However, sometimes a work-out cannot be contemplated, no other avenue is open and the mortgagee is left with no other choice.

A complication can arise when the vessel still contains cargo. A mortgagee who forecloses will face the cost of discharging the cargo and often for transporting the cargo to its original destination and he may well be the subject of claims made by the cargo owner. A further realistic danger which the financier as mortgagee needs to consider is being faced with the responsibilities of being a 'mortgagee in possession'. In this respect the pollution legislation in the US comes to mind. A mortgagee in possession is fully responsible, as the 'owner' of a vessel, should the vessel cause any pollution during the period of his perceived ownership.

These kind of considerations should be weighed against the benefits when the financier decides to take action. If the vessel arrested is part of a larger fleet financed by the same financier, he must carefully consider the geographic positions of all vessels, the jurisdictions in which they will be arrested and the question of cargo remaining on board. Of course the amount of debt outstanding against the vessel or vessels, and their value in relation to this debt, will be an important factor in the decision process.

19 Conclusion

The financing of shipping projects should be seen as a co-operative partnership between the equity provider and the debt provider, with a proper balancing of the rights and rewards based on the relative risks to be borne by each of these partners.

Both the equity provider and the debt provider have a responsibility for their own due diligence when structuring the transaction, but as a result of the nature of things, the equity provider will tend to be more optimistic, while the debt provider will want to cater for the worst case scenario. Both need to address the issues at hand in a professional and mature way. They will need to listen to each other's arguments, but the equity provider should always realise that the debt provider has the choice to invest or lend his money elsewhere and that his return is based upon a debt risk and not an equity risk. More projects have failed as a result of over-optimism than as a result of conservatism and this is what both parties should realise.

The financier has the responsibility of structuring the financing in such a way that his risk is minimised and that he has the flexibility of action if the project does not go as planned. In this chapter some of the issues he will need to deal with have been mentioned, although by no means exhaustively. The financier will need to build up his own understanding of the fascinating industry of shipping and the particular ways and means by which to structure adequately the financing of a shipping project. He will also need to realise that understanding the shipping industry cannot go without understanding the people within this industry, who make it the special industry it is and who, together with the appropriate structuring of transactions, can make ship finance an exciting and rewarding experience in every sense of the word.

Taco Th van der Mast, a Dutch national born in 1949, was trained at business school in Neuchatel, Switzerland and at Leyden University in the Netherlands where he obtained a Masters Degree in Law, specialising in contract, company and civil law. He spent ten years at the Dutch transportation concern Van Ommeren, initially as a lawyer, later as a shipping executive, with postings in the Netherlands, Indonesia and London. Having switched to banking, Mr van der Mast today is head of the London-based European shipping group at the US banking house of J P Morgan, one of the world's leading shipping banks, active both in ship financing and shipping related advisory business.

4 Mining: extractive and processing

Dr Keith Palmer, N M Rothschild & Sons Ltd

Introduction

In this chapter the primary focus is on recent developments in project finance as applied to the mining industry. It will be shown how the emergence of the acute Third World 'debt crisis' and consequent drying up of 'new money' lending by commercial banks to many countries – even where projects have very attractive economics – has created new financing problems requiring new project finance solutions. On the other hand, in developed countries the traditional project finance techniques have, in some circumstances, been broadened reducing the residual project risks left with sponsors.

The other theme of note is the emergence of new approaches to financing mining projects. These new approaches arise out of the 'debt crises' in many countries – leading to increased interest in privatisation of state mining investment and greater use of debt-equity swap instruments. The observations will draw heavily on the experience of Rothschilds' Natural Resources Group which over many years has acted as financial adviser to project sponsors seeking to finance and develop major mining projects around the world. Our perspective – often different to that of the commercial lender – is to devise a financing plan for a project that is feasible and, as far as possible, meets the financing objectives of the sponsors.

Project finance has always been important in the mining industry primarily because of the particular characteristics of mining projects. Investors cannot choose where mines are located – they have to be where the quality deposits are and this is, all too often, not where managements would prefer them to be! When major investments are to be made in countries where the political and commercial environment raise concerns, it is natural that management should look to project finance techniques as a means of sharing project risks. Moreover, the nature of modern mining ventures – low grade ores and heavily capital intensive mining methods – is such that project costs are often very large in absolute terms and relative to the balance sheets of the sponsors. Another good reason to seek to share project risk!

Acknowledgement: The author would like to acknowledge the assistance and contributions of his colleagues Charles Mercey and Hugo Dryland who are also senior members of Rothschilds' Natural Resources Group. The bulk of the observations in this article are based on their experiences advising project sponsors on project financings around the world over the last decade.

Without doubt, the most important development of the 1980s was a much greater concern to shed country or political risk and, as a result of the withdrawal of commercial bank lenders, to find new sources of project finance for viable projects in developing countries. It is to the topic of shedding political risk that we turn first.

Country or political risk

Under this heading we are primarily concerned with the following risks:

- expropriation, either outright or 'creeping' without fair and reasonable compensation;
- non-expropriatory adverse changes in the host country's fiscal and/or regulatory regime;
- interference with the investor's ability to export, to retain foreign currency sales proceeds abroad and/or to convert domestic currency proceeds and remit them;
- insistence by the host government that a project lender (or its guarantor) lend 'new money' to the government as part of a sovereign debt rescheduling;
- damage to property and/or inability to operate due to war or political violence; and
- abrogation by the host government of contractual arrangements entered into (by it or its predecessor) with the investor.

The list is not exhaustive but encompasses many of the risks which are commonly understood as political, rather than commercial, risks. Other actions, eg the inability of the investor to operate because of actions by local landowners in dispute with both the investor and the national government, eg Bougainville Copper in Papua New Guinea, fall into a grey area and serve to emphasise the potential difficulty in some circumstances of distinguishing political from commercial risk – a consideration that, we shall see, can have very material implications.

Concerns about political risk have tended to focus primarily on developing countries. This is not necessarily because these risks are peculiar to, or indeed always greater in, these countries. For certain risks, the opposite may be the case – for example, the frequency and magnitude of tax changes is probably greater in developed countries (witness changes in European oil tax regimes over the last two decades – not to mention the US windfall profits tax!). However, certain circumstances which tend to prevail in some developing countries do raise particular 'political' concerns. Depending on the country, these may include:

- a history of unconstitutional changes of government;
- political violence (and perhaps lack of central government control);
- lack of an independent judiciary; and
- chronic problems with remitting interest, profits and capital.

Of course, the last of these has become the dominant concern in view of the forced debt reschedulings which have prevailed throughout the 1980s in many countries. Respect for investment agreements by the government are of little use to sponsors if the central bank simply does not have the foreign exchange to meet project obligations on a timely basis.

We can consider how to deal with political risk under three headings:

- defining sponsor rights via an investment agreement with government;
- considering methods of sharing political risk between sponsors and third parties; and
- identifying third parties able/willing to share political risk.

1 Sponsor rights

An investment agreement is a contract between the project sponsors and the government defining certain investor rights and obligations – most notably in the areas of convertibility, non-discrimination, termination of rights and 'economic stabilisation'. Some governments will not agree to enter into investment agreements – arguing that the investor should be prepared to rely on the general statutory protections available in the country – but this can be fatal for inward investment where specific political risk concerns are acute.

The value of an investment agreement to the project sponsor is threefold:

- first, there is the perception that the existence of the agreement in itself reduces the likelihood of adverse government interference in those areas covered by the agreement. This perception may or may not turn out to be valid but management of mining companies may frequently regard contractual commitments by government as an essential demonstration of good faith;
- second, the investment agreement may extend or clarify statutory rights in ways which allow the sponsors to lay off a significant element of project risk with third parties. In particular, the right to maintain offshore proceeds accounts – if not clearly provided for in acceptable general statutory provisions – can be critical in ensuring the financeability of the project without full sponsor guarantees. This in turn may determine whether or not the investment proceeds at all;
- third, an important benefit of the investment agreement is that, by establishing contractual rights, it creates an insurable risk, namely the risk of abrogation of those rights. Losses (or loan defaults) arising from breach of an investment agreement can, in many cases, be insured with the major institutional political risk insurers – as described later. Similarly, breach of an investment agreement may (where this can be negotiated) be excluded from sponsor guarantees of project loans – thus transferring the risk (to the extent of the loan amount) to lenders.

The content of an investment agreement will be specific to the country concerned and influenced by the nature of the statutory protections offered and the track record of the country in applying those protections. However, certain common elements can be identified as set out below.

Foreign exchange

Many mining and energy projects in developing countries are export-oriented with hard currency sales proceeds. In this case, classic convertibility/transferability risk only arises if and to the extent that the mining company is required to bring sales proceeds onshore (or if government has discretion to curtail exports). Thus, a key element in reducing convertibility/transferability risk in an export project is to obtain rights, within the investment agreement:

- to export and sell the products overseas; and
- to retain the foreign currency sales proceeds offshore to the extent not required to meet local expenditures (including fiscal obligations).

These rights are commonly granted in many developing countries. However, there are numerous countries (particularly in Latin America) where there is strong resistance to granting such rights. In some countries the resistance originates with government-owned (monopoly) marketing boards unwilling to see their powers diluted; or from the central bank which fears that such arrangements will spread and be exploited to weaken its management of the country's (often desperate) foreign exchange position; and sometimes the resistance is political since the arrangements may appear to confer benefits on foreign multinational investors which are not available to smaller national investors. Whatever the source of the resistance it needs to be overcome in countries with debt problems – because in the absence of these rights project financing may be impossible and vital investments deferred indefinitely, to the cost of the country itself.

The converse of this is also valid – that where rights to export and to hold proceeds offshore are granted, project finance techniques may very often be used to fund productive mining projects in countries where commercial bank lending is otherwise totally terminated.

Non-discrimination

Certain government actions, while falling short of expropriation, may be intended selectively to impose high costs on a mining project as an indirect and discriminatory form of taxation. Examples might include levying of penal charges for government services or very high rates of duty on items specific to the mining industry. Investment agreements often seek to deal explicitly with this issue although the treatment differs between countries. The superficially attractive route of blanket exemptions from charges is simple – but may often be seen as discriminatory in favour of the foreign mining investor and thus increase the risk of future adverse political actions. Perhaps the more common (and more politically defensible) route is to include non-discrimination provisions which state that the charges levied on the project will not exceed those generally applicable (or applicable to local investors). To avoid argument over the interpretation of this provision it may be possible to quantify thresholds or benchmarks against which 'discrimination' may be tested – and/or to combine such provisions with an overall cap on the charges.

Termination of rights

Termination of rights over a mineral property by government following development is the ultimate disaster for a mining company – potentially wiping out the entire investment value. It will also, of course, be a major concern for project lenders whose loan security depends on continuing rights over the property. The problem for lenders is that most mining laws and/or investment agreements confer termination rights on the host government in circumstances of a major breach by the investor of his contractual or statutory obligations and/or of insolvency – and understandably this is an ultimate deterrent that most governments wish to retain. However, this leaves lenders in a position where a highly-leveraged project finance vehicle, if the project runs into severe difficulties, finds itself in breach of contractual obligations to government (and/or insolvent) – and thus potentially subject to termination of rights – at just the moment that the banks may seek to exercise their security over the project (because of a loan default).

For investors (and lenders), the most that can normally be achieved in the investment agreement is to make termination by government subject to, first, an appropriate grace period during which the investor may remedy the default; second, acceptance by government of international arbitration under one of the generally accepted sets of arbitration rules; and third, agreement that, in the event of an arbitration decision in favour of government, it would grant a further grace period during which project-secured lenders may appoint a receiver-manager to operate the project on their behalf (and remedy the default to government) whilst the banks seek a buyer for the project. This final provision is much valued by lenders as one last chance to save their security through their own efforts if the borrower has been unable (or unwilling) to rectify the default.

Economic stabilisation
The most controversial provisions in investment agreements are 'economic stabilisation' clauses which seek to cap the total government 'take' from royalties, profits, taxes etc, to some maximum percentage of profit. Non-discrimination clauses only provide protection against government action directed at a single investor but are of little benefit where very high fiscal charges are imposed – ex post – on a sector. The economic stabilisation provisions seek to compensate investors for any non-discriminatory increase in total charges eg by rebating payments in excess of the specified cap.

Governments differ considerably in their approach to these provisions; some (including most developed countries) see them as an infringement of their sovereign rights; while others (usually countries most seriously concerned to attract foreign investment) are prepared to agree to such provisions for 'nationally important' major investments. The presence of such a provision will significantly enhance project lenders' confidence that project economics will not be undermined by changes in the fiscal rules – and hence increase their willingness to lend (particularly for projects where fiscal payments have an important impact on project cash flow).

Investment agreements are contracts between the host country government and the (foreign) investor. Some agreements are subsequently ratified so as to become part of the law of the host country. The supposed advantage is that this entrenches the agreement terms – which can then be overridden only by express legislation. This may be necessary to establish a negotiated fiscal agreement different from the terms in the law of general application, but is a mixed blessing. Ratification by the national political assembly – particularly of a favourable investment package – may well attract criticism from opposition politicians and heighten, rather than reduce, concerns about the longevity of the agreement.

2 Sharing of political risks

Here we are concerned with methods of sharing political risk between sponsors and third parties who may include lenders, guarantors and insurers. Before doing so, however, it is worth asking why mining companies seek to lay-off political risk by means of project financing. There are several possible reasons:

- Some mining companies in developed countries are concerned that exposure to developing country political risk will in itself harm the performance of their share price. Management may need to demonstrate that they have laid off the political risk.
- Some mining companies have a strong desire, on commercial, financial and/or accounting grounds, to have project loans go wholly non-recourse to the parent following completion of the project. Here the issue of political risk-shedding is just one (important) aspect of risk-shedding rather than a particular concern in itself.
- Some mining companies take the view that sharing political risk between sponsors and lenders itself significantly reduces the likelihood of certain types of political event occurring. The reasoning is that governments may be less inclined to incur the displeasure of both investors and lenders particularly if the lenders have leverage over government in other areas of the economy. In today's circumstances, this still seems a good argument for sharing risk with official agencies and institutions – but commercial banks in indebted countries today have minimal leverage.

These are valid reasons for sharing political risk. However, we should not overlook the high and relatively fixed cost of structuring, implementing and administering such loans, and the considerable time and senior management effort that this involves. Project financing in developing countries will normally make most sense where the exposure that the sponsor is seeking to shed is large relative to the company itself.

In the past, when sponsors sought to share project risk, it was natural for them to turn to the international commercial banks with expertise in evaluating project risks – but today this is much less the case. Many of the international commercial banks are quite able to assess and assume mining project risks of a commercial nature. However, when projects are located in developing countries with a history of debt problems and reschedulings the banks are often unable to accept any additional country exposure no matter how attractive the economics of the project. In these circumstances, means must be investigated of splitting political from commercial risk exposure and sharing the political risks with participants which are not banks.

First, however, consider situations where the banks will/can take political risk. The simplest method of transferring political risk to lenders is to structure the financing so that loans are made to a sole-purpose project company with the loans entirely non-recourse to the sponsors following completion ie the point where the project is commissioned and operating and the lenders' completion tests have been met. Lenders assume all risks at completion including political risks – and so it is not necessary to worry too much about whether the cause of any loan default is political or commercial – a distinction which can be quite a 'grey area' when things go wrong and everyone is pointing a finger at everyone else.

The problem with this simple structure is that in developing countries lenders will usually require pre-completion loan guarantees from sponsors. The commercial risks of developing a mining project in a developing country are such that non-recourse project loans prior to completion are not usually obtainable (see below). From a political risk-shifting perspective, the problem for the sponsor is that while he may be prepared to guarantee project loans pre-completion against commercial risks (which he can to some extent control) he may be unwilling to take the political risk. In order to have lenders share in political risks pre-completion it is necessary to negotiate an exclusion or 'carve-out' from the completion guarantee to cover defaults arising from defined 'political events'. This was the approach adopted for the Ok Tedi copper/gold project in Papua New Guinea and for the Escondida copper project in Chile. The 'carve-out' can take the form either of an exclusion to the terms of the guarantee or its suspension (and ultimate termination). In either case, the pre-completion situation is such that there is scope for dispute over the cause of the default. However, so long as lenders require pre-completion guarantees for commercial risks then this may be inevitable and the objective for the financial adviser must be to provide as clear and precise distinctions between types of risk as possible to minimise dispute if and when things go wrong.

The situation is more complex when, as is increasingly common, lending banks are unwilling to bear political risks themselves and instead require that these be laid off with political risk insurers. For the project sponsors, the preferred situation must be that the banks themselves are the insured parties. Post-completion – when the loans are fully non-recourse to the sponsors – the banks would look only to their insurers if a default arose from a political event, and pre-completion, the terms of the political risk 'carve-out' to the completion guarantee would match the terms of the political risk insurance available to lenders. This is difficult to achieve in practice; as a result banks become very concerned about differing dispute resolution mechanisms required under the guarantee and the insurance policy and the risk of ending up both uninsured and unguaranteed. If this problem is resolved eg by a common arbitration mechanism, sponsors will still have to resist the banks demands for collateralisation of the defaulted sums while arbitration proceeds.

The additional problem with this approach arises where the project financing is in a country where 'new money' risk is considered to be significant. This is the risk that, in the event of a sovereign debt rescheduling, banks making project loans may find themselves subject to a demand for a 'new money' contribution calculated by reference to an overall country exposure which includes project loans (even though the contractual rights conferred by an investment agreement may mean that the loans themselves are not subject to the rescheduling). Both the commercial banks and the major institutional political risk insurers are very reluctant to bear this risk. In these circumstances, it may be necessary to structure the financing excluding commercial banks entirely or alternatively involving them via an IFC[1] 'B' loan facility as discussed below. Some sponsors have

---

1 The International Finance Corporation (IFC) is an affiliate of the World Bank group involved in lending to, and investing alongside, the private sector in developing countries.

dealt with the issue by providing to the banks a free-standing guarantee against new money risk, or a blanket guarantee against all political risk which the sponsors have then sought to lay off (excluding new money risk) with political risk insurers. This leaves major residual risks with the sponsors – the risk of non-collection from insurers, the risk that lenders will seek recourse from sponsors following any default with a vaguely political aspect and, of course, the (unquantifiable but potentially very significant) new money risk.

3 Who will share the political risk?

Different lenders have different attitudes to different countries and the same lender can have a different attitude to different types of projects in the same country. Moreover, attitudes are changing constantly – one thing the financial adviser adds to a project financing is the knowledge of who will have appetite for the project, on what terms and how best to present it to obtain the most positive response.

Some generalisations are possible. The traditional source of limited recourse project finance for mining projects were the international commercial banks. Until the debt crisis took hold they would, in many cases, bear all commercial and political risks post-completion and, in certain cases, defined political risks pre-completion. The current situation is very different. In countries which have rescheduled their sovereign debt – and in many developing countries that have not – there is no meaningful appetite for project lending by the commercial banks even where sponsors are first-rate and project economics excellent; and such appetite as may exist is focused on a small number of countries. The deterioration of credit availability in the 1980s worsened further in the early 1990s with the worldwide tightening of credit and in particular the sharp reduction of interest from Japanese commercial banks.

With the virtual disappearance of commercial bank project lending to mining projects in developing countries it has become necessary to involve other sources of funds willing to take political risk and/or to involve the banks in a way that eliminates their political risk. The latter course has involved political risk insurance agencies as well as the IFC. The public sector political risk insurers include the US Overseas Private Investment Corporation (OPIC), the World Bank's Multilateral Investment Guarantee Association (MIGA) and the export credit agencies of various developed countries. These organisations have played valuable roles in a number of successful financings principally in countries where 'new money' risk is not the banks' principal concern. Their involvement, however, is limited by the restrictions under which they operate; OPIC is limited to insuring only US banks (a requirement which becomes more restrictive as US banks appetite for new assets reduces); MIGA's maximum exposure to any project is relatively small (currently US$50 million); and the export credit agencies frequently restrict cover to bank loans tied to procurement of goods and services from their own countries. The private political risk insurance market adds little; the market is shallow, short-term and significantly more expensive than institutional cover. Finally, the attraction to banks of providing finance on an insured basis is often undermined by the failure of many central banks to make any distinction in the provisioning requirements as between insured and uninsured loans even where the insurance cover is written by the public sector insurers.

The alternative method of involving commercial banks has been through involvement with the IFC. Under the IFC's 'B' loan structure, banks lend alongside the IFC (the 'A' loan) on identical terms to the IFC and with the IFC as 'lender of record'. Although the banks bear all the risks on the 'B' loan – including political risk – they take considerable comfort from the knowledge that no IFC loan ('A' or 'B') has ever been rescheduled, nor has a project to which IFC has lent been expropriated. The absence of any history of rescheduling has meant that banks see involvement via 'B' loans as giving adequate protection against 'new money' risk. It has also led some central banks (including those of the UK, France and Japan) not to require banks to provision against 'B' loans to countries where they would otherwise require a mandatory write-down. The shortcomings of the 'B' loan structure are: firstly, IFC will not underwrite participation in 'B' loans so sponsors cannot be sure of obtaining the funds and hence prudence dictates that the finance plan must provide additional, fallback finance; secondly, involving the IFC means that the project has to meet IFC's non-economic criteria and guidelines and be subject to their lengthy appraisal/approval procedures; and, finally, the IFC will usually press for equity participation which may not always be welcome.

The IFC will also lend on its own account (the 'A' loan) without a 'B' loan tranche and bear the political risk. This is very valuable in 'difficult' countries. 'A' loans are limited to 25% of the total project cost (and US$75 million per project). However, the 'A' loan involvement makes it easier to obtain parallel participation from bilateral institutional sources.

Export credit agencies were not seen as a source of limited recourse project finance until the 1980s. They will of course take the political risk for countries which are 'on cover' (this is their principal role) but in their early forays into project finance, they were willing to bear the political but not the commercial risks. They required sponsor guarantees for the full term of the loans but with a political risk exclusion. Since then, however, a number of major export credit agencies (eg US EXIM, EDC, EFIC) have lent on the basis of assuming both political and commercial risks post-completion. It is notable, however, that this has often been in situations where either commercial banks or the IFC have lent alongside the agencies – and they have drawn comfort from the appraisal processes of those more experienced project lenders. The main drawback of export credit finance is that it is tied to procurement of goods and services from the country concerned. As a result, the sponsor's financing plan must provide for flexible access to export credit 'cover' to avoid being forced by financing considerations into procuring goods and services from high-cost sources. This can be achieved by arranging aggregate 'cover' from countries of potential procurement in excess of total requirements; and then drawing on facilities in countries from which lowest cost bids are received.

The last major source of non-bank project finance for mining projects is 'import finance'. The governments of certain major Western countries operate financing programmes for projects in developing countries which will provide new sources of 'strategic' raw materials for their economies. The key requirement to accessing this finance is a long-term sale/purchase contract for the output of the project with a processor/user in the country from which import finance is to be obtained. Equity participation by the offtaker may also be a condition of securing finance in some countries. The programmes are normally run through the same agencies as the export-credit programmes but the requirements are different. Import finance may be lent on a fully non-recourse basis post-completion and with political risk exclusions to pre-completion guarantees. Import finance represents a very major potential source of limited recourse finance for large base metal mining projects in particular; the greater part of Escondida's foreign exchange financing requirement was met by import finance linked to offtake contracts with Japanese, German and Finnish concentrate smelters in circumstances where commercial banks were unwilling or unable to lend. The principal drawback with import finance is that it constrains the projects product marketing flexibility and inevitably creates an (at least implicit) link between the terms of the finance and the terms of the smelting and refining charges for concentrates. Nonetheless, in many countries import finance is essential to a successful base metal project financing.

Project finance in developed countries

We have dwelt at length on political risk and problems of project finance in developing countries. This is because so many greenfield projects have been located in that type of country – and because the financing problems are so intractable. However, there has been plenty of mining project finance in developed economies – most notably North America and Australia – and there the issues and developments have been very different. The two areas of interest here relate to:

- completion risk and completion guarantees
- price risk.

Completion risk

As noted earlier, in developing countries it is normal for lenders to require full sponsor guarantees of project loans until a defined completion test is achieved – at least in respect of commercial risks. In developed countries, however, there has been an increasing willingness by project lenders to accept undertakings which are not so strong from sponsors – thus reducing sponsor residual risks (and potentially permitting more rapid corporate expansion than would otherwise be possible). Although lenders have accepted weaker sponsor undertakings they have *not* sought to take more risk themselves. The trick has been to unbundle the completion risk and allocate (for a price) those risks to third parties.

Completion risk can be unbundled into various specific risks: the cost overrun risk ie that the capital cost will turn out higher than budget; the risk of delay in completing the project with consequent increases in financing and inflation-related costs; the risk that initial output will be lower or operating costs higher than planned; and force majeure risks ie adverse circumstances arising beyond the control of the sponsors.

The sponsor is able, in principle, to lay-off some or all of these risks. It may be possible to contract the construction and commissioning of the mine facilities on an essentially fixed-price basis – and to include performance guarantees and liquidated damages provisions in the contract which effectively compensate the project for any delays incurred by the contractor. This will only be possible in certain circumstances: the project needs to be 'standard' with technology which is well understood, and with limited exposure to 'ground conditions' risk; contractors must be keen for the business (usually implying a large contract and/or quality sponsor); and, of course, the contractor will charge a 'risk premium' for taking the risk. To the extent that an acceptable 'fixed-price' contract is executed, project lenders will be more relaxed about cost over-run and delay risk.

Inevitably, even with a fixed-price construction contract there are many residual risks that remain. These may be covered through a combination of some or all of:

- a stand-by finance facility (often ranging from 10–25% of the base financing requirement) which may be drawn in adverse circumstances. Lenders will wish to reassure themselves that loan cover ratios remain acceptable if the stand-by facility is fully drawn;
- a full insurance package, often including business interruption/loss of profits cover (whose availability will depend on the nature of the project);
- a performance covenant from the sponsors committing them to take all reasonable steps to ensure timely completion of the project. Although not a financial guarantee this is a strong commitment intended to avoid premature abandonment by the sponsors.

In North America, a substantial number of projects have been loan financed without sponsor pre-completion guarantees – the basic requirements (other than the arrangements noted above) being a standard and well understood type of project and robust project economics.

From this discussion it should also be apparent why in developing countries completion guarantees are invariably required. There are few situations where major contractors will accept liability for commissioning a mine for a fixed price (in view of the many administrative/practical problems that can cause delay and the problem of predicting inflation) and if they did so the 'risk premium' would undoubtedly be prohibitive! Thus, in developing countries the focus of negotiation in relation to completion risk has been to seek an objective physical completion test rather than a wider 'economic test' which can potentially give lenders wide discretion in the timing of release of pre-completion sponsor guarantees.

Price risk

The largest post-completion risk faced by lenders is often the price risk – and many minerals have shown significant price volatility over the past two decades. Typically, lenders deal with price risk simply by adopting very conservative metal price assumptions and limiting the amount they will lend to the sum that is 'covered' adequately in projections of project cash flow using these conservative assumptions. They may further supplement this conservatism by seeking 'cash deficiency undertakings' from sponsors in the event that product prices fall below some threshold level.

More sophisticated approaches to price risk first developed in the gold market. Gold is a form of money as well as a metal; and holders of gold may deposit it with banks to earn a (gold denominated) return. Since banks can access gold deposits they can also lend gold and gold loans have consequently emerged as the most important form of commodity-finance. Sponsors with gold projects can borrow gold (selling in the spot market for cash to finance mine development) and thereby accept an obligation to repay a given amount of gold over a period of years. Since the (gold-denominated) liability matches the (gold) stream of future production the sponsor has, in effect, hedged the price risk in relation to repayment of the loan – falling gold prices will not make repayment more difficult because the dollar cost of the liability also falls; of course, the corollary is that the sponsor has 'sold' a portion of the gold price upside.

The gold market has also evolved a whole range of sophisticated gold-denominated financial instruments. There is an active and liquid forward and futures market for gold with maturities of three and up-to-five years; put and call options can be bought and sold; and recently it has become feasible to fix gold loan interest rates forward. This creates further scope for hedging price risk. It has become standard in gold project financing for borrowers to sell forward gold sufficient to finance estimated operating costs over the first three or four years of project operations. Thus, if spot gold prices fall the ability of the project to generate sufficient revenues to meet operating costs is not jeopardised. Similarly, the (gold-denominated) cost of gold borrowing can be locked in through the forward interest-rate market. The availability of these price-hedging instruments has meant that borrowers have been able to shed price risk and as a result gold lenders have been able/willing to accept tighter loan cover ratios and other covenants.

The gold lending market offers another interesting example of risk splitting. The banks with access to gold deposits (and hence the ability to make gold loans) are not always the same banks that feel comfortable taking project risk – particularly without financial completion guarantees. As a result, over the past decade it was not uncommon for a gold loan facility to be split between two groups of banks – project risk banks which issued L/Cs in favour of the project sponsors for a fee and gold lending banks which funded the gold loans but did not take any project risk. In the event of a project default the project risk banks would be obliged to meet repayment obligations to the gold banks.

In principle, the same price risk management techniques are applicable to other minerals and to oil. In practice, however, they have not evolved significantly because banks do not normally have metal (or oil) deposits against which they can lend. Individual commodity swap transactions rely on end-consumers of the product accepting a medium-term fixed price deal for metal which is passed back to the project sponsors via financial intermediaries. Several fixed price deals have been publicised in the mining or energy sectors eg the Cananea copper project financing in Mexico and the Sovereign-Emerald oil financing in the UK North Sea. Situations may arise where this type of commodity financing can be utilised to hedge price risk (particularly in the oil sector where reasonably liquid forward and futures markets exist) but it is likely to continue to be the exception rather than the rule.

Structuring the project finance vehicle

Thus far the discussion of project finance has focused principally on risk sharing. There are, however, many other issues to be addressed which relate to the structuring of the project finance vehicle. These include:

- optimising the tax position of the sponsor(s) taking account of both host and home country tax rules;
- achieving the balance sheet accounting treatment sought by the sponsor(s);
- providing protection for sponsors, where more than one sponsor is involved, against defaults by other sponsors (particularly when they have very different credit ratings and/or one partner is the host government); and
- defining an acceptable security package for the banks.

While it is difficult to generalise in these areas, several points are worth mentioning. The ownership structure of a project will have important tax and accounting implications for the project vehicle and for the sponsors. The choice of corporate vehicle – whether a company, contractual joint venture or other partnership arrangement; whether the vehicle is incorporated onshore or offshore (and, if so, where); and the level of participation by each sponsor in the various vehicles created – all will have an impact on total tax liability and on the parent companies balance sheet treatments. Optimising the overall position requires a detailed understanding of the host and home country tax and accounting rules and of the (often very different) objectives and requirements of the sponsors.

Multiparty joint ventures are the most common feature of major mining investments in developed and developing countries. The basis of the partnership (and the identity of the partners) will have an important influence on the decision as to whether each partner is separately responsible for its own share of financing ('separate financing') or whether finance is to be raised for the venture as a whole ('common financing') backed by 'several' undertakings of the sponsors and appropriate inter-partner default clauses. Without going into details here, I would note that this decision is of great importance where sponsors have different credit standing.

The composition of the security package to be offered to lenders will vary depending on the nature of the project and on whether a separate or common financing approach is adopted. Three elements are common to practically all project financings, however:

- a completion undertaking (or guarantee) from the sponsors which may take the form of several undertakings or a joint undertaking in proportion to the sponsors respective interests;
- a security interest or charges in favour of the lenders over the sponsors 'equity' or joint venture interest in the project including the mining concessions/licences/investment agreement and possibly over the underlying project assets; and
- the establishment and maintenance of an 'offshore account' into which loan and export sales proceeds will be deposited and from which debt service can be effected directly. In the event of default, lenders (typically through a trustee) would have the right to take control of this account and apply project cash in priority to service their loans.

Processing industries

Most of the previous discussion relates to mining rather than processing of minerals. This is because there have been very few examples of greenfield smelting/refining complexes in recent years and even fewer that have been project-financed. However, in principle, the same financing approach could be adopted – indeed completion risk is considerably lower for a manufacturing facility than for a mine – and the key issue will always be the nature and extent of user/owner obligations. Throughput volumes and the processing margin determine the economics of processing industries and spot margins are highly volatile and uncertain. Project financing, therefore, depends on commercial user agreements with concentrate suppliers and/or end-users which on the one hand stabilise project cash flows and, on the other, do not diverge so far from market terms as to prove unsustainable once the plant is operating. Thus, the challenge in the project financing of processing plants lies not only in the financing but also in the design of sustainable underlying commercial terms.

New approaches to financing mining projects

The debt crisis in developing countries has stimulated financial innovation and the emergence of new approaches to financing mining investment. As so often, the stimulus has been necessity. Governments who, in the past, would have supported public-sector investment simply have not been able to raise the required finance and have increasingly turned to the private sector to manage existing operations and to develop new properties.

One notable development has been the spread of privatisation of state industries – latterly with a heavy emphasis on debt-equity swaps. This latter development arose from a recognition by international banks that they may be better off accepting equity in a privatised company rather than continuing to hold 'bad loans'. Of course, the debt-equity swap route does not generate new resources for financing new mining investment – the transaction is simply a transfer of existing assets from one owner to another (in return for a debt write-off). However, with the transfer goes a transfer of the obligation to finance future investment (sometimes with quantified obligations) – and this should generate additional future project finance opportunities – and challenges!

In some developing countries, the debt crisis has resulted in the development of new means of raising local currency financing for mining projects on attractive terms – through debt swap programmes. Although in detail these vary immensely (depending on the local rules) the essence is simple. International banks have made loans to private sector borrowers in developing countries. The local borrower has deposited local currency with the central bank to repay the loan but the central bank has failed to provide foreign currency to repay the international bank. The international bank has written-down the value of the loan in his books and is prepared to sell the loan at a (deep) discount to reduce its country exposure to further sovereign rescheduling. The mining investor buys the loan at a discount and receives the corresponding local currency amount from the central bank to finance local expenditure costs by way of equity or subordinated loans to the project vehicle. In effect, the investor accesses local currency at a very favourable exchange rate. The official programmes vary tremendously between countries but all have a common theme: there are repatriation restrictions on dividends, interest and capital originating from these transactions. This form of finance is potentially inflationary for the local economy and so access to the funds is normally rationed, and the central bank will typically levy charges on the transaction which will transfer part of the financial benefit to the state. In each individual project financing the availability and total cost of this type of financing needs to be understood as part of the development of the project financing plan.

Conclusion

If there is a conclusion to this chapter, it is that project financing of mining projects in developing countries has been greatly complicated by the 'debt crisis' and reduction in credit availability in the early 1990s. However, financing can be arranged that meets sponsors' objectives if close attention is paid to hedging political risk. In developed countries, mining project finance lives on and creates interesting new challenges as commodity-related financial derivatives become more sophisticated. The debt crisis will create new opportunities for private sector mining investment in developing countries – as well as new financial instruments that can generate low cost local currency funding.

Keith Palmer is a Director and member of the Executive Committee of NM Rothschild & Sons Limited. He is the head of the Natural Resources and Utilities Group which specializes in providing corporate and project finance advisory services to the energy and mining industries. He has degrees in geology and economics and has spent more than 20 years involved in the financing of energy and mining projects. Prior to joining Rothschilds he spent six years working for the World Bank Energy Department.

5 Aircraft and other mobile assets

Ian Hosier, The Sanwa Bank Limited

1 Introduction

Despite the heading of this chapter, it is written almost entirely in relation to aircraft, although there are a few references to other 'mobile' assets, such as computers. Also, although the book itself is about 'project finance', this chapter is largely (but not wholly) written in 'asset finance' terms.

This is not out of a perverse pleasure in ignoring the brief! Rather it is for the following combination of reasons:

(*a*) aircraft are about the most mobile (in terms of 'market', as well as physically) of the assets which will be covered in this chapter;

(*b*) most of the key concepts/considerations which are described later apply (in some form or other) to non-aircraft mobile assets; and

(*c*) with regard to aircraft, the term 'project finance' translates more nearly to asset finance – because that requires assessment of the individual case against the background of the overall market, and then taking risk against that (which is the author's understanding of project finance).

Although it is intended to provide a broad (and fairly comprehensive) analysis of the background to (and application of) asset-based aircraft finance, it is *not* intended to be an exhaustive study of all issues and aspects – if, indeed, such a study were practicably possible anyway.

It cannot be said too often that each case must be reviewed on its individual merits: in that way, the degree of relevance/focus of attention on the key factors can properly be determined and arranged.

An important example is the regular question as to 'how much one should finance, as a percentage of the initial aircraft cost?': *there is no one certain answer* – because it depends upon so many factors (including factors such as the competence of the operator, the asset itself, the price being paid, the security available, the amortisation period, and the amortisation profile).

Similarly, there is no single standard numerical answer which can be given to questions regarding the 'cost of repossession', or the 'amount that will be achieved upon the resale of an asset'. However, you *can* pre-determine the likely steps and procedures involved, the sources of professional assistance, and some broad parameters for possible net sale proceeds and, consequently, for appropriate asset exposure positions.

The approach of this chapter

The approach taken in this chapter is:

- to review the general background to, and development of, commercial aviation;
- to focus upon the current position, and the recent trends which have brought us to this position;
- using that information, to consider how the commercial aviation business might grow over the next 10/15 years;

(note: the above three topics together comprise the 'market' review aspect of project finance)

- next, to consider the use and value of the aircraft asset itself to an asset-financier;
- then, to review the key conceptual issues/principles behind asset-based finance of aircraft; and
- finally, give some examples as to how those issues/principles can be tailored for individual cases.

Certain matters (eg aircraft future value forecasts) which are discussed herein are taken from studies prepared for Sanwa by independent expert appraisers, which are confidential to the bank – although similar studies can of course be acquired.

2 The commercial aviation market

A The general development of commercial aviation

Although man has had an obsession with flying right back to prehistory, his history of powered flight goes back just under 90 years.

On 17 December 1903, Orville Wright made what is generally accepted as the first controlled power flight (in fact, he and his brother made four flights that day, the longest lasting approximately one minute). Then, on 14 May 1908, Wilbur Wright recorded the first known passenger flight, when he took up one Charles Furnas for just under 30 seconds. The first daily international scheduled services began in 1919 (London/Paris), quickly followed by many other scheduled services in Europe and elsewhere.

So, the commercial aviation business has progressed enormously in the 80 or so years since then, with commercial airline flights for 350 plus passengers lasting 15 hours or more now a regular feature.

Although growth has been continuous (with the obvious exception of the Second World War period – albeit aircraft design and capability did progress dramatically in those few years), the really large-scale developments have taken place since jets arrived in commercial service in the early 1950s.

Let us now look in more detail at the last 20 years, and the trends which have developed/established in that period.

B Commercial aviation business development since 1970

As mentioned above, the first regular international daily services began in 1919, and they gradually developed all around the world over the next 30 years. However, it was not until the arrival of commercial jets in the early 1950s that the volume growth really became substantial – the jets offered greater range, speed and efficiency (and passenger comfort).

By the beginning of the 1970s, the world's major airlines were almost all jet-powered on their primary routes, and so 1970 is a useful base from which to consider business development and growth.

As in most widely-diversified international business, it is not easy to select just one undoubted measure of activity, so let us consider three possible measures (between them, they must say something!).

Please note that the following figures relate just to the non-Communist countries for the obvious twin reasons of lack of reliable information and the lack of normal economic development. However, it is thought that substantial volume growth opportunities are available in these regions.

Year	Total passengers Number millions	% change on previous	Total RPM* Number billions	% change on previous	Total Jet Aircraft Number	% change on previous
1970	350	–	250	–	3900	–
1980	710	+105%	650	+160%	5800	+50%
1989	1150	+60%	1100	+70%	8000	+40%

* RPM = Revenue Passenger Miles

The above table shows:

- the explosive growth seen in the 1970s, due to the impact of the jet aircraft, coupled with increased internationalisation of business generally, and increased personal leisure time;
- the increased range and capacity of the jet fleet is evident from the much slower growth in numbers of aircraft (+105% over the period) compared with either total passengers (+230%) or total RPMs (+320%);
- also, average RPM/passenger has grown (from 715 miles in 1970 to 955 in 1989) ie the average passenger is flying further per flight.

As an example of how the business volumes have increased, world airline traffic now grows each year by an amount which is greater than one and a quarter times the *entire* market volume in 1960.

Growth trends

A great deal of analysis has been done on this subject. In particular, with regard to forecasting future business trends, it is interesting to see if there has been any relation between general economic activity and commercial aviation growth.

Aircraft and other mobile assets 83

Intuitively, one would expect that there should be some connection, since changes in economic growth impact not only on business activity (and therefore business travel), but also on individuals' personal income (and therefore on personal travel inclination/affordability). Detailed statistical research shows that there is indeed a close relationship between annual changes in world gross domestic product (GDP) and total commercial aviation RPMs as is shown by the following graph:

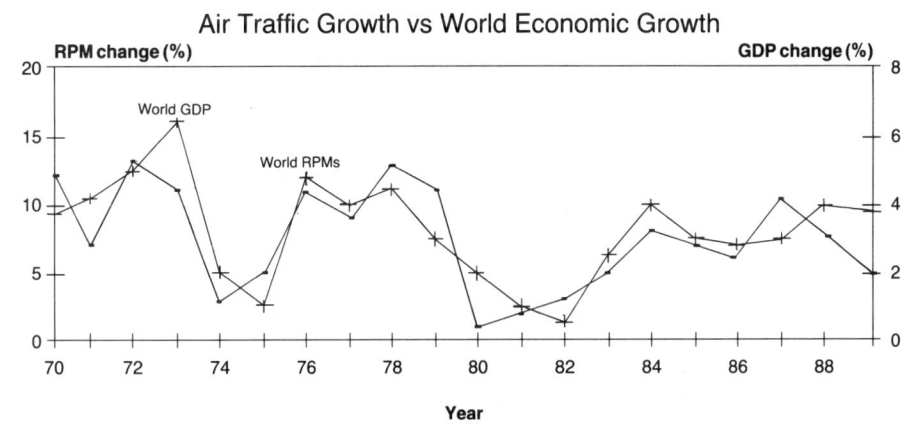

Air Traffic Growth vs World Economic Growth

[Graph showing RPM change (%) and GDP change (%) from 1970 to 1988, with curves labeled "World GDP" and "World RPMs", plotted against Year on the x-axis.]

The statistical analysis shows total RPMs growing at 2.5% pa for every 1% pa GDP growth (the higher growth for RPMs being largely attributed to increased efficiency causing real reductions in costs, which has encouraged more travel).

Using knowledge of that historical trend, we can now consider how one can project commercial aviation growth over the next 10/15 years.

C Commercial aviation business growth prospects

(a) Traffic volume growth

A number of detailed studies of growth forecasts are prepared each year (eg by the main aircraft manufacturers, by the major aircraft leasing companies such as GPA, and by various independent forecasters). These usually go into a great deal of detail, analysing the market into geographic sectors, and also product sectors (eg cargo). However, one can obtain a fair idea of the possible overall picture by simply looking at the global figures – although always acknowledging that growth is not likely to be at an even rate across the world.

Therefore, taking an expected average world GDP growth rate of 2.5% pa, then we would anticipate RPM growth in the range 5.5 to 6.5% pa – which would mean that traffic volumes should at least double from the present level by the year 2000.

(b) Aircraft fleet growth

How do these overall traffic growth figures translate into aircraft fleet numbers?

A combination of higher load factors and greater efficiency of use is expected to be able to absorb RPM growth of about 1% pa. Also, average aircraft size is expected to grow, although by not much more than about 10% of the present size (by reviewing the manufacturers' production capacity, and the present fleet composition, one can estimate this factor quite closely over a 10/12 year period).

Balancing all these factors together implies a fleet growth of at least 60% (to 12,500 jet aircraft) by the year 2000. Allowing for likely aircraft retirements over that period (estimated at around 2,500), this points to a production need of some 7,000 new jet aircraft (and – by similar analysis – some 3,500 new turboprops).

Assuming cost inflation of around 4% pa, these figures point to a total cost of new aircraft over the next 10 years of *over $430 billion – ie about $40 billion per annum* (which is equivalent to over 300 new B747-400 jumbos every year).

Again, as with all of the earlier figures, these numbers do not include the majority of the Communist world's aviation activity (which are not available to the same degree of reliability). However, it is thought that inclusion of that substantial market could increase the overall totals by one-quarter, or more.

(c) Warning

The aviation industry is a truly global industry, and has much less local or sectoral variations than, say, property or even shipping. Also, the growth trends discussed above are strong, and established over a reasonable period.

However, that very consistency of past performance can be dangerous, in that it can tempt one into assuming that it will continue, and always be upwards.

A safer analysis would be that there is a high potential for future growth, but that it will not come in smooth patterns.

This has been graphically illustrated by the recent events in the Gulf. Prior to the Iraqi invasion of Kuwait in August 1990, the airline industry had seen almost eight years of strong growth – which is fairly long as a bull market in any circumstances, and so a correction was probably due anyway.

However, the Iraq/Kuwait situation served to focus sharply a set of highly negative factors (ie increases in fuel and insurance costs, and reductions in passenger volumes). This produced very adverse cash flow conditions for the airlines, causing (or accelerating) various bankruptcies, and lowering resale values – especially for the older equipment (some of which would normally have been retired several years earlier, but for the previous strong business growth levels).

It is expected that the past pattern of cyclicality will continue, and that will have a direct impact on future asset values – which are considered next.

3 The suitability of the aircraft asset for an asset-financier

A Necessary criteria

For *any* asset to be suitable for use in any asset-based finance situation, it must:

- be readily identifiable, and allow the financier's interests in it to be effectively registered;

- be (legally and physically) recoverable in the event of default or expiry of the financing;
- have a continuing income-earning ability, thus ensuring a ready resale market, and have a good continuing future resale value over its estimated useful life.

B Comparison with other major assets

At least to date, aircraft have met the above criteria as well as almost any other asset, and these issues will be considered in a little more detail shortly. But first, here is a brief comparison with some other assets.

Of the other major categories of asset-financeable assets:

Freehold land has generally also performed well: although it would generally be expected to maintain its real value (whereas aircraft are expected to gradually decline in real value as they get older), land has the major disadvantage (compared to aircraft) of not being moveable, and subject to local economic changes;

Ships[1] have proven a much more volatile asset (and anyway tend to have a shorter full economic life, at 15/20 years against 30 years plus for aircraft).

Computers have a relatively short useful life, and tend to be rendered technologically obsolete even more quickly than that. Therefore, other than for full pay-out finance leases to good-quality lessees, computers (and other high-technology, mass-produced equipment) are unlikely to prove the most suitable assets for leasing.

C Meeting the necessary 'asset-based finance' criteria

(a) Identification

An aircraft consists of an airframe plus fitted engines, each of which has a unique manufacturer's serial number (note: the airframe itself has many parts, the more valuable of which, such as the avionics and the undercarriage, also have unique serial numbers).

Therefore, at any time, a commercial aircraft can be uniquely identified and determined, by reference to the airframe serial number (and other parts, if necessary), and to the recent national registration mark.

(b) Registration of the financier's interest

This is necessary to establish *public notice* of the financier's rights over the asset, in case of need.

---

1 As compared with aircraft, ships are relatively low technology and issues such as safety and after-sales product support are less demanding upon the manufacturer. Therefore, it is much easier, cheaper and quicker for new manufacturing capacity to be introduced into the shipping market, causing possibly severe imbalances between supply and demand – and hence causing asset values (in the short term) to fluctuate wildly, although this would be less so for the best quality assets, such as tankers with good anti-pollution design.

Aircraft operate in just about every country of the world, and therefore there is the widest possible range of legal and regulatory situations which could possibly apply to this question: hence, there is no one simple answer.

Because aircraft are valuable and expensive assets, and because financiers are so frequently involved with them, it is almost always going to be possible for the interest of the financier to be registered, for both legal and public notice purposes. Unfortunately, there is no one universally complete approach (although it is always advisable to ensure that suitable plaques are affixed to the aircraft and engines, advising the financier's involvement).

In some countries, it is possible to record publicly a mortgage interest in the aircraft, whereas in others it is not. On the other hand, it is usually easier to register ownership interests. Additionally, even if one can perfect and register a mortgage over the aircraft (as one can for example, in the UK or the US), that may not be very useful if you have to enforce the security when the aircraft is in another country, which may not recognise those mortgage rights.

The whole subject of taking legal interests in an aircraft is very complex and wide-ranging, and should always be reviewed with the assistance of expert legal counsel.

However, as mentioned above, it is safe to conclude that – one way or another – the financiers' interests should be capable of being satisfactorily established: if it is not possible in any particular case, then the financing should not be done (at least, not on an asset-backed basis).

(c) Recoverability following default, or other expiry/termination of the financing

Clearly, this subject is closely related to the previous one. However, the practical aspects of enforcing one's rights are sufficiently important to warrant separate discussion.

Although there is very little experience of major airlines or flag-carriers going into uncorrectable default, there have been a substantial number of cases involving smaller carriers like Air Europe and TEA in Europe (and a few medium-sized carriers, such as the recent examples of Braniff, Eastern and PanAm in the US).

Again, as with the subject of rights in the aircraft, there is no one standard procedure for enforcing one's rights; it has to be done with careful regard to the relevant legal and other considerations. For example, it is essential that – in close conjunction with local legal counsel – you establish precisely what notices of action must be given, and when; also, you must know what possession rights you, the lessee, and any other parties (eg local airports) may have.

In some jurisdictions (eg the US), the position is reasonably clear, with the well-established special provisions of the Bankruptcy Code dealing with leased aircraft – albeit that even there, decisions of individual judges can cause surprise, as happed in 1989/90 to GPA over its Braniff leases. Elsewhere, the legal situation can be less clear, often with the local courts being given a high level of individual discretion. Again, GPA encountered this when repossessing aircraft leased to Spanish Carriers Spantax and Hispania.

Provided that it is done promptly and carefully, repossession/enforcement against an aircraft asset should always be possible (provided also of course that the rights were properly and appropriately established in the first place). However, it should also be recognised that timing and co-ordinating of the action will be crucial, and that there will be costs involved (including especially items such as legal fees, and – usually – payment of local possessory liens etc).

Aircraft and other mobile assets 87

As a final comfort on this subject, it is now possible to purchase full insurance cover against failure to recover the asset in certain countries: this matter is reviewed post, pp 90ff under 'other available tangible security'.

(d) Resale potential over useful life

This is the area where aircraft assets can be clearly distinguished from almost all others – including ships, which (whilst also moveable) generally do not have the same degree of homogeneity of use around the world. For example, a car transporter ship will have very limited other applications, whereas a B737 flying with BA could – with minimal amendment – be operated by almost any other airline with short/medium range routes.

This 'market flexibility' is often very useful for the airlines themselves, in situations where a carrier has a long-term need for certain aircraft in its fleet (and so does not want to dispose of them), but possibly does not have a pressing need for them for a few weeks/months – regular examples of such situations are seen in the charter airlines who normally have much lower usage of their aircraft in the winter months.

The modern jet aircraft is built with an indefinite design life: however, maintenance and operating costs will mount as it gets older, so it is generally thought the useful economic life is around 30 years. There are many aircraft in current use that are well over 20 years old, and some of those are traded from time to time, at sales prices well above scrap value.

Also, in comparison with real estate, although aircraft are depreciating assets, they have the great advantage of being moveable – so they can be moved to escape a locally-depressed situation.

As with repossession, the remarketing effort should be done in close conjunction with independent expert advisers – each individual case has to be carefully addressed in the light of its own circumstances. However, the general process and procedures are well established, and there are expert professional advisers who can advise on all aspects.

The key steps are to identify the airlines/lessors who already use the particular aircraft type (or who are known to be considering it), and then to present them with a detailed specification of the aircraft, and its usage history. Thereafter, it will be a matter of negotiating prices (and any other terms and conditions, such as correcting any maintenance deficiencies) with any interested parties.

(e) Resale value

Obviously, this is an adjunct of the previous item – but it has been separated here so as to highlight the specific numerical information which is available in this regard. First, we can review actual *past* resale experience, and then consider prospective *future* values.

(i) Actual resale values The following graph shows actual resale performance achieved for the best selling jet aircraft model type (namely, the B737-200 series): similar results are shown for all the main commercial jet types over the last 20 years.

88 Tried and true, and still valid

Historic resale performance B737-200 ADV

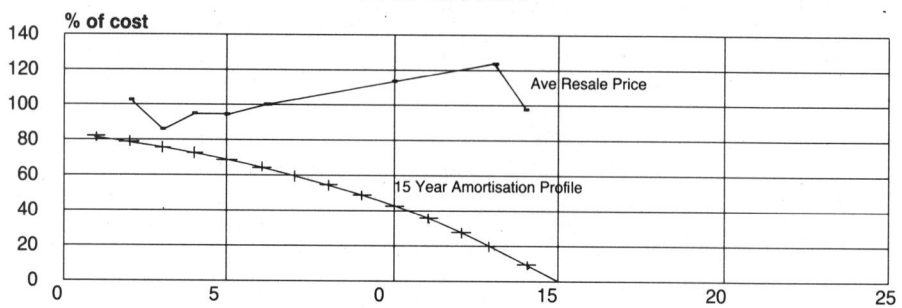

Graph showing % of cost vs. years (0-25), with "Ave Resale Price" curve around 80-120% and "15 Year Amortisation Profile" declining from ~80% to 0%.

When considering such analysis, it is important to remember that monetary inflation rates have varied so widely over the past 20 years, that one cannot simply compare a resale value achieved in, say, 1978 with one five or ten years later. Instead, we have removed the actual inflation impacts, and replaced them with a constant 3% pa assumption for consistent comparison. The graph also shows for comparison the amortisation profile for an 85% (of cost), 15-year financing.

It will be seen that – in almost every case – if one had provided such a financing, without any other substantial security, then resale of the asset would have repaid the financing.

(ii) Prospective future values Again, expert independent studies are readily available on this important aspect. The result of such a study (again, for the B737 aircraft, although this time for the latest variants) is summarised in graphic form below.

Future value forecast B737-300; B737-400

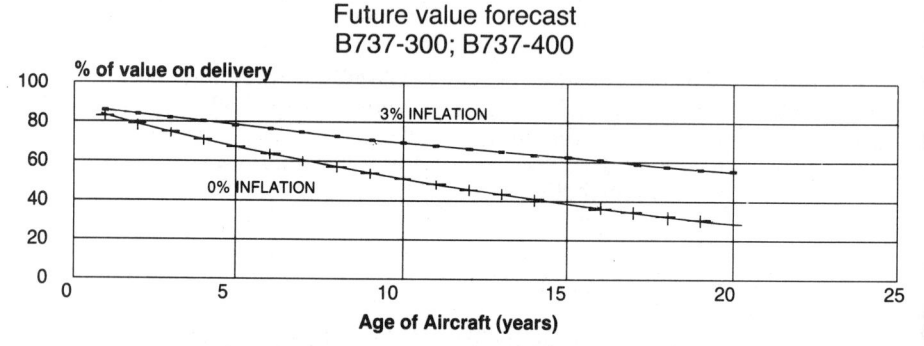

Graph showing % of value on delivery vs. Age of Aircraft (years) (0-25), with two curves: "3% INFLATION" and "0% INFLATION".

In preparing their studies, the appraisers take into account a wide range of factors, including:

- The aircraft's design life
- The aircraft's income generation ability
- Enforced obsolescence
- Care and maintenance
- Marketability

When using these studies, it must of course, be remembered that they are forecasts – *not* guarantees. However, the appraisers are well-qualified to produce these forecasts, and the evidence of history gives a great deal of comfort that such values can indeed be achieved. Indeed, to date there appears to be a much greater level of consistency and predictability for aircraft asset values than for other major capital items such as ships or property.

Nonetheless, it would be unwise for a commercial bank to place total reliance on achieving *100%* of the forecast values: prudence dictates that a lower level (*say 70/75%*) of reliance should be used – in that way one can be reasonably sure of recovering the financing, after making fair allowance for possible market conditions, and also the inevitable costs of realising the value.

As was mentioned earlier, severe world economic/political situations (such as the Iraq/Kuwait conflict) can cause quite sharp downward fluctuations in values. Although past experience suggests that such fluctuations do get ironed-out over time, it is nonetheless the case that they must be anticipated when estimating appropriate asset-value cover levels. Any exposure which is taken above a 70/75% rate of asset value has to be justifiable against the creditability of the relevant obligor, and/or any other available security/credit support/relevant factor.

This matter is further discussed below, when the key conceptual issues/principles behind the application of asset-based finance to aircraft are considered.

4 Key issues/principles of aircraft asset-based finance

An attempt is now made to review key principles; then outlines of some specific cases will be given (see section 5, pp 93ff), showing how those general requirements have been applied in particular transactions.

Before moving on to these key principles it should be stressed again that asset-based finance is (like project finance in general) *a supplement* (not a *replacement*) to 'conventional' credit facilities. Indeed, the first stage of the analysis for an asset-based finance is exactly that for a 'conventional' credit (ie the competence, capability and commitment of the owners and managers, and the feasibility of the particular project). Only when reasonably satisfied on these matters can you move on to see how the available asset(s) could support the required financing, where the 'conventional' credit-standing of the parties does not in itself provide the necessary reassurance.

The key issues for the 'asset-based' part of the assessment are assessing, preserving and accessing the maximum value of the assets. These breakdown into the following main factors:

(a) the current/prospective value of the financed asset(s);
(b) other tangible security available (eg third-party guarantees, export credit agency cover, security deposits, other aircraft, etc);
(c) the transaction structure, with particular reference to the security options available, and the relevant local legal/tax/accounting considerations; and
(d) preserving/ensuring the value of the asset during the financing.

These will now be looked at in a little more detail.

A The current/prospective value of the financed asset(s)

This was discussed at some length in the previous section. However, it is worth repeating the point about not relying 100% upon of the forecast values – because that takes the bank into the 'equity risk' area of the asset value, which is not appropriate for a commercial banking margin. That 'equity' (or 'top slice') risk is properly for the airline or true lessor (such as GPA or ILFC) who are geared to assess, manage and control such risks, in return for the much higher rewards which should accompany those risk levels.

One other important issue here is *'what if the asset is not new?'*. Used aircraft assets are not – in themselves – a problem: indeed, if in good condition, are often a better asset for 'asset-finance', because they do not carry the 'newness' premium that a new aircraft (like any other new asset) inevitably carries. However, if the asset is not new, you must have your advisers make two additional steps (as compared with the new asset):

- *the existing legal title* (and any rights or interests held over it) for the asset must be clearly established (for a new aircraft, the manufacturer will warrant good title – and you know that will be acceptable and reliable);
- *the physical condition (and technical records)* must be examined in detail by an expert inspector, and a specific current value given in the light of that inspection.

This is very important: if the aircraft (and/or its technical records) are in poor condition, then it can cost several millions of dollars to put right – which might severely damage your valuation assessments, if you have not allowed for it.

B Other available tangible security

The most commonly seen examples here are as follows:

Manufacturer's deficiency guarantee These are given reluctantly, and only if there is no other way of achieving the financing required by the purchaser. Typically, these guarantees would range between 15 and 30% of the amount financed, declining as the financing is repaid.

Export credit agency guarantee If this is given in the full amount allowed under the international rules (ie 85% of equipment cost), then the financing is unlikely to be truly asset-based – even if you are financing the other 15% for the airline. However, there are occasions where – for reasons of the agency's own credit limits – they will not make the maximum amount available. Also, they have recently begun to issue their guarantee for 'non-repossession' risk only, thus leaving the asset value/airline credit risk with the financier. In such cases, it will be an asset financing.

Security deposits An operating lessor will almost always take – as a pre-condition to his lease – a certain number of months' (usually between two and six) rental in advance, as additional collateral for any failure by the lessee airline. At present lease rent rates, such security deposits translate into 3 to 9% of aircraft value.

It is unusual to see such deposits in a commercial bank financing because – unlike the operating lessor – we are not normally financing 100% of the asset value. However, the concept is occasionally used for very difficult credits, or where regular delays, but not full default, in rental payments are anticipated.

Other guarantees   These might include parent company guarantees (which we probably would wish to take) and governmental guarantees – which we probably would *not* want, since we would usually be looking to distance the financing from the local country risk.

Also, there may be asset value underwriting (or 'slice') guarantees available at certain specified dates, if the structure featured 'walk-away' options for the airline, at various times during the financing. Such 'slice' guarantees are usually provided either by the relevant manufactuer or specialist asset risk takers, although – depending upon the level of risk involved – they are also provided on occasions by commercial banks.

The purpose of these guarantees is to enable an otherwise full pay-out financing to be stopped well short of its natural maturity (say year five of 15), but without requiring the long-term financiers to take the full asset risk exposure at the early termination date. Such 'early termination' arrangements are normally designed to enable the lessee to treat the lease as off balance sheet for his Accounts.

Other undertakings   For a difficult country risk situation, it is useful to seek:

- Finance Ministry confirmation that the financing payments were approved for foreign exchange payments;
- undertakings/confirmations from the relevant ministries/bodies that the aircraft would be released free and clear (and de-registered, if necessary) in the event of a lease termination.

Repossession insurance   In recognition of the difficulty which the banks have in achieving complete removal of any adverse country risk from a financing, even if all of the above protections/approaches have been employed, the London Insurance Market has developed a special form of cover, to ensure payment of an agreed sum, should repossession not prove possible following a default. This insurance originally developed from the general 'contract frustration' insurance market, but has now become a specific product in its own right, with a well-developed policy wording, and experienced brokers/underwriters.

Of course, the general rule still applies that insurance cannot make a bad deal good. However, the major benefit of repossession insurance is that it is a clear-cut and accepted way of achieving full risk transfer away from the particular country (which is crucial for escaping the need for automatic bad debt provisioning under present regulatory systems).

C The transaction structure

In the absence of any other consideration, the financier will want to get the most direct control possible over his assets, and the revenues arising therefrom. But, because the financier's requirements cannot be viewed in isolation, the key point here is how to achieve the best security position for the financier, after having full regard for the requirements/constraints imposed by the financing form(s) available in the particular case.

For example, if *tax-based finance* is available to enhance the cost-effectiveness of the overall structure, then that tax-based finance may require ownership to be with certain parties, or in a certain jurisdiction (or both). Also, if there are issues such as *avoidance of withholding tax*, then again this will have implications for payment flows, including possibly the need for lease/sub-lease structures, etc. Additionally, *local legal or regulatory requirements* must be allowed for: for example, in some countries, for an aircraft to be registered locally, it must be owned locally.

A flexible approach is therefore essential – although this does *not* mean that the financier's security interests must be of secondary importance to the financial/fiscal issues. However, it is normally the case that those security interests can be protected in more than one way – albeit that there may be some difference in effectiveness of the alternative routes, but that can usually be addressed by variations in risk pricing (at least, as between alternatives which are in themselves acceptable).

As mentioned previously, it is important that the 'structuring' considerations take place with the assistance of appropriate legal/tax/accounting advice.

D Preserving/ensuring the value of the asset

Having assessed future asset value exposures, and attempted to ensure that you can access the asset in case of need, it is also crucial to know that the asset is being properly looked after whilst it is out of the financier's control.

It is, of course, a fact that any projections of future values of any asset will be made upon assumptions regarding the relative condition of the asset at any time – usually, the assumption is that the asset is in the condition that it should be for its age and usage, *if maintained in accordance with manufacturers and regulators approved programmes/procedures*.

This can be a very important assumption, should repossession be required following a lessee default. Failure to maintain the aircraft properly (and the related technical records) might result in substantial cost for the financier – possibly as much as 10% or more of the aircraft value. For example, if a wide-body aircraft is repossessed in a condition that requires a major overhaul (perhaps a full 'D' check), that might well cost up to $5 million (or more, if expensive items – like the engines – require major repair).

The financier can deal with the 'satisfactory maintenance' issue in one of two main ways – ie the airline can be allowed to perform (or arrange) maintenance itself, or it will be required to contract maintenance to an acceptable third-party, such as a major airline like Swissair or Alitalia. In either case, but especially the latter, the airline can be required to pay regular sums into a maintenance reserve account charged in favour of the financier. Also, in every case, the financier must have the documentary right to inspect the aircraft at any time (subject to reasonable notice, prior to default).

In addition, it is also usually crucial that – should the asset be damaged or destroyed – *sufficient insurance proceeds* are both available and paid directly to the financier (or to his order), and that suitable liability risk insurances are held to cover damages which can arise from incidents with the aircraft. Aircraft

Aircraft and other mobile assets 93

insurance is a complex issue in itself, and – as with other matters such as legal advice – it is essential to enlist the services of an expert adviser (most aviation insurance brokers offer this service).

Therefore, the maintenance and insurance aspects of an asset-based financing are very much more than just mere 'technicalities'. Again, as has been stressed in this chapter:

- each case has to be reviewed and assessed on its merits (there is no one 'standard' answer); and
- where necessary, independent expert advice should be sought.

Next, some specific cases will be considered, including how the maintenance arrangements in particular can be established in a variety of ways, with particular reference to how reputable third party maintainers (frequently major airlines, or their subsidiaries) can be involved in this process.

5 Examples of aircraft asset-based finance

As mentioned previously, 'asset-based' financing techniques are used in aircraft finance for a range of reasons, including not only the obvious 'credit enhancement' purposes, but also for balance sheet or other 'financial structuring' reasons, including situations which are more akin to general project (or quasi-project) finance.

The following brief outlines describe a variety of situations where asset-based approaches have been employed to achieve a range of objectives. The outlines used are all from actual transactions, but (for obvious reasons) the details have been limited to those which are matters of general public information.

A Credit enhancement

There are two main categories here, namely *corporate* credit enhancement, and *country* credit enhancement (which latter category generally includes the former too!).

(a) Corporate credit enhancement
The most frequently seen examples of this category are for new aircraft acquisitions by airlines with (relatively) limited credit-standing operating in an acceptable country risk area, with the relevant aircraft manufacturer supplying some form of credit guarantee to the financiers.

In 1987, at Chemical Bank ('Chemical') we completed just such a transaction for what was then a brand-new 'start-up' airline called Air 2000 – the in-house airline of the specialist travel group, Owners Abroad Group ('OAG') (which specialised in 'seat-only' travel for the increasing number of people owning or renting property outside the UK, in addition to providing services to people looking to acquire such property). Owners Abroad was publicly-quoted, but with a market value of considerably less than the over-$40 million cost of the new B757 aircraft which the airline planned to acquire (with 2/3 others to follow). Therefore, the transaction could not be supported on pure 'corporate credit' grounds.

Although the new airline was a complete 'start-up' (and so had no performance track record), the senior management all had good previous airline experience: in particular, the managing director had previously started up Air Europe for the International Leisure Group. So, we were able to satisfy ourselves with the *competence of the management*, and the *commitment of the shareholders*. Also, *the feasibility of the project was acceptable* given that the airline was going to obtain a good 'feed' from its parent, but was not going to rely wholly on that (for instance, they had negotiated contracts with other travel companies for a substantial number of seats).

With regard to the transaction structure, the airline required:

(a) UK tax-enhanced financing (because they would not be able to use the tax allowances themselves in their first few years); and

(b) to limit the impact on the parent company's balance sheet (remember that the parent was a quoted company, and did not want its balance sheet 'blown-up' by the aircraft assets of its new subsidiary).

Therefore the following structure was put in place:

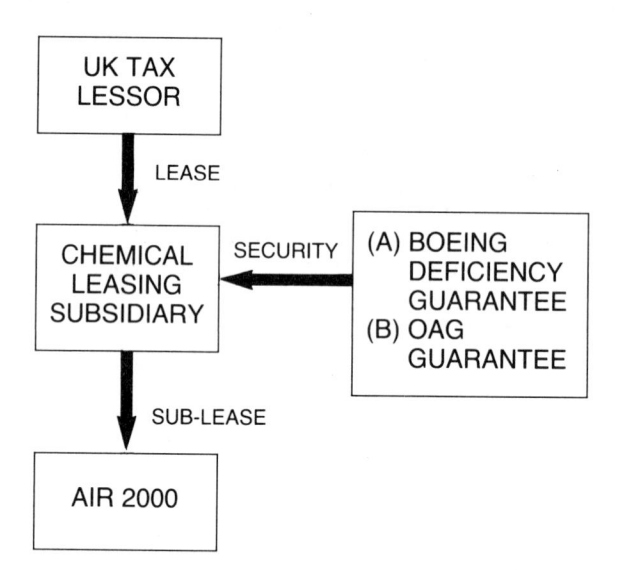

```
           ┌──────────────┐
           │  UK TAX      │
           │  LESSOR      │
           └──────┬───────┘
                  │ LEASE
                  ▼
    ┌──────────────┐  SECURITY  ┌──────────────────┐
    │  CHEMICAL    │◄───────────│ (A) BOEING       │
    │  LEASING     │            │     DEFICIENCY   │
    │  SUBSIDIARY  │            │     GUARANTEE    │
    └──────┬───────┘            │ (B) OAG          │
           │                    │     GUARANTEE    │
           │ SUB-LEASE          └──────────────────┘
           ▼
    ┌──────────────┐
    │   AIR 2000   │
    └──────────────┘
```

Comments

(a) *The 'lease/sub-lease' structure* was designed to enable the head tax lease to remain in place if the airline either defaulted or exercised its return option (although any replacement sub-lease would have had to be a suitably qualifying UK operator if it was desired to keep the tax lease in place).

Aircraft and other mobile assets 95

(b) *The sub-lease contained 'window dates'* on which the aircraft could be returned, but where the full lease outstanding did not have to be repaid (the levels of payment to which the airline was committed on the return dates were set so as to ensure that the sub-lease qualified as an 'operating lease' for the purposes of the UK accounting standards). Of the amounts which were not payable by the airline on such 'window dates', the risk was shared between the bank and the aircraft manufacturer;

(c) Because UK tax leases are written in pounds sterling, whilst aircraft are generally valued in US dollars, clearly there was a *potential currency exposure* for Chemical, in addition to the pure asset value risk.

There are a number of ways of handling such situations, but the usual approach, where (like here) there was no substantial credit party prepared to cover the risk, is to require the airline to provide some form of additional collateral should sterling appreciate against the dollar.

(d) *The maintenance of the aircraft* was easier for the bank to consider than in some 'country risk' situations (see below), because – although the airline was new – its management were very experienced and, as the aircraft was UK-based, its condition could be readily inspected.

(b) Country credit risk enhancement

As discussed previously, the difficult country risk situations have a great deal of similarity with the difficult corporate risk cases, such as that described above – but they introduce the additional considerations such as repossession, de-registration and maintenance (the latter because inspection/checking may well be less easy).

At Chemical, through both the London and the New York offices, we had a great deal of experience with African and South American carriers. To help illustrate the earlier point that one must tailor each case to its own merits (and in particular to recognise that different airlines have different levels of capability), there is shown below a brief comparison of new aircraft financings done by Chemical for two African carriers.

Item	Royal Air Maroc	Zambia Airways
Aircraft	2 × B757-200 ($85m)	1 × DC 10-30 ($50m)
Finance format	Lease	Lease
Ownership	Chemical UK subsidiary	Chemical US subsidiary
Additional security	Limited support from Boeing	Limited support from McDonnell Douglas
Registration	Morocco	USA
Maintenance	Airline	Contracted to Alitalia
Government undertakings	To return free and clear, de-registered	To return free and clear

Comments

(a) Although Morocco and Zambia were both re-scheduling countries at the time of the respective financings, the two airlines fairly reflected the difference in the relative development (economic and political) between the two countries.

(b) Royal Air Maroc ('RAM') was a long-established and profitable carrier, with an all-Boeing jet fleet of over 20 aircraft, whereas Zambia Airways had just a couple of jet aircraft, with a rather less developed system and structure.

(c) RAM had a substantial maintenance base, certificated to full US Federal Aviation Authority standard for all work on its fleet, except for the major checks on its two B747s (for which substantially-larger physical facilities are required – which is not economic for just two aircraft).

(d) Zambia on the other hand had limited maintenance capability, other than for the basic day-to-day work.

(e) However, both airlines were able to demonstrate the economic need and feasibility for the proposed aircraft acquisitions (which have both been more than borne out by actual experience).

(f) With regard to aircraft registration, Morocco had always had theirs registered locally, and non-local registration would have been difficult for them to accept, whereas – for Zambia – there was no substantial local precedent as this was their first major external financing.

(g) The experience of Chemical Bank under those transactions was excellent, as was the case with all other similar financings they had, including in South America.

(h) For example, the Mexican government ensured that all financiers were paid in full on a timely basis (and also kept regularly informed of developments) when they put their national carrier into bankruptcy in 1988 (a publicly acknowledged union-breaking action, designed to force the carrier into a new, efficient and profitable basis).

B Balance sheet enhancement

There are a number of such examples of aircraft financing, although not as many as of the 'credit enhancement' category, because balance sheet considerations are usually only of concern to carriers which are – or which are targeted to become – privately owned.

Given that, until quite recently, any form of lease finance was not shown on the face of balance sheets, then avoidance of adverse balance sheet impact was fairly simple (especially in the US, where tax-based leases were frequently the most attractive form of aircraft finance, anyway). There have been a number of UK-based examples of such 'balance sheet' finance, partly because the UK accounting standards were amongst the first to toughen up on 'leasing commitments' accounting, and also because the UK was amongst the first (outside the US) to privatise its principal airline.

British Airways has enjoyed three major facilities of this type (totalling over $5 billion), which are the most prominent examples of this type. Elsewhere in the UK, there have also been off balance sheet structures for private carriers such as ILG/Air Europe, Horizon Travel/Orion Airways, and (as already reviewed above) Air 2000.

Examples outside the UK are much less common, because (other than in the US), fewer airlines have been fully exposed to private ownership, and so there is much less concern over the balance sheet ratios and general condition. The US carriers have traditionally financed a substantial portion of their fleet on US tax-based leases, which are closer to operating leases (because it is not normally possible for the airline to have anything but a fair market value purchase option at lease expiry).

The majority of these 'off balance sheet' financings have been completed under what are frequently known as *asset value underwriting ('AVU')* facilities, the typical structure of which will include the following features:

- the aircraft will be leased to the airline (sometimes as the sub-lease under head/sub-lease structure for tax purposes);
- at various dates (return option dates or window dates) during the lease period, the airline will have the option to either terminate the lease (without having to pay off the outstanding finance), or to extend the lease for a further period;
- on such 'return' dates, the airline will usually be required to make some payment if it does decide to return the aircraft, *but* such payment will be well short of the whole outstanding amount at that time;
- for example, if the first return date were Year 5, and if the finance balance outstanding then were 85% of the initial amount, then the airline (or possibly the airlines and other parties, such as the manufacturer) may be required to pay sufficient to reduce the outstanding to 55 or 60% (of initial amount);
- the remaining balance would then be a risk for the asset-financiers to take against the aircraft value at the time;
- generally, it is the case that provided the present value of the aggregate of:
    (a) the lease rentals for the period to such a return date, and
    (b) the required payment at such date
  is less than a certain percentage of the asset cost (such percentage being determined in accordance with relevant accounting practice), then the airline will not have to 'capitalise' the lease onto its balance sheet;
- there are usually several such 'return' dates during the lease term, enabling the off balance sheet treatments to continue during the lease term; and
- the asset-risk takers in these transactions will generally receive a separate fee for this risk (in addition to any normal financing margin which they might also earn, as in a conventional transaction).

C Other 'financial structuring' reasons

This is a deliberately wide category, because – as should already be evident – there is a large set of circumstances which might lead to an asset-based approach to aircraft finance, which may involve credit or balance sheet factors, but which may well be primarily driven by other considerations.

Into this category would come things such as GPA's financings for their joint venture companies ('JVCs'), one specific objective of which is to limit the impact on GPA's balance sheet. This was achieved by arranging these financings through the JVCs themselves, in which GPA has a 50% stake, but not management control. The financings were recourse only to the JVCs and neither GPA nor their joint venture partners gave any guarantees or any other support (except GPA undertook to provide the management of the JVCs). Therefore, the lenders had to rely on the (limited) balance sheet resources of the JVCs plus the assets financed.

Project financing in its more general sense is also possible in relation to aircraft – although we are not aware of any situations where the concept has actually been converted into real financing. However, it has been considered in a number of cases, especially in conjunction with development finance for aircraft (eg Airbus A321) or engines (eg Rolls Royce Tay) which are *derivatives* of existing equipment (note: a brand new model would be too high risk for commercial bank finance). Project-finance concepts are also possible for related financing situations, such as airports.

However, the particular example which is featured here involves an aircraft manufacturer, who was seeking *'sales aid' finance* – ie he wished to be able to offer finance as a part of his sales package.

Short Brothers: US sales finance facility

This facility was first developed in 1982, by Citibank, with the particular assistance of NatWest: subsequently, NatWest and Citi developed similar facilities for Shorts UK/Europe sales, and Westland Helicopters (discussions as to similar concepts were also held with most commuter aircraft manufacturers).

Short Brothers (now acquired by a Canadian manufacturer) was wholly-owned by the UK government, and was the major employer in Northern Ireland (an area of high unemployment). Therefore, politically it was very sensitive, but had been heavily subsidised for years, and had had a very poor financial position (indeed, it was technically insolvent, and only able to continue to trade because of UK government public support of its business obligations).

However, it had suddenly found itself in the early 1980s as the earliest entrant into production of the 30/36 seat commuter aircraft sector, for which there was a sharply-growing demand, especially in the USA, following airline deregulation there. Unfortunately, of course, the majority of its potential customer base were small-scale (sometimes even 'start-up') operators, for whom even the relatively modest cost ($5 million) of these small aircraft was not possible to finance on a conventional basis.

A full Shorts (and UK government) guarantee was not appropriate, as Shorts was intended as a privatisation candidate. Therefore the solution developed was a *limited recourse 'umbrella' credit facility* (available by way of loans, guarantees etc), for Shorts (via a suitable US subsidiary or subsidiaries) to provide finance for their US customers.

The whole concept was of a *'pool' of risk* for the banks, and so all security in the aircraft involved was cross-collateralised. Shorts' recourse was limited (to about 30% of outstanding financing), but was available (subject to that limit) on a 'first-loss' basis across the whole outstanding amount at any one time. Shorts were fully responsible for all aspects of documentation and repossession (note: if there were any losses arising from these aspects, then they became 100% liable for the relevant outstanding amount). Shorts were also responsible for servicing the relevant financing from default until repossession, and for a period thereafter; and to ensure that the banks did enjoy a good spread of airline risk, there was a strict limit on how many aircraft could be acquired by any one airline (or group of airlines).

Overall, the facility was successful, and was closer to a 'project' risk than an 'asset' risk, as one had to form a view of the whole commuter airline market, and not just the particular aircraft, or airline.

The concept can be applied in a number of situations, but – for larger aircraft – the problem is being able to write a large enough facility (in monetary terms) to ensure the necessary spread of risk.

D Can aircraft asset-based financing go wrong?

As aircraft asset-based financings are not 'risk-free' situations – the answer to the above question must be 'yes it is possible'. Against that, it must also be said that such financing does offer the financier the potential to give himself as good a level of protection as is available in almost any long-term financing.

Airlines do go into bankruptcy – especially the smaller, privately-owned carriers in Europe or the US. Very few examples exist of national flag-carriers becoming unrecoverably insolvent (although a fair number in LDC countries have inevitably had short periods of cash-flow problems).

Clearly, anyone who lent unsecured to Braniff in the US, or to Air Europe in the UK (or – in 1981 – to Laker Airways), would have suffered a substantial percentage loss of their financing. However, even in those private-carrier collapses, I believe that those who were properly asset-secured recovered (or will recover) most, if not all, of what was owed to them.

6 Summary and conclusions

I hope that this chapter has shown that the aircraft asset can be – and has been – successfully financed in a variety of ways which rely to a greater or lesser extent upon the continuing value of the asset, and the market in which it operates.

However, it is also important to note that those 'asset' assessments do not remove the crucial need to assess the competence of the relevant project managers, and the reasonable economic feasibility of the project. Additionally, it is also crucial that suitable legal and other professional advice be obtained, so as best to achieve the desired combination of flexibility and security – including, especially, unwinding the structure should a termination occur.

As stated in the introduction, this review is focused very much upon aircraft asset/project finance, although many of the basic points and concepts will apply to any moveable asset which has a reasonable market life and value. The review is also intended as a fairly brief consideration of the various key aspects, and to show how they can be handled and combined. However, the principal message is that 'asset-based' finance is a generic name for a very wide set of possibilities, which (in risk concept) are similar to the general field of project finance, which is what this book is about.

Although they can seem somewhat complex and daunting on occasions, asset-based financings are not – in themselves – something to be afraid of: indeed, they can be a very useful part of a bank's range of services and capability – enabling it to improve some transactions, and to tackle some others that it would not otherwise be able to do.

Ian Hosier is Deputy General Manager, and Head of Aerospace Finance at Sanwa Bank's London Branch.

He was educated at Colchester Grammar School and Bristol University, receiving an Honours Degree in Mathematics. He is an Associate of the Chartered Institute of Bankers.

He joined National Westminster Bank in 1972, where he held a variety of appointments in Head Office – including Personal Assistance roles for both the Finance Director and the Group Chief Executive – and in the Aerospace Group of the International Division, concentrating on manufacturer and asset financing.

In January 1986, he moved to Chemical Bank, where he was the deputy head of the Special Finance Group (which specialised in asset-based financing, especially of aircraft, until it was sold off in the second half of 1989).

He joined Sanwa in November 1989 as an Assistant General Manager, and has particular responsibility for the development of Sanwa's aerospace finance activities in Europe, Africa and the Middle East. He now heads a team of seven in London and was promoted to his present status in April 1991.

He wishes to acknowledge specific thanks to Kay Jiggins, for her help and patient assistance in preparing this chapter.

6 Leasing and tax-based project finance

Peter J Whitney, Lloyds Leasing Limited

The fundamental risks involved in project financing, whether of assets or of complex projects, will be very much the same where project financing techniques are used with the addition of leasing or a tax base.

The addition of either of these products will be undertaken with a view to reducing the financing costs either by impacting directly on the funding or by providing additional benefits to the project. The purpose of this chapter is to set out what benefits may be available through leasing, tax-based structures and to identify both the additional costs (direct) and the additional risks involved (mainly indirect).

Leasing

Where are the additional risks and what value is added by the project sponsor accepting these additional risks?

The simplest answer to the question 'what is the added value' will be that leasing offers a more cost-effective means of financing and the tax-based route is being followed for the same reason.

'Cost-effective' in this context is to be regarded as providing funds at a rate below that otherwise available. The addition of the financing medium will have a direct effect on the underlying finance of the project sufficient to enable the provider of the finance to extract a reward (margin) and provide the borrower with a worthwhile benefit. The quantification of the benefit is dealt with in the appropriate section of this chapter.

In contemplating leasing it will be useful to appreciate the connotations attaching to the word leasing – a lease may be defined as:

> 'a contract between a lessor and a lessee for the hire of an asset selected from a manufacturer or lender of such assets by the lessee. The lessor retains ownership of the asset. The lessee has possession and use of the asset on payment of specified rentals over a period.'

The permanent separation of ownership and use is central to the whole concept of equipment leasing and distinguishes it from other payment by instalment types of transactions.

The implications of the separation of ownership from use may be of significance to a project financing where it is usual for the project banks to seek to obtain charges over the equipment of the business (in this case the equipment is owned by the lessor who may regard the equipment as his first security). A further significant point is that the lessor as owner has potentially to face the third-party liabilities inherent in ownership.

Although the foregoing is a basic definition of leasing, leasing may be broken down into other areas of which the following are examples:

- Finance leasing
- Operating leasing
- Lease purchase
- Vendor leasing (sales aid)
- Contract hire
- Rental, hiring and plant hiring

For the purpose of this chapter we will consider finance leasing and lease purchase as being the most appropriate for large projects.

In finance leasing the equipment is selected by the lessee before being bought by the lessor. That it is to say, the lessor buys and leases whatever equipment it is that the lessee wants to use. In operating leasing rental contracts, the goods are not necessarily selected by the lessee from the manufacturer or vendor, and in hiring the equipment is normally supplied by a business specialising in the hire of a particular range of goods on regular contract terms.

The operating lessor offers a wider service: choosing or advising on the best equipment for the lessee's needs, sometimes the equipment he has in stock, perhaps after an earlier operating lease. Thus he knows more about the market for the equipment and the likely market at the end of the primary period; he provides greater skill as well as taking greater risk to justify the extra profit on the secondary lease. A similar situation arises with regard to contract hire where a knowledge of the equipment is essential.

Finance leasing

Finance leasing or 'full pay-out leasing' is a contract involving payment over a period (usually referred to as the primary period) of specified sums sufficient in total to amortise the capital outlay of the lessor and to provide for the lessors' borrowing costs and profit. The lessee is normally responsible for the maintenance and insurance of the asset. Usually leases may be extended after the expiration of the primary period by a secondary period, when it is usual for the rentals to be significantly reduced (this will be the case where the lease has been a 'full pay-out lease') in the primary period. If a lump sum has remained outstanding at the end of the basic primary period (because the lessor has been able to take a view on residual value) the secondary rental will of necessity be a figure somewhat larger than nominal.

Finance leases are normally full pay-out so that after the primary period the lessor has no need to recover further large amounts. Rent in the secondary period is therefore usually nominal. In the few cases where the lessor has been able to take a view on residual value, he will need a higher rent in the secondary period to give a full return.

Operating leasing

An operating lease is a contract under which the asset is not wholly amortised during the primary period and where the lessor does not rely wholly upon the rentals in that period for his profit but looks for recovery of the balance of his costs and of his profit from the sale or release of the returned assets at the end of the lease. Operating leasing is common for goods where technological or other changes may mean that the lessee would not wish to retain the asset for its full working life and where there exists a good secondhand market. The classic examples of this are the car and computer leasing markets.

Sales-aid leasing

In 'sales-aid' leasing there is usually a connection between the lessor and the manufacturer or the vendor whereby the lessor or the vendor offers a leasing package as an alternative form of finance on the particular goods for whose distribution he is responsible. Sales-aid leasing may be used in connection with both financial and operating leasing.

Contract hire

Contract hire is a form of lease used most often for fleets of motor vehicles where commonly the lessor may contract to provide not the use of certain vehicles but the use of an agreed number of a specified type for a term generally shorter than the life of the asset. The lessor may therefore provide the repair, maintenance and servicing, and replacement of the vehicles. The lessee knows that for the payment of specified sums he will have the service of the fleet he requires.

Rental, hiring, and plant hire

These forms of leasing are different from those previously described, in that plant or equipment is pre-purchased by the lessor and is let out from stock on a short-term basis. Such items may vary from civil engineering equipment such as excavators and other items required on a short-term basis to those items hired in the consumer market such as television sets.

The specialisation of the lessor is likely to mean that he will acquire the equipment at a favourable price, and the equipment will be made available to the lessee on a short-term basis, the lessee having no interest in the economic life of the asset, the lessor assuming all ownership risks on the basis that the lessee market is constant/reliable and that the lessee is willing to pay a premium for the short-term use of the equipment.

Taxation benefit

Finance leasing involves a lessor utilising the ownership of the assets to obtain the benefits of tax depreciation/acceleration/or grants and reflecting the receipt of these benefits in the lease rental. Lease purchase, as its name suggests, involves the lessor in providing funding to the lessee on the basis that the lessee may acquire title to the equipment at the end of the lease period and does not necessarily provide for the inclusion of any additional benefits.

Capital allowances are claimed by the lessor and are normally reflected in the form of reduced rentals from the start of the lease. This reduction is particularly beneficial to those capital-intensive companies whose earnings may not be sufficient to obtain immediate and full benefit from the allowances which would be available to them if an asset were purchased. This situation is particularly likely to arise when project financing is involved. Leasing converts the deferred benefit of allowances into the immediate cash advantage of reduced rentals. An indication of the scale of the capital allowances available in two different jurisdictions is set out in Table 1. It should be noted that in the case of the US equipment is allocated a class life of three, five, seven or ten years which determines the rates of depreciation available and a class life of seven years has been used as applicable to manufacturing equipment and aircraft.

Table 1

	UK	USA
Tax rate	33%	34% (Federal)
Cost	100	100
Depreciation year 1	25.00	14.25
Depreciation year 2	18.75	24.49
Depreciation year 3	14.06	17.49
Depreciation year 4	10.55	12.49
Depreciation year 5	7.91	8.93
Depreciation year 6	5.93	8.93
Depreciation year 7	4.45	8.93
Depreciation year 8	3.34	4.46
Depreciation year 9	2.50	—
Balance remaining to be written off	7.51	Nil

Purchase options

In the UK and in the US a nominal purchase option may not be included in a finance lease as by so doing the lessor will be unable to claim the taxation benefits inherent in ownership. However, in the US a fair market purchase option may be included. In other jurisdictions, for example, France and Japan, a nominal or residual value may be assumed in the lease and the lease therefore is capable of resembling a lease purchase facility, but the benefits of a finance lease will be reflected in the pricing. The effect of this is normally that the lessee will receive a discount below the underlying cost of funds by way of the lease.

Lease purchase is more common in other jurisdictions and as its name suggests, involves the payment of lease rentals to a lessor and the deferral of the transfer of ownership until the end of the lease period. The lease may be brought to an end either by means of a single payment representing the lessors' best guess of the residual value at the end of the lease period (this 'best guess' fixed at the outset) or it may involve a transfer for a nominal sum at the end of the lease period; the lessor having fully amortised his financing costs. In different jurisdictions leasing may also be on or off the balance sheet and the off balance sheet aspect may be one of its attractions. In view of the range of benefits it is intended to endeavour to identify both the risks and the rewards for the varying/various schemes which are available although it should be appreciated that the list of schemes highlighed in this chapter is not intended to be exhaustive.

Third-party risk

In any project financing the lender is at risk in the event that the assets or project founder. For this reason a project financing will concern itself with the insurance protections which are available to the lenders – these protections concentrating primarily upon cashflow and asset protection. Where leasing is utilised the leasing company (usually a financial institution) is the owner of the asset, and in addition to the normal project financing risks there will be substantial concerns regarding the third-party risks which will automatically accrue against the owner of the equipment. If the lessor is a substantial financial institution, the possibility and concern will exist that the 'deep pocket syndrome' may apply, causing the lessor (financier) to be involved in any litigation in the event of the equipment being responsible for damage or injury to third parties. The project financing banks, if called upon to guarantee a lessor, must be aware of the lessor's sensitivity on this issue. The insurance risk will apply whether the equipment is leased under a finance lease or in lease purchase facility.

Direct benefit

The finance lease will offer benefits to the borrower by way of a lower interest rate and/or advantageous cashflows. The approach to leasing varies from jurisdiction to jurisdiction although two main types of finance leases may be identifed 'leveraged lease' and the 'single investor lease'.

The 'single investor lease' involves one lessor who provides both the tax base and the funding; he thus takes both commercial/project risk and tax risk, but also takes the full return.

The 'leveraged lease' separates the tax base provider and the main source of funding. It is most widely used in the US. The tax provider supplies between 20% and 30% of the value of the facility, in the form of the net value of the tax depreciation, after he has taken his profit. He takes 100% of the tax allowance, but none of the project risk. His leverage thus consists of obtaining tax deferral on 100% of the cost of the equipment while providing only about 30% of the funds. He gets his return almost entirely in the tax benefits. The majority of the rent goes to the debt provider, who takes the whole of the project risk, often on a non-recourse basis.

Power project

The most active finance-lease project financings in the UK, in the recent past, have involved greenfield power generation plants. Such plants typically involve a construction period of three years and pay-back period (debt amortisation period) of between 12 and 15 years. The risks and rewards of leasing will vary from jurisdiction to jurisdiction and the basic principles which emerge from this UK example will apply in most areas.

The example now given is based on the financing of a private power generation plant which will be constructed in a greenfield site and it is assumed that the project sponsors will be financing the element of the project upon which favourable tax deductions cannot be obtained from equity, or from other project funds. Such items will include the land cost and infrastructure costs. The pay-back period is assumed to be 12 years.

Throughout the example it is assumed that the plant cost of £100m is incurred over two and a half years and that the repayment occurs on an equal instalment (annuity) basis. For illustrative purposes a commencement date of 1 January 1990 has been used:

Start date 1 January 1990

£15m expenditure incurred 30.06.1990
£15m expenditure incurred 31.12.1990
£15m expenditure incurred 30.06.1991
£15m expenditure incurred 31.12.1991
£20m expenditure incurred 30.06.1992
£20m expenditure incurred 31.12.1992

Repayment commences on 1 January 1993 with the first payment of principle and interest due on 30 June 1993.

Loan profile

Table 2 illustrates the basic cash flow required to service the project assuming a pay back over a period of 12 years and a cost of funding of 10%. The project sponsor will be required to prove to the lenders that the repayments of £8.14m will be available semi-annually over the life of the facility.

Lease profile

Table 3 is a simple example of the cash flow within a UK finance lease, which assumes that tax depreciation is available on the whole facility.

The finance lease has reduced the cash required from the project sponsor by £1.24m per annum – the semi-annual payments being reduced from £8.14m to £7.52m. The overall financing cost has reduced from 10% to a little over 8.7%.

In the example the underlying cost of funding the lease has been shown as

Table 2

Period	Expenditure	Repayment	Interest (at 10%)	Balance
1	15.00	—	—	15
2	15.00	—	.75	30.75
3	15.00	—	1.54	47.29
4	15.00	—	2.36	64.65
5	20.00	—	3.23	87.88
6	20.00	—	4.39	112.27
7	—	8.14	5.61	109.74
8	—	8.14	5.49	107.09
9		8.14 etc		

Table 3

Period	Expenditure	Repayment	Interest	Taxation relief (payment)	Balance
1	15.00	—	—	—	15.00
2	15.00	—	0.83	—	30.83
3	15.00	—	1.70	—	47.53
4	15.00	—	2.52	2.91	62.14
5	20.00	—	3.43	—	85.57
6	20.00	—	4.52	6.07	104.02
7	—	7.52	5.74	—	102.24
8	—	7.52	5.34	9.73	90.33
9	—	7.52 etc			

increasing from 10% to 11% to reflect the fact that in the main the lessor will seek to increase his yield in recognition of the introduction of the tax benefits. In the example although the lessor's yield has increased by 1% the lessor has effectively shared tax benefits with the project sponsor by reducing the cost to the sponsor by 1.3% per annum.

Participators

Where the lessor has no or limited experience in the project finance arena a syndicate of guaranteeing banks with project financing experience may be put together to carry the project forward. This has several advantages in that:

(a) The guarantors are able to spread their risk; and
(b) The guarantor banks may advance funds under a project finance line to the project sponsor or may guarantee the commercial risks of the lessor from a single facility. This is particularly advantageous where the project may involve expenditure upon which the lessor is unable to obtain or provide any worthwhile taxation benefits.

Benefit

The funding benefit in the foregoing example (Table 3) represents an obvious and immediate 'added value'; however, it must be recognised that the added value is being secured by virtue of the tax deferral available to the lessor. The funding benefit is therefore provided by the lessor on the assumption that his tax liability will be deferred to a later date, and in the event that it is necessary to pre-pay to terminate the lease, the capital sum required to accomplish this will be somewhat higher than the outstanding cash balance which would otherwise be outstanding under a loan facility.

Provided the lessor or project financier giving a guarantee is confident of the long-term cash flow prospects this pre-payment option may be of little consequence. However, where the project requires a guarantee of the project financier to a lessor who is unfamiliar with project financing techniques the costs of the guarantee (bearing in mind that the guarantee will be for sums greater than those which would otherwise be outstanding under a loan) will reduce the otherwise obvious funding advantage of the lease.

Table 4 provides a comparison between the outstanding cash balance in the loan from Table 1 and the lease termination sum required in terms of Table 3.

Table 4

Period	Loan balance	Lease balance	Additional risk
	£m	£m	£
2	30.75	30.83	80,000
4	64.65	64.87	220,000
6	112.27	112.43	160,000
8	107.09	107.86	770,000
10	101.38	102.30	920,000
12	95.09	95.85	760,000
14	88.15	88.57	420,000
16	80.50	80.48	20,000
18	72.07	71.61	—
20	62.77	61.91	—
22	52.52	51.38	—
24	41.22	39.97	—
26	28.76	27.65	—
28	15.02	14.34	—
30	—	—	—

Lease risk

In addition to the potentially higher risk in the event of early termination, the approach of project finance lessors will also vary as the effect of the recovery of the taxation benefits will vary if there is a taxation change.

For example, if tax decreases, as it did in the UK in the period of 1984–1987 (falling from a rate of 52% to 35%), the recovery of the outstanding balances, subject to lower taxation rates, will have the effect of reducing the project sponsors' costs. If however corporation tax rates rise the reverse will occur which could of course have a substantial detrimental effect upon the economics of the project. For this reason it is necessary for any project contemplating utilising finance leasing to consider the sensitivities of the project lease financing to the possibility of corporation tax changes.

Taxation

In the UK market it is usual for lessors to seek to recover the effect of any corporation tax rate changes from the lessee; this of course means that the up-side and down-side of tax rate changes will be reflected.

The example in Table 3 assumes a corporation tax rate of 35% throughout; however, if corporation tax should increase to 40% on 1 April 1994 the lessor will find it necessary to increase the rentals to £7.62m payable semi-annually and the overall interest rate within the lease will increase to 8.93% (an increase of 0.23%). The lease outstanding balances as reflected in Table 4 will increase.

If the reverse of the foregoing were to occur ie if corporation tax rates were to decrease with effect from the same date from 35% to 30% the rentals would decrease to £7.43m payable semi-annually and the interest rate in the lease would amount to 8.53% (a decrease of 0.17%).

In Table 5 the line £0 represents the outstanding balance in the loan. The extent to which a change in corporation tax rates affects the project financiers liabilities by way of the lease is highlighted in the graph.

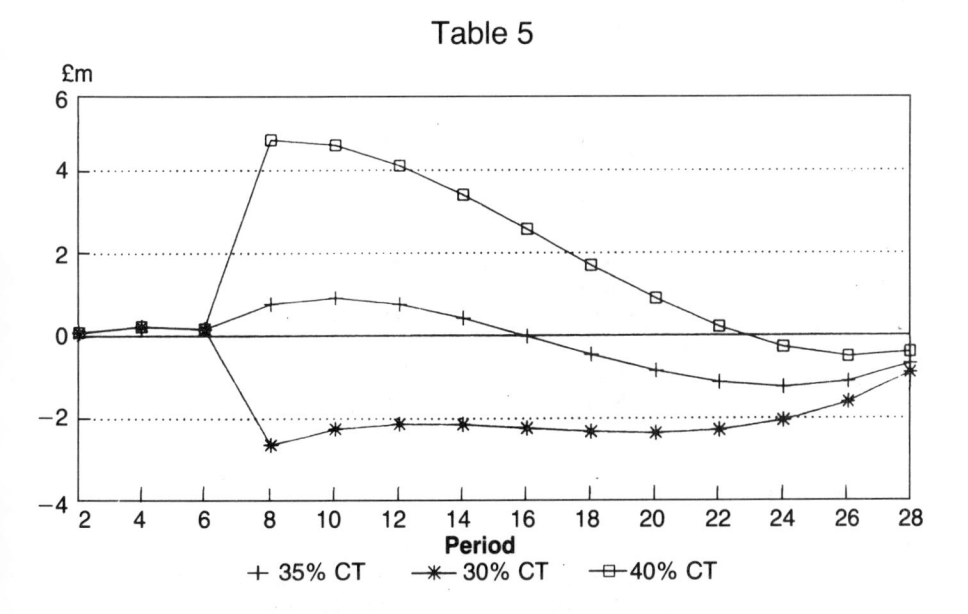

Table 5

The loan profile which is represented by the zero line in Table 5 is illustrated in graphical form in Table 6.

Table 6

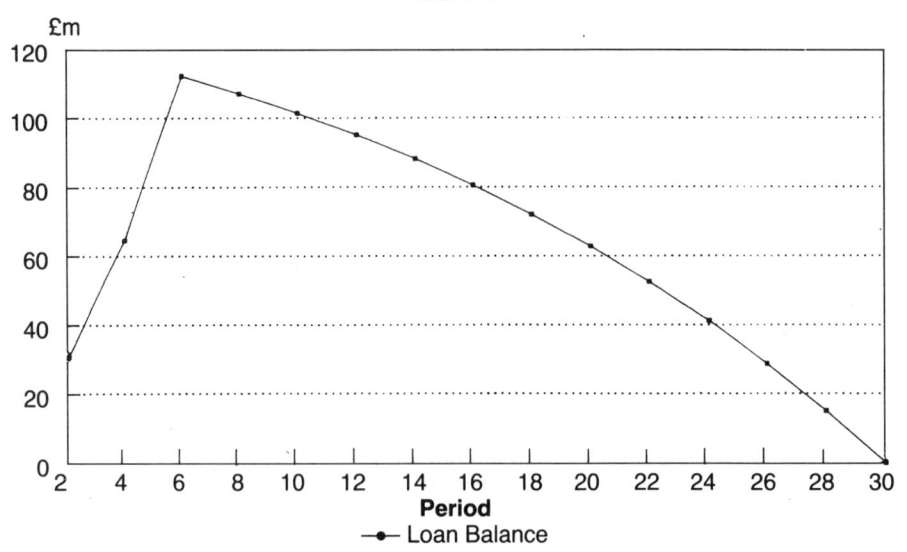

Loan Balance chart, £m vs Period (2–30)

Non-UK

In other areas where project financing may be utilised whether because of market pressures or because the taxation environment has remained stable, the leasing market may be willing to accept the risks of changes in taxation rates. In the Japanese market the stability has meant that it is not usual for the lessor to seek to introduce the concept of a tax rate change, although in the UK market as rates have been subject to change in the recent past there is a tendency for lessors to seek to place the risk of tax rate change uon the lessee.

Plant

The foregoing examples and comments are all made on the assumption that the project financing involves fixed equipment in the jurisdiction of the lessor. In addition to fixed plant, project financing techniques may apply to mobile plant, such as aircraft and shipping, and increasingly jurisdictions are limiting the use of their own tax base in what is seen as the financing of external assets. The utilising of allowances in different jurisdictions will be specifically commented upon under cross-border leasing, post, p 112.

Special areas

Where the new ventures are proposed in areas in which governments are offering specific tax advantages, leasing may offer a way in which a new venture (which otherwise will be unable to take advantage of these benefits) may establish itself utilising the benefits to provide substantial savings in some funding costs.

The examples already given use general plant depreciation allowances in the

UK and the effects of depreciation in other major industrialised coutries are not dissimilar.

One example of a specific substantial benefit being provided to encourage investment – albeit in a very limited area, is the designation of areas in the UK as Enterprise Zones. Businesses investing in these designated Enterprise Zones were permitted to depreciate 100% of the cost of their commercial premises immediately the expenditure was incurred. London Docklands is perhaps the most highly publicised Enterprise Zone and in that area the investment has concentrated upon office buildings. However, the Enterprise Zones in the centre of the UK have been very successful in stimulating both manufacturing and distribution depots. Several distribution companies have succeeded in financing their developments using project financing approaches because they have secured long-term distribution contracts for household names. The effect of the 100% depreciation is to reduce the apparent cost of funding by in the region of 4% per annum.

Property

The tax deferral available through leasing may be enhanced by the cash flow benefits as leasing lends itself more easily to varied cash flows and once again the tax deferral may provide an additional benefit. This has been particularly the case in the UK market where leasing has become an attractive method of property financing as property yields have been in the range of 6% to 8% and funding costs range between 10% and 14%. In many cases borrowers have sought lease financing and the lessor has accepted a fixed growth pattern in the rentals to effect the overall funding in line with the market.

Two shopping malls in the UK have both been financed using finance leases to take maximum advantage of the cash flow advantages of this medium. The first shopping mall in the UK was the Metro Centre constructed in Gateshead in an Enterprise Zone, and the Enterprise Zone allowances were of substantial benefit in the establishment of the project.

The Meadowhall shopping mall which was constructed in Sheffield, has also been financed by means of a lease and although the mall is not situated in an Enterprise Zone, the lease syndicate was able to use the underlying strength of the pre-lets to provide the base for a leasing cash flow which would enable the project to proceed.

Off balance sheet

The 'off balance sheet' advantages of financing are mentioned elsewhere in this book and the advantages of leasing may be aligned with the inherent advantages of 'off balance sheet' financing, which may be similar as regards cash flow and the impact on profit and loss. The advantages of a finance lease may be geared to an off balance sheet structure, and in many cases a lease may itself be structured 'off balance sheet'.

Accounting standards in both the UK and the UK require that where a company has the risks and rewards of ownership of an asset it is required to place that asset on its balance sheet even though the asset may not be owned but may be used through a lease.

The standard 'full pay-out' finance lease would therefore normally appear as an asset (with the lease financing costs appearing as a loan) in the balance sheet and one of the ways in which the lease finance may be amended to remove the asset from the balance sheet of the lessee is by the lessor accepting an element of asset risk. By so doing sufficient of the risks of ownership will be transferred to the lessor and the finance lease will effectively be converted into an operating lease for accounting purposes.

The simplest example of such an 'off balance sheet' lease is the lease of an aircraft where the lessor will be willing to accept asset risk and may therefore provide the lessee with a 'window' at which the aircraft may be returned to the lessor without penalty.

Such a lease, as it would not transfer the benefits of ownership to the lessee, would in most jurisdictions ensure the asset remained off the balance sheet of the airline. If the lease financing package is a full pay-out lease with a 'window' the possibility exists that the asset will be 'off balance sheet' during the period from purchase of the aircraft up to the 'window' date (as the lessee may during that period choose to return the aircraft). As the lessee will be fully amortising the equipment cost after the 'window' date the asset will probably then be re-categorised as being on balance sheet. The possibility is however that as at that time the borrowings will be less substantial the lessee will be willing to accept the cost of borrowing onto its balance sheet. In major aircraft financings it is not unknown for aircraft to be financed over a period of in excess of 20 years and for 'windows' to be provided at five, nine, 11 and 15 years from the purchase date of the aircraft.

Cross-border leasing

Cross-border leasing is viewed as the lease financing of equipment from one country to another. It may also involve the utilising of allowances in one country to provide subsidised finance elsewhere. The classic example of a direct financial subsidy was the Japanese Samurai lease. In 1978 Japan's trade balance was recording a substantial surplus and the Export–Import Bank of Japan funded leasing companies with foreign currency and concessionary rebates of interest. The funds were used to purchase aircraft from the US which were then leased to third country airlines. This programme was not a success for the Japanese government because IMF accounting regulations required the leases to be treated as export transactions at their inception. The effect on the financial trade balance was therefore that which was sought by the Japanese government but the global effect of the scheme was neutral.

The Japanese leasing companies were by this means however introduced to the concept of cross-border leasing, and when foreign currency regulations were revised in the early 1980s the Japanese leasing companies entered the cross-border leasing market using the tax allowances available to them and to other Japanese companies to effectively subsidise aircraft leases. This market when it commenced was known as the Shogun lease market and it has been heavily utilised by avaiation financiers as the Japanese government has only recently taken steps to limit the extent to which the Japanese tax reliefs could be used to subsidise external aircraft operators. As that particular market has developed, the US leverage lease concept has gained in popularity which has brought more funding to the Japanese leasing market.

In the same manner in which the Japanese market has provided substantial funds for aircraft finance the tax allowances available from various Scandinavian jurisdictions have provided opportunities for ship leasing over the past few years.

As has previously been mentioned the benefits available through local jurisdictions may easily be upset by changes in domestic legislation or because local governments have specifically targeted what they perceive to be an abuse of their system. Over the past ten years both the UK and Hong Kong have been perceived as areas from which cross-border leasing could advantageously be utilised, and in both cases government action has ultimately brought the markets to a close (the UK in March 1982; Hong Kong in November 1990).

Re-classification

Other forms of leasing (other than finance leases) are unlikely to provide substantial benefits in a domestic environment. Before considering tax-based financing, excluding leasing, it is appropriate to mention the potential re-classification of debt which may occur by using a lease or a lease structure as a cross-border financing medium. We will for this purpose ignore the cross-border finance lease benefits and concentrate solely on a lease purchase facility.

(a) *Off balance sheet for the IMF* – it is not unknown for a country to enact specific legislation to encourage lending to be reconfigured as a lease. The Brazilian government enacted specific legislation reducing import duties and reducing the withholding taxes on interest in respect of financial transactions which were amended to resemble leases. It is believed that transactions which were entered into within the Brazilian leasing parameters were not reported to the IMF as they fell outside the scope of the IMF definition of borrowing. Several other countries have enacted similar legislation.

(b) *Withholding tax savings* – it is common for cross-border lending to involve the lender in accepting that the interest payments will suffer a withholding tax. Before accepting the inevitability of such a liability it is worthwhile considering whether the re-classification of a loan into a lease could reduce the burden of the local withholding tax. In considering this possibility care should be taken to ensure that by so doing the ownership of the asset will not involve the lender/lessor in additional local taxes because of a liability to import duties or because of being regarded as a local business.

(c) In exceptional circumstances it may well be that the local jurisdiction will not recognise the existence of a mortgage or charge but that a foreign owner will be recognised thereby making a deferred purchase or leaseholder more secure as regards his title.

Other tax considerations

Withholding tax

Withholding tax is the tax deducted from various sources of income in the country in which it arises on its remittance abroad. The tax is typically levied upon dividends, interest and royalties. (The definition of royalties includes consideration for the use of or the right to use artistic or scientific work including films etc and in many cases also extends to payments of any kind for the use of or the right to use industrial, commercial or scientific equipment.) The royalty definition in many cases will therefore encompass leasing.

In project financing by means of loans a withholding tax may be regarded as a local tax deducted from interest payments and in most cases will be regarded as an additional borrowing burden for a project lending. The project financier must consider whether the double taxation agreements of a country of the project offer any scope for minimising the level of withholding tax (which in OECD countries ranges from 0% to 30%).

A copy of a double taxation agreement is provided in the Appendix to this chapter (pp 119ff) and it will be noted that the agreement in addition to stipulating the level of withholding tax to be applied to income also specifies the location in which it is anticipated that the major tax burden will fall. The double taxation agreement may offer assistance by:

(a) exemption;
(b) reduction; or
(c) sparing

depending on the classification of the overseas remittance. The previous section has addressed the possible benefits of re-classifying a loan into a lease or indeed of re-classifying a lease into a loan. The categorising of a lease payment as a royalty may in this respect be useful as a loan may be converted into a lease purchase agreement with the focus being upon the use of the equipment or alternatively a lease purchase agreement may be presented as a loan with the focus being upon the elements of principle and interest involved in the overseas remittances.

Having considered the opportunities the project lender may minimise the effects on the project costs.

(a) Both exemption and reduction may involve the project lender in endeavouring to ensure that the project is financed by or through a jurisdiction with beneficial treatment. In the case of exemption the objective will be to ensure that the foreign taxes are eliminated.

(b) In the case of reduction the objective will be to reduce the liability and also to consider whether the project banks are prepared to absorb any of the withholding tax.

As a lending bank will be paying tax in its base country on its worldwide profits and the majority of OECD countries permit the off-setting of foreign taxes arising abroad on income taxed in the home country against tax liabilities in the home countries, this should be successful. Many countries however limit

Leasing and tax-based project finance

the home country credit for overseas tax to the income earned overseas on the specific transaction (The UK and US for example) and the effect of this full and partial set-off are given below.

Table 7

Lenders' cost of funds 10%
Local tax rate 50% (Country A) – Project lender
Overseas tax rate 15% (Country B)
Project loan 10,000

Country A

Local other income		10,000	Tax at 50%	5,000
			Net income	5,000
Less: cost of funds at 10%		1,000		
		9,000		
Add: gross interest		1,100		
		10,100	Tax at 50%	5,050
			Net income	5,050
			Increase in net income	50

Note Tax charge comprises due 5,050
Less: credit for overseas taxes 165
Payable 4,885

Country B
10,000 loan to project at 11% 1,100
Less: 15% Withholding tax
(local tax) 165
Net interest 935

The project-lending bank has received a net margin of 0.5%. The cost of the borrowing to the project will be 11%. The project itself will pay 11% passing only 9.35% to the project lending bank.

However, if the lending bank had only been able to set off the overseas tax against the overseas income the position would have been as follows:

Country A
Gross interest 1,100 (Foreign tax 165)
Less: cost of funds 1,000
Profit 100

Tax at 50% 50
Foreign tax credit 165
Unutilised credit 115 (Credit limited to tax due)

Net profit (loss)
Net interest	100
Less: tax at 50%	50
	50
Less: unutilised Credit	115
Loss	(65)

In this scenario it is essential for the project-lending bank to increase its margin substantially to recover the overseas tax charged.

To maintain the post-tax margin of 0.5% the cost of funds to the borrower must increase from 1,100 to 1,235:

Gross interest	1,235 (Foreign tax 185.25)
Less: cost of funds	1,000
Profit	235
Tax at 50%	117.50
Net profit	
Net interest	235
Less: tax at 50%	117.50
	117.50
Less: unutilised Credit	67.75
Net profit	49.75

Country B
10,000 loan to project at 12.35%	1,235
Less: 15% withholding tax (local tax)	185.25
Net interest	1,049.75

The project-lending bank has received a net margin of 0.4975%.
The cost to the project borrowers has increased to 12.35% from 11%.

(c) Sparing or tax-sparing involves the overseas country providing a credit advice to the lending bank as if a withholding tax had been applied without actually imposing such a tax. The objective of the double taxation agreement which gives such benefits is usually to stimulate investment in the country granting tax-sparing – it is often at present negotiated as an alternative form of aid. The agreements between:

(a) Germany and India and
(b) France and India

contain a tax-sparing clause regarding interest which has been utilised in the financing of Airbus aircraft into India. This has been possible because Airbus parts are supplied from the countries listed and banks in each of those countries have participated in the loan agreements necessary to fund the aircraft to India. The effect of the tax sparing agreement is to further reduce the borrowers' costs and an example is given below in Table 8.

Table 8

Lenders' cost of funds	10%		
Local tax rate	50% (Country A) – Project lender		
Overseas tax rate	15% (Country B)		
Project loan	10,000		

Country A

Local other income	10,000	Tax at 50%	5,000
		Net income	5,000
Less: cost of funds at 10%	1,000		
	9,000		
Add: gross interest	1,161.50		
	10,161.50	Tax at 50%	5,080.75
		Net income	5,080.75
		Increase in net income	80.75

Note Tax charge comprises due	5,080.75	
Less: credit for overseas taxes	151.50	
Payable	4,929.25	

Country B

10,000 loan to project at 10.1%	1,010.00
Add: assumed 15% withholding tax (local tax spared)	151.50
Gross interest	1,161.50

The project-lending bank has increased its net margin from the basic cost in Table 7 from 0.5% to 0.8075% and the project borrower has reduced his effective borrowing cost from 11% to 10.1%.

Mining

Where mineral or extraction projects are involved the project sponsors may find it preferable to receive royalties rather than 'interest or other consideration' although care must be taken to ensure that the project financier is not 'caught' by article 3 of the general OECD convention.

Quasi-equity

One other heavily utilised tax-based financing method involves ensuring that the funding to the project resembles equity such as a preference share rather than either a loan or a royalty payment.

This approach may be attractive to the project lenders where (once again) the double taxation agreements stipulate that the income having been taxed in one country cannot be taxed in the other. The objective of the project financier in this situation is to ensure that the preference share interest (which is not subject to tax on its remittance to the main office) is subject to tax outside that jurisdiction at a rate substantially below the domestic rate of taxation (if indeed it is subject to taxation at all). Table 9 outlines the effect of such a scheme on the project costs. The agreements between the Republic of Ireland, Austria, Belgium, Canada or Germany (this list is not exhaustive) contain provisions permitting this approach.

Table 9

Lenders' cost of funds 10%
Local tax rate (A) 50%
Overseas tax rate (B) 5%

Lender subscribes for 10,000 shares

Country A
Local income	10,000	Tax at 50%	5,000
		Net income	5,000
Less: borrowing cost of share capital 10%	1,000		
	9,000	Tax at 50%	4,500
		Net income	4,500
Add: non-taxable dividend distribution	855		
	9,855	Tax at 50%	4,500
		Net income	5,355

Country B
10,000 loan to project at 9%	900
Less: 5% overseas tax	45
Net dividend distributed	855

It will be seen from the above that the project facility has achieved a cost of funds of 9% and the lending bank has achieved a net of tax return on its lending of 3.55%.

Peter J Whitney is Assistant Chief Manager, Lloyds Leasing Limited. He left HM Inspectorate of Taxes in 1969 and spent 10 years involved as a tax specialist in the banking industry. With effect from 1979 he concentrated on the corporate sector with an international bias and since 1981 has specialised in asset finance and leasing.

Appendix 1977 text of OECD model agreement

Title of the Convention

Convention between (State A) and (State B) for the avoidance of double taxation with respect to taxes on income and on capital.

Preamble of the Convention

Note
The Preamble of the Convention shall be drafted in accordance with the constitutional procedure of both Contracting States.

Article 1

Personal scope
This Convention shall apply to persons who are residents of one or both of the Contracting States.

Article 2

Taxes covered
1 This Convention shall apply to taxes on income and on capital imposed on behalf of a Contracting State or of its political subdivisions or local authorities, irrespective of the manner in which they are levied.
2 There shall be regarded as taxes on income and on capital all taxes imposed on total income, on total capital, or on elements of income or of capital, including taxes on gains from the alienation of movable or immovable property, taxes on the total amounts of wages or salaries paid by enterprises, as well as taxes on capital appreciation.
3 The existing taxes on which the Convention shall apply are in particular:

(a) (in State A)
(b) (in State B)

4 The Convention shall apply also to any indentical or substantially similar taxes which are imposed after the date of signature of the Convention in addition to, or in place of, the existing taxes. At the end of each year, the competent authorities of the Contracting States shall notify each other of changes which have been made in their respective taxation laws.

CHAPTER II   DEFINITIONS

Article 3

General definitions
1 For the purposes of this Convention, unless the context otherwise requires:

(a) the term 'person' includes an individual, a company and any other body of persons;
(b) the term 'company' means any body corporate or any entity which is treated as a body corporate for tax purposes;
(c) the terms 'enterprise of a Contracting State' and 'enterprise of the other Contracting State' mean respectively an enterprise carried on by a resident of a Contracting State and an enterprise carried on by a resident of the other Contracting State;
(d) the term 'international traffic' means any transport by a ship or aircraft operated by an enterprise which has its place of effective management in a Contracting State, except when the ship or aircraft is operated solely between places in the other Contracting State;
(e) the term 'competent authority' means:

   (i) (in State A): ....
   (ii) (in State B): ....

2 As regards the application of the Convention by a Contracting State any term not defined therein shall, unless the context otherwise requires, have the meaning which it has under the law of that State concerning the taxes to which the Convention applies.

Article 4

Resident
1 For the purposes of this Convention, the term 'resident of a Contracting State' means any person who, under the laws of that State, is liable to tax therein by reason of his domicile, residence, place of management or any other criterion of a similar nature. But this term does not include any person who is liable to tax in that State in respect only of income from sources in that State or capital situated therein.
2 Where by reason of the provisions of paragraph 1 an individual is a resident of both Contracting States, then his status shall be determined as follows:

(a) he shall be deemed to be a resident of the State in which he has a permanent home available to him; if he has a permanent home available to him in both States, he shall be deemed to be a resident of the State with which his personal and economic relations are closer (centre of vital interests);
(b) if the State in which he has his centre of vital interests cannot be determined, or if he has not a permanent home available to him in either State, he shall be deemed to be a resident of the State in which he has an habitual abode;
(c) if he has an habitual abode in both States or in neither of them, he shall be deemed to be a resident of the State of which he is a national;
(d) if he is a national of both States or of neither of them, the competent authorities of the Contracting States shall settle the question by mutual agreement.

3 Where by reason of the provisions of paragraph 1 a person other than an individual is a resident of both Contracting States, then it shall be deemed to be a resident of the State in which its place of effective management is situated.

Article 5

Permanent establishment
1 For the purposes of this Convention, the term 'permanent establishment' means a fixed place of business through which the business of an enterprise is wholly or partly carried on.
2 The term 'permanent establishment' includes especially:

(a) a place of management;
(b) a branch;
(c) an office;
(d) a factory;
(e) a workshop, and
(f) a mine, an oil or gas well, a quarry or any other place of extraction of natural resources.

3 A building site or construction or installation project constitutes a permanent establishment only if it lasts more than twelve months.
4 Notwithstanding the preceding provisions of this Article, the term 'permanent establishment' shall be deemed not to include:

(a) the use of facilities solely for the purpose of storage, display or delivery of goods or merchandise belonging to the enterprise;
(b) the maintenance of a stock of goods or merchandise belonging to the enterprise solely for the purpose of storage, display or delivery;
(c) the maintenance of a stock of goods or merchandise belonging to the enterprise solely for the purpose of processing by another enterprise;

(d) the maintenance of a fixed place of business solely for the purpose of purchasing goods or merchandise or of collecting information, for the enterprise;
(e) the maintenance of a fixed place of business solely for the purpose of [carrying on, for the enterprise, any other activity of a preparatory or auxiliary character];
(f) the maintenance of a fixed place of business solely for any combination of activities mentioned in sub-paragraphs (a) to (e), provided that the overall activity of the fixed place of business resulting from this combination is of a preparatory or auxiliary character.

5 Notwithstanding the provisions of paragraphs 1 and 2, where a person – other than an agent of an independent status to whom paragraph 6 applies – is acting on behalf of an enterprise and has, and habitually exercises, in a Contracting State an authority to conclude contracts in the name of the enterprise, that enterprise shall be deemed to have a permanent establishment in that State in respect of any activities which that person undertakes for the enterprise, unless the activities of such person are limited to those mentioned in paragraph 4 which, if exercised through a fixed place of business, would not make this fixed place of business a permanent establishment under the provisions of that paragraph.

6 An enterprise shall not be deemed to have a permanent establishment in a Contracting State merely because it carried on business in that State through a broker, general commission agent or any other agent of an independent status, provided that such persons are acting in the ordinary course of their business.

7 The fact that a company which is a resident of a Contracting State controls or is controlled by a company which is a resident of the other Contracting State, or which carried on business in that other State (whether through a permanent establishment or otherwise), shall not of itself constitute either company a permanent establishment of the other.

Article 6

Income from immovable property
1 Income derived by a resident of a Contracting State from immovable property (including income from agriculture or forestry) situated in the other Contracting State may be taxed in that other State.

2 The term 'immovable property' shall have the meaning which it has under the law of the Contracting State in which the property in question is situated. The term shall in any case include property accessory to immovable property, livestock and equipment used in agriculture and forestry, rights to which the provisions of general law respecting landed property apply, usufruct of immovable property and rights to variable of fixed payments as consideration for the working of, or the right to work, mineral deposits, sources and other natural resources; ships, boats and aircraft shall not be regarded as immovable property.

3 The provisions of paragraph 1 shall apply to income derived from the direct use, letting, or use in any other form of immovable property.

4 The provisions of paragraphs 1 and 3 shall also apply to the income from immovable property of an enterprise and to income from immovable property used for the performance of independent personal services.

Article 7

Business profits
1 The profits of an enterprise of a Contracting State shall be taxable only in that State unless the enterprise carries on business in the other Contracting State through a permanent establishment situated therein. If the enterprise carries on business as aforesaid, the profits of the enterprise may be taxed in the other State by only so much of them as is attributable to the permanent establishment.

2 Subject to the provisions of paragraph 3, where an enterprise of a Contracting State carried on business in the other Contracting State through a permanent establishment situated therein, there shall in each Contracting State by attributed to the permanent establishment the profits which it might be expected to make if it were a distinct and separate enterprise engaged in the same or similar activities under the same or similar conditions and dealing wholly independently with the enterprise of which it is a permanent establishment.

3 In determining the profits of a permanent establishment, there shall be allowed as deductions expenses which are incurred for the purposes of the permanent establishment, including executive and general administrative expenses so incurred, whether in the State in which the permanent establishment is situated or elsewhere.

4 Insofar as it has been customary in a Contracting State to determine the profits to be attributed to a permanent establishment on the basis of an apportionment of the total profits of the enterprise to its various parts, nothing in paragraph 2 shall preclude that Contracting State from determining the profits to be taxed by such an apportionment as may be customary; the method of apportionment adopted shall however, be such that the result shall be in accordance with the principles contained in this Article.

5 No profits shall be attributed to a permanent establishment by reason of the mere purchase by that permanent establishment of goods or merchandise for the enterprise.

6 For the purposes of the preceding paragraphs, the profits to be attributed to the permanent establishment shall be determined by the same method year by year unless there is good and sufficient reason to the contrary.

7 Where profits include items of income which are dealt with separately in other Articles of this Convention, then the provisions of those Articles shall not be affected by the provisions of this Article.

Article 8

Shipping, inland waterways transport and air transport
1 Profits from the operation of ships or aircraft in international traffic shall be taxable only in the Contracting State in which the place of effective management of the enterprise is situated.

2 Profits from the operation of boats engaged in inland waterways transport shall be taxable only in the Contracting State in which the place of effective management of the enterprise is situated.

3 If the place of effective management of a shipping enterprise or of an inland waterways transport enterprise is aboard a ship or boat, then it shall be deemed to be situated in the Contracting State in which the home harbour of the ship or boat is situated, or, if there is no such home harbour, in the Contracting State of which the operator of the ship or boat is a resident.

4 The provisions of paragraph 1 shall also apply to profits from the participation in a pool, a joint business or an international operating agency.

Article 9

Associated enterprises
1 Where

- (a) an enterprise of a Contracting State participates directly or indirectly in the management, control or capital of an enterprise of the other Contracting State, or
- (b) the same persons participate directly or indirectly in the management, control or capital of an enterprise of a Contracting State and an enterprise of the other Contracting State,

and in either case conditions are made or imposed between the two enterprises in their commercial or financial relations which differ from those which would be made between independent enterprises, then any profits which would, but for those conditions, have accrued to one of the enterprises, but, by reason of those conditions, have not so accrued, may be included in the profits of that enterprise and taxed accordingly.

2 Where a Contracting State includes in the profits of an enterprise of that State – and taxes accordingly – profits on which an enterprise of the other Contracting State has been charged to tax in that other State and the profits so included are profits which would have accrued to the enterprise of the first-mentioned State if the conditions made between the two enterprises had been those which would have been made between independent enterprises, then that other State shall make an appropriate adjustment to the amount of the tax charged therein on those profits. In determining such adjustment, due regard shall be had to the other provisions of this Convention and the competent authorities of the Contracting State shall if necessary consult each other.

Article 10

Dividends
1 Dividends paid by a company which is a resident of a Contracting State to a resident of the other Contracting State may be taxed in that other State.

2 However, such dividends may also be taxed in the Contracting State of which the company paying the dividends is a resident and according to the laws of that

State, but if the recipient is the beneficial owner of the dividends the tax so charged shall not exceed:

(a) 5% of the gross amount of the dividends if the beneficial owner is a company (other than a partnership) which holds directly at least 25% of the capital of the company paying the dividends;

(b) 15% of the gross amount of the dividends in all other cases.

The competent authorities of the Contracting States shall by mutual agreement settle the mode of application of these limitations.

This paragraph shall not affect the taxation of the company in respect of the profits out of which the dividends are paid.

3 The term 'dividends' as used in this Article means income from shares, 'jouissance' shares or 'jouissance' rights, mining shares, founders' shares or other rights, not being debt-claims, participating in profits, as well as income from other corporate rights which is subjected to the same taxation treatment as income from shares by the laws of the State of which the company making the distribution is a resident.

4 The provisons of paragraphs 1 and 2 shall not apply if the beneficial owner of the dividends, being a resident of a Contracting State, carried on business in the other Contracting State of which the company paying the dividends is a resident, through a permanent establishment situated therein, or performs in that other State independent personal services from a fixed base situated therein, and the holding in respect of which the dividends are paid is effectively connected with such permanent establishment or fixed base. In such a case the provisions of Article 7 or Article 14, as the case may be, shall apply.

5 Where a company which is a resident of a Contracting State derives profits or income from the other Contracting State, the other State may not impose any tax on the dividends paid by the company, except insofar as such dividends are paid to a resident of that other State or insofar as the holding in respect of which the dividends are paid is effectively connected with a permanent establishment or a fixed base situated in that other State, nor subject the company's undistributed profits to a tax on the company's undistributed profits, even if the dividends paid or the undistributed profits consist wholly or partly of profits or income arising in such other State.

Article 11

Interest

1 Interest arising in a Contracting State and paid to a resident of the other Contracting State may be taxed in that other State.

2 However, such interest may also be taxed in the Contracting State in which it arises and according to the laws of that State, but if the recipient is the beneficial owner of the interest the tax so charged shall not exceed 10% of the gross amount of the interest. The competent authorities of the Contracting State shall by mutual agreement settle the mode of application of this limitation.

3 The term 'interest' as used in this Article means income from debt-claims of every kind, whether or not secured by mortgage and whether or not carrying a

right to participate in the debtor's profits, and in particular, income from goverment securities and income from bonds or debentures, including premiums and prizes attaching to such securities, bonds or debentures. Penalty charges for late payment shall not be regarded as interest for the purpose of this Article.

4 The provisions of paragraphs 1 and 2 shall not apply if the beneficial owner of the interest, being a resident of a Contracting State, carries on business in the other Contracting State in which the interest arises, through a permanent establishment situated therein, or performs in that other State independent personal services from a fixed base situated therein, and the debt-claim in respect of which the interest is paid is effectively connected with such permanent establishment or fixed base. In such a case the provisions of Article 7 or Article 14, as the case may be, shall apply.

5 Interest shall be deemed to arise in a Contracting State when the payer is that State itself, a political subdivision, a local authority or a resident of that State. Where, however, the person paying the interest, whether he is a resident of a Contracting State or not, has in a Contracting State a permanent establishment [or a fixed base] in connection with which the indebtedness on which the interest is paid was incurred, and such interest is borne by such permanent establishment [or fixed base], then such interest shall be deemed to arise in the State in which the permanent establishment [or fixed base] is situated.

6 Where, by reason of a special relationship between the payer and the beneficial owner or between both of them and some other person, the amount of the interest, having regard to the debt-claim for which it is paid, exceeds the amount which would have been agreed upon by the payer and the beneficial owner in the absence of such relationship, the provisions of this Article shall apply only to the last-mentioned amount. In such case, the excess of the payments shall remain taxable according to the laws of each Contracting State, due regard being had to the other provisions of this Convention.

Article 12

Royalties

1 Royalties arising in a Contracting State and paid to a resident of the other Contracting State shall be taxable only in that other State if such resident is the beneficial owner of the royalties.

2 The term 'royalties' as used in this Article means payments of any kind received as a consideration for the use of, or the right to use, any copyright of literary, artistic or scientific work including cinematograph films, any patent, trade mark, design or model, plan, secret formula or process, or for the use of, or the right to use, industrial, commercial, or scientific equipment, or for information concerning industrial, commercial or scientific experience.

3 The provisions of paragraph 1 shall not apply if the beneficial owner of the royalties, being a resident of a Contracting State, carries on business in the other Contracting State in which the royalties arise, through a permanent establishment situated therein, or performs in that other State independent personal services from a fixed base situated therein, and the right or property in respect of which the royalties are paid is effectively connected with such permanent establishment or fixed base. In such a case the provisions of Article 7 or Article 14, as the case may be, shall apply.

4 Where, by reason of a special relationship between the payer and the beneficial owner or between both of them and some other person, the amount of the royalties, having regard to the use, right or information for which they are paid, exceeds the amount which would have been agreed upon by the payer and the beneficial owner in the absence of such relationship, the provisions of this Article shall apply only to the last-mentioned amount. In such case, the excess part of the payments shall remain taxable according to the laws of each Contracting State, due regard being had to the other provisions of this Convention.

Article 13

Capital gains
1 Gains derived by a resident of a Contracting State from the alienation of immovable property referred to in Article 6 and situated in the other Contracting State may be taxed in that other State.

2 Gains from the alienation of movable property forming part of the business property of a permanent establishment which an enterprise of a Contracting State has in the other Contracting State or of movable property pertaining to a fixed base available to a resident of a Contracting State in the other Contracting State for the purpose of performing independent personal services, including such gains from the alienation of such a permanent establishment (alone or with the whole enterprise) or of such fixed base, may be taxed in that other State.

3 Gains from the alienation of ships or aircraft operated in international traffic, boats engaged in inland waterways transport or movable property pertaining to the operation of such ships, aircraft or boats, shall be taxable only in the Contracting State in which the place of effective management of the enterprise is situated.

4 Gains from the alienation of any property other than that referred to in paragraphs 1, 2 and 3, shall be taxable only in the Contracting State of which the alienator is a resident.

Article 14

Independent personal services
1 Income derived by a resident of a Contracting State in respect of professional services or [other activities of an independent character] shall be taxable only in that State unless he has a fixed base regularly available to him in the other Contracting State for the purpose of performing his activities. If he has such a fixed base, the income may be taxed in the other State but only so much of it as is attributable to that fixed base.

2 The term 'professional services' includes especially independent scientific, literary, artistic, educational or teaching activities as well as the independent activities of physicians, lawyers, engineers, architects, dentists and accountants.

Article 15

Dependent personal services
1 Subject to the provisions of Articles 16, 18 and 19 salaries, wages and other similar remuneration derived by a resident of a Contracting State in respect of an employment shall be taxable only in that State unless the employment is exercised in the other Contracting State. If the employment is so exercised, such remuneration as is derived therefrom may be taxed in that other State.

2 Notwithstanding the provisions of paragraph 1, remuneration derived by a resident of a Contracting State in respect of an employment exercised in the other Contracting State shall be taxable only in the first-mentioned State if:

- (a) the recipient is present in the other State for a period or periods not exceeding in the aggregate 183 days in the fiscal year concerned, and
- (b) the remuneration is paid by, or on behalf of, an employer who is not a resident of the other State, and
- (c) the remuneration is not borne by a permanent establishment or a fixed base which the employer has in the other State.

3 Notwithstanding the preceding provisions of this Article, remuneration derived in respect of an employment exercised aboard a ship or aircraft operated in international traffic, or aboard a boat engaged in inland waterways transport, may be taxed in the Contracting State in which the place of effective management of the enterprise is situated.

Article 16

Directors' fees
Directors' fees and other similar payments derived by a resident of a Contracting State in his capacity as a member of the board of directors of a company which is a resident of the other Contracting State may be taxed in that other State.

Article 17

Artistes and athletes
1 Notwithstanding the provisions of Articles 14 and 15, income derived by a resident of a Contracting State as an entertainer, such as a theatre, motion picture, radio or television artiste, or a musician, or as an athlete, from his personal activities as such exercised in the other Contracting State, may be taxed in that other State.

2 Where income in respect of personal activities exercised by an entertainer or an athlete in his capacity as such accrues not to the entertainer or athlete himself but to another person, that income may , notwithstanding the provisions of Articles 7, 14 and 15, be taxed in the Contracting State in which the activities of the entertainer or athlete are exercised.

Article 18

Pensions
Subject to the provisions of paragraph 2 of Article 19, pensions and other similar remuneration paid to a resident of a Contracting State in consideration of past employment shall be taxable only in that State.

Article 19

Government service
1 (a) Remuneration, other than a pension, paid by a Contracting State or a political subdivision or a local authority thereof to an individual in respect of services rendered to that State or subdivision or authority shall be taxable only in that State.
   (b) However, such remuneration shall be taxable only in the other Contracting State if the services are rendered in that State and the individual is a resident of that State who:

   (i) is a national of that State; or
   (ii) did not become a resident of that State solely for the purpose of rendering the services.

2 (a) Any pension paid by, or out of funds created by, a Contracting State or a political subdivision or a local authority thereof to an individual in respect of services rendered to that State or subdivision or authority shall be taxable only in that State.
   (b) However, such pension shall be taxable only in the other Contracting State if the individual is a resident of, and a national of, that State.

3 The provisions of Articles 15, 16 and 18 shall apply to remuneration and pensions in respect of services rendered in connection with a business carried on by a Contracting State or a political subdivision or a local authority thereof.

Article 20

Students
Payments which a student or business apprentice who is or was immediately before visiting a Contracting State a resident of the other Contracting State and who is present in the first-mentioned State solely for the purpose of his education or training receives for the purpose of his maintenance, education or training shall not be taxed in that State, provided that such payments arise from sources outside that State.

Article 21

Other income
1 Items of income of a resident of a Contracting State, wherever arising, nor dealt with in the foregoing Articles of this Convention shall be taxable only in that State.

2 The provisions of paragraph 1 shall not apply [to income, other than income from immovable property as defined in paragraph 2 of Article 6], if the recipient of such income, being a resident of a Contracting State, carried on business in the other Contracting State through a permanent establishment situated therein, or performs in that other State [independent personal) services from a fixed base situated therein, and the rightor property in respect of which the income is paid is effectively connected with such permanent establishment or fixed base. In such case the provisions of Article 7 or Article 14, as the case may be, shall apply.

CHAPTER IV   TAXATION OF CAPITAL

Article 22

Capital
1 Capital represented by immovable property referred to in Article 6, owned by a resident of a Contracting State and situated in the other Contracting State, may be taxed in that other State.
2 Capital represented by movable property forming part of the business property of a permanent establishment [which an enterprise of a Contracting State has in the other Contracting State or by movable property pertaining to a fixed base available to a resident of a Contracting State in the other Contracting State for the purpose of performing independent personal services, may be taxed in that other State].
3 Capital represented by ships and aircraft operated in international traffic and by boats engaged in inland waterways transport, and by movable property pertaining to the operation of such ships, aircraft and boats, shall be taxable only in the Contracting State in which the place of effective management of the enterprise is situated.
4 All other elements of capital of a resident of a Contracting State shall be taxable only in that State.

Article 23A

Exemption method
1 Where a resident of a Contracting State derives income or owns capital which, in accordance with the provisions of this Convention, may be taxed in the other Contracting State, the first-mentioned State shall, subject to the provisions of paragraphs 2 and 3, exempt such income or capital from tax.
2 Where a resident of a Contracting State derives items of income which, in accordance with the provisions of Articles 10 and 11, may be taxed in the other Contracting State, the first-mentioned State shall allow as a deduction from the tax on the income of that resident an amount equal to the tax paid in that other State. Such deduction shall not, however, exceed that part of the tax, as computed before the deduction is given, which is attributable to such items of income derived from that other State.
3 Where in accordance with any provisions of the Convention income derived or capital owned by a resident of a Contracting State is exempt from tax in that

State, such State may nevertheless, in calculating the amount of tax on the remaining income or capital of such resident, take into account the exempted income or capital.

Article 23B

Credit method

1 Where a resident of a Contracting State derives income or owns capital which, in accordance with the provisions of this Convention, may be taxed in the other Contracting State, the first-mentioned State shall allow:

(a) as a deduction from the tax on the income of that resident, an amount equal to the income tax paid in that other State;

(b) as a deduction from the tax on the capital of that resident, an amount equal to the capital tax paid in that other State.

2 Where in accordance with any provision of the Convention income derived or capital owned by a resident of a Contracting State is exempt from tax in that State, such State may nevertheless, in calculating the amount of tax on the remaining income or capital of such resident, take into account the exempted income or capital.

Article 24

Non-discrimination

1 Nationals of a Contracting State shall not be subjected in the other Contracting State to any taxation or any requirement connected therewith, which is other or more burdensome than the taxation and connected requirements to which nationals of that other State in the same circumstances are or may be subjected. [This provision shall, notwithstanding the provisions of Article 1, also apply to persons who are not residents of one or both of the Contracting States.]

[2 The term 'national' means:

(a) all individuals possessing the nationality of a Contracting State;

(b) all legal persons, partnerships and associations deriving their status as such from the laws in force in a Contracting State.]

3 Stateless persons who are residents of a Contracting State shall not be subjected in either Contracting State to any taxation or any requirement connected therewith, which is other or more burdensome than the taxation and connected requirements to which nationals of the State concerned in the same circumstances are or may be subjected.

4 The taxation on a permanent establishment which an enterprise of a Contracting State has in the other Contracting State shall not be less favourably levied in that other State than the taxation levied on enterprises of that other State carrying on the same activities. This provision shall not be construed as obliging a Contracting State to grant to residents of the other Contracting State

any personal allowances, reliefs and reductions for taxation purposes on account of civil status or family responsibilities which it grants to its own residents.

5 Except where the provisions of paragraph 1 of Article 9, paragraph 6 of Article 11, or paragraph 4 of Article 12, apply, interest, royalties and other disbursements paid by an enterprise of a Contracting State to a resident of the other Contracting State shall, for the purpose of determining the taxable profits of such enterprise, be deductible under the same conditions as if they had been paid to a resident of the first-mentioned State. Similarly, any debts of an enterprise of a Contracting State to a resident of the other Contracting State shall, for the purpose of determining the taxable capital of such enterprise, be deductible under the same conditions as if they had been contracted to a resident of the first-mentioned State.

6 Enterprises of a Contracting State, the capital of which is wholly or partly owned or controlled, directly or indirectly, by one or more residents of the other Contracting State, shall not be subjected in the first-mentioned State to any taxation or any requirement connected therewith which is other or more burdensome than the taxation and connected requirements to which other similar enterprises of [the] first-mentioned State are or may be subjected.

7 The provisions of this Article shall, notwithstanding the provisions of Article 2, apply to taxes of every kind and description.

Article 25

Mutual agreement procedure
1 Where a person considers that the actions of one or both of the Contracting States result or will result for him in taxation not in accordance with the provisions of this Convention, he may, irrespective of the remedies provided by the domestic law of those States, present his case to the competent authority of the Contracting State of which he is a resident or, if his case comes under paragraph 1 of Article 24, to that of the Contracting State of which he is a national. The case must be presented within three years from the first notification of the action resulting in taxation not in accordance with the provisions of the Convention.

2 The competent authority shall endeavour, if the objection appears to it to be justified and if it is not itself able to arrive at a satisfactory solution, to resolve the case by mutual agreement with the competent authority of the other Contracting State, with a view to the avoidance of taxation [which is] not in accordance with the Convention. Any agreement reached shall be implemented notwithstanding any time limits in the domestic law of the Contracting States.

3 The competent authorities of the Contracting States shall endeavour to resolve by mutual agreement any difficulties or doubts arising as to the interpretation or application of the Convention. They may also consult together for the elimination of double taxation in cases not provided for in the Convention.

4 The competent authorities of the Contracting States may communicate with each other directly for the purpose of reaching an agreement in the sense of the preceding paragraphs. When it seems advisable in order to reach agreement to have an oral exchange of opinions, such exchange may take place through a Commission consisting of representatives of the competent authorities of the Contracting States.

Article 26

Exchange of information
1 The competent authorities of the Contracting States shall exchange such information as is necessary for carrying out the provisions of this Convention or of the domestic laws of the Contracting States concerning taxes covered by the Convention insofar as the taxation thereunder is not contrary to the Convention. The exchange of information is not restricted by Article 1. Any information received by a Contracting State shall be treated as secret in the same manner as information obtained under the domestic laws of that State and shall be disclosed only to persons or authorities (including courts and administrative bodies) involved in the assessment or collection of, the enforcement or prosecution in respect of, or the determination of appeals in relation to, the tax covered by the Convention. Such persons or authorities shall use the information only for such purposes. They may disclose the information in public court proceedings or in judicial decisions.

2 In no case shall the provisions of paragraph 1 be construed so as to impose on a Contracting State the obligation:

(a) to carry out administrative measures at variance with the laws and administrative practice of that or of the other Contracting State;

(b) to supply information which is not obtainable under the laws or in the normal course of the administration of that or of the other Contracting State;

(c) to supply information which would disclose any trade, business, industrial, commercial or professional secret or trade process, or information, the disclosure of which would be contrary to public policy (*ordre public*).

Article 27

Diplomatic agents and consular officers
Nothing in this Convention shall affect the fiscal privileges of diplomatic agents or consular officers under the general rules of international law or under the provisions of special agreements.

Article 28

Territorial extension
1 This Convention may be extended, either in its entirety or with any necessary modifications to any part of the territory of (State A) or of (State B) which is specifically excluded from the application of the Convention or, to any State or territory for whose international relations (State A) or (State B) is responsible,

which imposes taxes substantially similar in character to those to which the Convention applies. Any such extension shall take effect from such date and subject to such modifications and conditions, including conditions as to termination, as may be specified and agreed between the Contracting States in notes to be exchanged through diplomatic channels or in any other manner in accordance with their constitutional procedures.

2 Unless otherwise agreed by both Contracting States, the termination of the Convention by one of them under Article 30 shall also terminate, in the manner provided for in that Article, the application of the Convention [to any part of the territory of (State A) or of (State B) or] to any State or territory to which it has been extended under this Article.

Article 29

Entry into force
1 This Convention shall be ratified and the instruments of ratification shall be exchanged at .... as soon as possible.

2 The Convention shall enter into force upon the exchange of instruments of ratification and its provisions shall have effect:

(a) (in State A): ....
(b) (in State B): ....

Article 30

Termination
This Convention shall remain in force until terminated by a Contracting State. Either Contracting State may terminate the Convention, through diplomatic channels, by giving notice of termination at least six months before the end of any calendar year after the year .... In such event, the Convention shall cease to have effect:

(a) (in State A): ....
(b) (in State B): ....

Part 3
Projects under the new influences

7 Transportation infrastructure: recent experience and lessons for the future

Chris Elliott, Barclays de Zoete Wedd

Introduction

This chapter deals with the most recent developments in the private sector financing of infrastructure within the UK and tries to draw conclusions which may be of relevance in other countries that wish to implement similar strategies. Private sector infrastructure finance in the UK is perceived as a relatively new dimension to project financing as there is still an overwhelming tendency to think of the responsibility for the infrastructure of the UK as lying in the public sector. This is also true in many other countries, however, some are beginning to emulate the UK and are considering how to involve the private sector. We should recall that in the Victorian era much of the UK's infrastructure was constructed and financed by the private sector, a good example being the railway system. The railway network was developed by private companies who were interested in making money out of the network as well as securing other benefits. An important benefit was being able to enjoy some of the collateral benefits from the development of the railway, such as the uplift in the value of land adjacent to the railway. By participating in the development of this land as well, these companies were able to enjoy the wider value which the construction of the railway brought. In addition, some of the companies who sponsored the railway construction had other interests in the railway, such as being producers of goods which would be carried by the railway. As the railway developed to become an integrated network it came to provide a service of value to the community and to society as a whole. Society came to appreciate the benefits of having a relatively cheap means of transport. The same process occurred for other utilities such as electricity, water supply and telecommunications. Government's interest in such assets increased to the point that they moved into the public arena and were taken over by government.

Government policy

The present government continues to re-evaluate whether these utilities should remain in the public sector. Major elements of infrastructure have already been sold back to the private sector, including telecommunication services, gas supply and distribution, water supply, electricity generation and distribution. The reasons for this are varied and generally lie outside the scope of this chapter. Major aims were to improve the economic performance of the industries, to raise finance for business development, to free managers from the sometimes conflicting requirements put on them in the public sector, and to increase competition and choice. The government's approach has been less forthright with regard to transport. It has privatised the major companies involved in air transport, British Airways and BAA. Some local authorities are looking at the possibility of privatising airports currently under their jurisdiction, but in relative terms, little has been done with regard to the basic infrastructure of road or rail transport. This could be due to the fact that privatisation has mainly involved mature companies. They have generally been required to achieve an adequate track record before being sold to the private sector, certainly if a public issue is the preferred method of privatisation. This structure does not exist in road transport, and the privatisation effort has taken place via a relatively small number of discrete projects. Therefore, private sector infrastructure finance can be seen as a combination of project financing and privatisation.

Experience to date

Infrastructure projects are defined in this context as being free-standing projects which the government wishes to have built, operated and financed by the private sector. Only a small number of these projects have been concluded so far. Most have had the requirement to finance via a concession company and eventually be transferred back to the public sector debt-free. The largest is the Channel Tunnel project. Two other projects are the third crossing of the Thames at Dartford and the second crossing of the Severn. The Dartfor project recognises the chronic congestion at the existing tunnels on London's M25 orbital motorway and will ease this by the construction of a cable-stay bridge to provide a third crossing.

Similarly, the construction of a cable-stay bridge over the River Severn will ease the periodic congestion which occurs at the current bridge carrying the M4 motorway and thereby linking England and Wales. These two projects are very similar in concept as both are expansions of existing facilities, albeit currently in the public sector, and both have been tolled crossings.

One light rail project has been concluded in Manchester, as has one airport project – London City Airport. None of the above projects can be regarded as a benchmark for future infrastructure projects. The Channel Tunnel was of such magnitude and importance that it was readily identified as a prestige project. The Dartford and Severn projects were both expansions: each had one or more existing crossings which generate an on-going revenue stream. The Manchester Light Rail project was based on securing government support through the allocation of a substantial amount of section 56 grant funding. Finally, the London City Airport was financed on an equity basis, wholly by the sponsor. Although each project completed to date is very different, the first four listed above are all structured on a concession basis where the operation of the project is limited in length by the period of the concession. The implications of this will be discussed later.

Risk profile of infrastructure finance

As indicated above, infrastructure finance within the UK is a subset of project finance combined with the desire to transfer from public to private ownership, and thus many of the principles of project finance apply. Moreover, there is no general set of rules or solutions and each project must be looked at separately. The starting point is, therefore, to identify the risks inherent in the project and to analyse what the likely effect of each risk will be. The risks can best be classified into two time periods: firstly, those which occur during the construction of the project which can jeopardise the successful completion of the project on time and within budget; and secondly, those which occur on an on-going basis thereafter during the operating phase which can affect the normal operating efficiency of the project. Some of the principal risks which can crystallise, for example, on road infrastructure projects, are listed in the table below.

Pre-completion phase	Operating phase
Parliamentary risk	Receipt of any necesary operating licences and approvals
Receipt of all planning and other approvals	Recruiting and retaining all staff within budget
Proper design of the project	Achieving the expected levels of traffic flows
Obtaining land and access to the site	Elasticities of demand to toll increases
Interest rate risk	Interest rate risk
Mobilising sufficient resources on time and to budget	Achieving budgeted maintenance and operating performance
Labour relations	Labour relations
Force majeure	Force majeure
Stable ground conditions	Political risk
Project management capabilities	
Credit risk of contractors	
Political risk	

It should be noted that all the operating risks are broadly similar whatever the country in which the project is located, with the exception of countries where foreign currency debt is used to finance the project and hence exchange rate risks are introduced. The parliamentary, political and planning risks are specific to each country.

Pre-completion risks

During the pre-completion phase these risks will affect the opening date and the cost of completion of the project. On a large road infrastructure project, strong project management capabilities are essential to estimate correctly the extent of these risks and also to manage them effectively during construction. The company which implements the project is usually a special purpose project company (SPPC). The financial structure and capitalisation of the company will depend on what degree of risk is taken by the project company. If it takes substantial pre-completion risks it will need to be structured with a significant equity base. If, on the other hand, it is able to avoid pre-completion risk it may be possible for the project company to have only nominal equity. The Dartford and Severn Crossing projects are examples of the second type of structure, where the project company sought to lay off as many of these pre-completion risks as possible. This was done by signing a design and build contract with a major construction company, the terms of which mirror the relevant provisions of the concession agreement between the SPPC and government. The construction company then becomes responsible for completing the project on time for a fixed sum and thus is primarily responsible for estimating and managing these risks. The SPPC acts as the conduit for contractual and financial services. Its role is basically to enable the project to happen, and is different from a traditional 'equity' based company. As mentioned above, it is the degree of risk taken by the SPPC which determines its capital structure. As the Channel Tunnel project carried risks in terms of its size, its complexity and uncertainty about future revenues, about cost and timing of completion, a significant equity contribution was essential. What remains to be seen is whether the uncertainty about revenues will work to Eurotunnel's advantage, in other words, whether future revenues will provide shareholders with an acceptable level of return (see 'Operating Risks' post).

A particular risk which has ocurred in the development of private sector infrastructure in the UK which rarely occurs in project financing of a general nature, is that the project requires specific legislation to be passed prior to commencement of construction. This sets the financiers specific new risks as the finance must generally be committed prior to the passage of any legislation. Additionally, long commitment periods are rare for certain types of financial instrument and can deter investors who are otherwise happy to accept the other risks in the project. The pricing of such instruments that are subject to such long commitment periods are also problematical as the underlying benchmark price could change over time, and additionally the market perception of the price of the risk could change. The requirements for certainty of finance as determined by the government and the absolute power of Parliament to amend a specific Bill during its process through Parliament, represent a risk area which is perhaps possible only to mitigate via the insurance markets.

Lenders and investors will not accept this level of political risk. However for other, less significant, changes lenders and investors will delegate some degree of judgement to pre-agreed panels who have well defined terms of reference.

For a project where the SPPC has only a nominal capital it is necessary to ensure that the responsibility for the successful completion of the asset, on time and on cost, is passed to the construction company. This results in the major obligations in the concession agreement being 'back to back' with those in the construction contract. Problems can arise in areas where this risk pass-through is not possible, such as securing the necessary approvals for the start of works and obtaining all necessary land rights. If the construction company is not able to start work within a specified period, the construction contract may allow for a re-negotiation of the contract price and timetable for completion. This could cause insoluble problems in road projects, if for example a set level of tolls was pre-determined in real terms for the project.

A second problem area would arise if during construction it became clear, for instance, that the design of a road bridge was inadequate due to errors in the design brief given by government to the promoter. However, the degree of attention given to the design brief by eminent firms is generally sufficient to reduce this risk to acceptable levels.

A final important area of risk is financial risk, and particularly interest rate risk. The SPPC will execute financing agreements with its financiers at the same time as it enters into the other principal agreements. These will be for sufficient amounts to cover all costs arising during the pre-completion phase and to provide adequate working capital for start-up. However, the concession company will have to estimate the amount of interest it will pay during the pre-completion phase. This will be easier if it is able to borrow at fixed rates of interest, or if it hedges its interest costs via the swap market. Timing delays between signing the financial agreements and eventual drawdown may cause fluctuations in estimated interest costs. Thus there should always be a significant contingency added to the amount of finance raised to cover this and other areas where estimates have to be made.

Notwithstanding these areas of difficulty, practice has shown that for correctly structured projects with sound economics, an SPPC can lay off the principal areas of pre-completion risk via a fixed price design and build contract, and a balanced finance structure with fixed, floating and index-linked debt.

Operating risks

For a road or bridge project, operating and maintenance costs form only a small fraction of revenues (in the order of 15%) and, in addition, the SPPC can, if it wishes, lay off its operating and maintenance responsibilities by entering into contracts with third parties. The principal costs which have to be met after completion, therefore, are those associated with debt service. As described earlier, debt service costs can be effectively fixed, thus avoiding the risk of rising interest rates increasing the cost of debt service, or can be linked to the same index that increases the toll (index-linked debt). The principal risk during the operating period will therefore be whether revenues reach their expected level. Revenues will be a function of the volume of traffic using the road and the level of toll being paid.

On monopolistic projects, such as the Dartford and Severn crossings, the level of toll and its escalation formula are agreed at the outset. Therefore, the SPPC has no flexibility to alter the level of tolls to increase their revenue. In these circumstances the principal determinant of revenues is the volume of traffic using the crossings. This is something that the SPPC is relatively powerless to influence since it depends on the overall level of economic activity. Therefore, lenders and investors must not only be in agreement with the projected specific traffic flows but must agree the basic assumption underlying these levels and the relationships of traffic growth to other economic indications. On non-monopolistic projects, such as the Channel Tunnel and tolled motorways, the SPPC is able to set the level of tolls and thus has the opportunity to be pro-active over the marketing and hence the revenue-generating ability of the project. This further explains the funding strategies of monopolistic and non-monopolistic projects. Given that the upside and downside earnings potential of monopolistic projects is limted, they are ideally suited to being funded by debt. Thus the SPPCs have only pinpoint equity. However, considerably more uncertainty exists on non-monopolistic projects which explains why Eurotunnel has a significant equity base. This equity helps to reassure lenders by providing higher debt service coverage ratios. At the same time equity holders are cognizant of the upside potential of the project, which they hope will lead to substantial returns over the medium to long term.

Characteristics of infrastructure finance

There are certain characteristics of infrastructure finance which mark it out as being quite different from other examples of project finance, such as those structures used for projects in the extractive or processing industries. An infrastructure project is generally a major element in a relatively limited market. Indeed, sometimes it has monopolistic characteristics as mentioned above. An extractive or natural resource project, in contrast, would provide only a marginal addition to the resource base of the industry. The Channel Tunnel will be the only project of its kind and it will offer a huge increase in the carrying capacity of the cross-Channel route. However, it will not have monopolistic powers since it will still face competition from the ferry operators and from airlines. The Dartford and Severn projects have strong monopolistic characteristics since each project takes over the operation of the existing crossing(s) at the relevant site. In addition, no close substitute crossing exists to provide competition. Therefore, each is subject to a large degree of regulation by the government which affects the operation of the project.

Whilst extractive projects have to price their goods to be competitive, generally in an international context, this is often not the case with the services provided by an infrastructure project. Infrastructure services may be priced to be competitive only in a local context, or, for the Channel Tunnel project in a bi-national context, or as above by national government regulation.

Infrastructure projects also have to be designed to last for much longer than most other types of projects. Roads and bridges are designed for a lifetime of 25–40 years and upwards. This poses an added complication to the financing of these projects since very long-term finance is needed to approximate to the useful life of the asset. It is rare for commercial banks to provide loans with a final maturity of more than 15 years. However, the UK is fortunate in having a bond market which extends to maturities of 25 years.

Given the very long life of infrastructure assets and the time, cost and frequent disruption associated with the construction, they have to be designed to meet the projected capacity of many years hence. There is, therefore, substantial over-capacity in the early years. This is slowly filled over the years as the growth in traffic occurs. This is again quite different from projects in other industries which would be designed to operate at capacity as soon as possible. Low usage in the early years sets another challenge to the project financiers since debt service would need to be commensurately low at this time. This can be achieved by structuring the financial plan to include finance with balloon or bullet repayments. The long-term sterling bond market is well suited to this form of profile since long-term investors are generally looking for investments with bullet repayments. However, care is needed to balance the risk and return available in each project. An alternative but less satisfactory approach to this problem is to re-finance the project's debt in the early years of project operation. This option is severely curtailed by the short concession periods encountered on some projects to date and the perceived objective of the government to transfer the project back into the public sector at the earliest possible opportunity.

Long-term bonds are usually secured on large pools of disposable fixed assets. Therefore, to attract this type of investment into a cash flow project takes great skill. The strength of the underlying economics and the risk allocation within the SPPC have enabled this to happen in both the Dartford and Severn projects. Investors rely on a stable cash flow stream to build up surpluses to pay off all the debt. In the early years there is cash flow from the existing crossing which helps minimise borrowing and in the later years the security package becomes valuable as cash surpluses accumulate in the concession company. However, for projects which do not benefit from monopolistic characteristics and have start-up risks, there is a dichotomy between the venture capital/development capital risk profile, and the long-term utility return which can be expected.

Role of the sponsor

The role and objectives of the sponsor in infrastructure finance are also different in a number of important ways from those of sponsors of other projects. Firstly, the identity of the sponsor is less clear cut. As infrastructure has been in the recent past completed in the public sector, there are no successful private sector operators to promote or sponsor projects. This leads to the problem that prior to provisional award the role of sponsor is frequently filled by contractor(s) and perhaps a bank, the interests of which are not primarily in the operation of the project but rather the construction and finance. The promoter is not, therefore, fully independent. The SPPC which implements the project is usually a shell company with, at the early stages, minimum resources. It implements the project by entering into contracts with a contractor to construct the project, an operator to run the project, a maintenance firm to maintain the project and financiers to finance it. These contracts have to be agreed by government before it will execute the concession agreement with the concession company. Under the concession agreement government will also have an on-going role during the lifetime of the project, to ensure standards are fulfilled. If these standards are not maintained to the extent that the concession company defaults in its obligations under the concession agreement, government has the right to terminate the agreement and take over the project.

There is, however, a further complication inasmuch as the government fulfils many of the early roles of a sponsor – project definition etc, and is simultaneously attempting to transfer risk, and therefore logically, control and management, to another party. As the government has statutory obligations to fulfil on the management of private as well as public sector roads, they also have an on-going role in the project. As indicated below this can be in conflict with the SPPC and the interface between the two needs to be clarified. This can lead to rather extensive documentation.

Secondly, in circumstances where monopoly power is invested in the private sector, it is, quite understandably, the government's objective to achieve the lowest possible level of toll commensurate with the standards of design, construction and operation which it has laid down. This objective of price minimisation is markedly different from that of a normal sponsor, who would seek to maximise revenues by charging what the market will bear and exploiting monopoly power.

Thirdly, the interest of the shareholders of the SPPC, if the company is nominally capitalised, is to enable the project to proceed rather than seek high equity returns. They will secure one or more of the contracts which the concession company enters into for the construction, financing, operation and maintenance of the project. Their profits are therefore designed to come through providing services to the concession company rather than from the profits of the concession company.

One further difference between infrastructure finance and other forms of project finance is what happens if things go wrong. Usually, as a final resort, lenders have the right to exercise their security, appoint a receiver and realise some value. To date lenders have not had an unfettered right to do this in infrastructure finance in the UK. It is of paramount importance to the government that the infrastructure asset is continually operative and also being managed and controlled by the parties who signed the original documentation. Indeed, any attempt to appoint a receiver would trigger default under the concession agreement and render the asset almost valueless.

Lessons to be learned

The absence of a normal sponsor coupled with the government's role as a sponsor and the requirement for specific legislation means that the process of concluding an infrastructure financing is slow. Although there have been the specific successes identified at the beginning of the chapter, the number of projects coming forward is disappointingly low and as yet the breakthrough to establish a private sector infrastructure 'industry' has not been achieved. For this to happen a critical mass of projects needs to be developed. This needs to occur in the short rather than the long term and a real equity base to the industry needs to be generated. The single-purpose project companies which have been been used to date have specific conditions which hinder this growth, namely:

- only the specific project is to be completed;
- there can be no transfer of expertise to other projects;
- there can be no balancing of the investment to manage the risk;
- the concession aspect whereby the assets are transferred debt-free to the public sector at the end, does not encourage highly profitable long-term operation; and
- monopolistic projects which have been expansions of existing facilities have led to nominally capitalised SPPCs.

Project finance is a technique which enables complex green and brown field transactions to be developed especially in the infrastructure areas as the risks can be identified, quantified and hence accepted by investors. Although some of these risks have been over time frames longer than those normally accepted by investors, the markets have shown the flexibility to adapt. What project finance has yet to show is that it is capable of transforming a discrete number of projects into a healthy industry, which in itself will spawn new projects.

The very nature of project finance is the exacting examination of the risks inherent in a project and the subsequent allocation of these risks to investors. The restriction in the covenants which lenders require to accept those risks may indicate that it is, as an independent technique, the wrong financing method to create the industry approach to private sector infrastructure financing. To generate a significant network of private sector road and rail corridors will, at the present rate, take a very long period of time. Therefore, for the potential for the private sector contribution in the country's infrastructure to be fulfilled additional catalysts ar required. What should these catalysts be?

Firstly, the time taken to implement projects must be significantly shortened. The extremely long commitment periods are deterring investors, and are increasing the cost of promotion to the sponsors. Secondly, the private sector is ill-equipped to fund the risks associated with public enquiries if funding must be committed beforehand. If the promoter loses at this stage, significant sums of money are lost; the return from infrastructure does not justify such a risk. Thirdly, the number of projects coming forward must be increased. For a few private sector toll roads to be set amongst a full network of 'free' roads will not encourage the success of the private sector road. A network of roads is necessary – motorists cannot be expected to pay to use a short stretch of private road simply to get to the next traffic jam more quickly; to fulfil this some roads could be privatised. Fourthly, the idea of short concession periods that terminate debt-free, will not encourage long-term equity investors and therefore an industry will not grow. Finally, the dual role of the public and private sectors must be recognised in the development, operation and finance of such projects. Government and the private sector should arrange joint funding programmes. This should apply to the conceptual development of projects as well as the construction. The subscription of government equity (or subordinated debt) should not be seen as either back door or creeping nationalisation, nor should the borrowings be defined as affecting PSBR.

The private sector is keen and able to play a significant part in the development of infrastructure projects. However, this will only happen if the risks taken are commensurate with the potential returns and the government and private sector work together.

Chris Elliott is a Director of Barclays de Zoete Wedd Limited where he runs the Project Advisory Unit. This unit concentrates on providing independent advice on the development of privately financed infrastructure projects. Mr Elliott led the BZW teams which were involved in the successful bid by John Laing/GTM Entrepose for the Second Severn Crossing and the successful Trafalgar House/Italstat for the development of the Birmingham Northern Relief Road, the first toll motorway in the UK.

Prior to joining BZW he worked for Bank of America where he was responsible for the financial structure for the third river crossing at Dartford. He has twice given evidence to the Transport Select Committee of the House of Commons on the introduction of private financing for UK transport infrastructure. He is a Graduate in Engineering and has a Masters Degree in Management Sciences.

8 Project finance in the utility industries

Dr Michael R Smith, Bank of America NT & SA

1 Introduction

This chapter is concerned with the specific issues surrounding the financing of projects in the utility industries. It will commence by discussing the reasons why utilities are often considered an ideal area for this type of financing, and the differences between utility projects and other types of project which lead to this conclusion.

Utility projects also lend themselves to particular types of funding, and the appropriate sources are also discussed.

A large portion of this chapter is devoted to the utility industries in the UK which have, of course, been largely privatised in recent years. This process has revealed a great deal about the structure of utility industries, their regulation and their financing. The UK experience will therefore be of great value when considering similar situations in other countries.

The UK privatisation process has in itself led to an increase in the opportunities for project financing, at least in the perception of many observers. However the road to large-scale project financing continues to be strewn with obstacles, in many cases caused by the nature of the privatisation process and the structures put in place by government and its advisers, mostly with an eye to the market value of the industries being sold and in the interests of some specific views about the nature of commercial competition.

The chapter concludes with a detailed look at the issues concerning the financing of projects in particular industries. Power, perhaps the best-trodden of all, is considered in the most depth, including a look at the rather chequered history of its financing in recent years. Other areas include pipelines, various types of telecommunications projects and the developing market of the waste disposal industry.

2 Utilities – an ideal area for project finance?

Why is it that the utility industries are so often held to be an ideal area for project financing, particularly when, in the UK at least, so little project financing has actually been done in these industries?

The reason stems mainly from considerations of risk and reward. At the most basic level, utilities can be seen as capital-intensive service industries whose operations are fundamental to the operation of the national economy. Demand for the services of the utility is therefore assured to a level which can be a relatively high proportion of the total demand to be provided for. Competition is frequently limited, either by regulation or licensing or by the physical difficulty or unattractiveness of duplicating services. The multiple competing sets of telephone poles and wires which once blocked out the light in Broadway, New York are an example of competition being found to be inconvenient and subsequently removed by regulation.

Regulators who make rules limiting competition normally extract a price from those fortunate enough to be granted licences, in the form of limits to profitability. To generalise, therefore, the whole utility business sector can be seen as one of a low risk, low return character which is well suited to a relatively high level of relatively low priced, risk-averse bank financing, rather than higher priced but more risk-tolerant equity funds.

A further factor which reinforces this low risk, low return characteristic for projects in these industries is the ability to provide firm offtake contracts. Projects in other industries often rely on large numbers of customers making individual buying decisions (e g choosing to use a toll road). Utility companies, however, can provide secure long-term offtake contracts and take the final market risk as a part of their normal business. Examples would be a power purchase agreement for a power station or a throughput agreement for a pipeline project.

Naturally these entities will not wish to pay high returns to project companies who they perceive are taking few risks, so the price at which they are prepared to enter into contracts will leave only slender margins. Thus again a low risk low return form of financing is required.

3 Sources of finance for projects

In considering sources of finance for projects, we can concentrate on debt funds rather than equity. As noted above, there is a relatively small requirement for equity in these projects and in general this is best satisfied by contributions from the project sponsors themselves. Many bankers regard a certain minimum level of equity as a sine qua non, as a means of ensuring that the sponsors are genuinely committed to the project and, if the worst comes to the worst, have something to lose as well as the bankers.

This slightly doctrinaire approach does not sit well with the normal project finance maxim that no two projects are alike and that universal solutions are dangerous. A better approach is to ascertain the level of commitment of the sponsors on the basis of the particular case presented, and then to set the level of debt available by means of coverage ratios which are themselves set according to the risks in the project, following a sensitivity analysis of the project cash flows. The amount of non-debt funds required is then the amount of additional funding required to meet the total project cost.

The major sources of debt for projects in the UK, as in most countries, are bank finance and leasing. Bank finance for projects is widely available as most major banks have some project lending expertise. This enables them to understand the requirements of the project and so produce appropriate financing structures. The terms that banks wish to see on projects are normally quite flexible and it is possible in many cases to vary such matters as repayment profiles to suit the requirements of the project. This flexibility can also be maintained during the life of the facility so that early payments, extensions and waivers of other terms can usually be negotiated provided lenders agree that they are in the best interests of the project.

Leasing, though in the UK an important source of finance for industry, is still in its infancy as a source of finance for projects. Despite the reductions in tax allowances for industrial investment (capital allowances) in recent years, there are still significant benefits to be gained. Tax benefits, and the way they can be utilised in leasing, vary country by country, and should be checked for each project. In the UK, the tax allowances are taken by the leasing company and reflected in the lease rentals which thereby become cheaper (in terms of effective interest rate) than the equivalent loan financing.

This effect can be particularly attractive to a typical single purpose project company which would have no taxable income during the project construction period, which is when the capital allowances are generated. The allowances cannot therefore be used until the project commences operation, usually after some years. If the allowances are taken by a leasing company, however, it will be able to use them as they are generated and their present value will therefore be that much higher.

The main difficulty with leasing as a source of finance for projects concerns the attitude of lessors to project credit structures. Lessors are for the most part used to standard corporate and public sector borrowers (lessees) and in general are not equipped or prepared to analyse and accept project risks. The conventional method of overcoming this problem is to provide a bank guarantee facility to take the project finance risk and provide a guarantee to the lessor. This facility is set up in the same way as a bank loan facility and the guarantee fee charged is equivalent to the margin on the equivalent loan. Indeed many facilities are set up as dual purpose facilities which can be drawn as either loans or guarantees.

Unfortunately the size of bank guarantee facility required is rather larger than the principal amount drawn because of the requirement to cover the stipulated loss value (SLV). The SLV is the amount required to unwind the arrangements, ir particular the lessor's tax situation, if required due to an event of default part way through the scheduled life of the facility. By having the SLV guaranteed, the lessor is able to provide an alternative return and so preserve its after-tax profit take out (ATPTO) even though the originally intended benefit from the tax allowances will cease.

A further problem concerns additional risks which may arise as a result of the lease itself, such as the risk of a change in taxation rates during the life of the facility. In conventional corporate leases, lessors normally pass risks such as this to lessees, and so they naturally look to do the same in project financings. From the standpoint of the bank guarantors however, the exposure to such risks is magnified by the lease structure and the overall effect is to add further risks to the conventional project risks. The net result may not be attractive.

While the above problems have been described in a manner appropriate to the UK, similar problems with the interface between leasing and project finance exist in the different systems in other countries. Again these must be examined on an individual basis.

As with all forms of finance, the cost of leasing is subject to market forces. In this case the governing factor is the tax capacity available to the lessors resulting from the profitability of their parent companies, compared with the number of transactions requiring lease financing. The terms and conditions available for lease financings vary according to this balance of supply and demand.

4 Project finance in the UK

Project financing is a relatively young business in the UK. While for many years both British and foreign banks based in London had done project financings overseas, the technique had never been applied in the UK itself until the arrival of North Sea oil and gas projects in the mid-1970s. At this point the oil companies, many of whom were accustomed to use this method of financing both in the US and elsewhere in the world, created the first largescale domestic demand for project finance in the UK.

The reasons why project finance had never been used to any extent elsewhere in the UK economy seem to be connected with the fact that for many years both the major utilities and some other major companies were in state ownership, and borrowing for these entities was tightly controlled by the Treasury. Possibly due to the resulting low level of demand, the UK clearing banks had never seen the need to provide project finance services and even the merchant banks had not promoted the product domestically to any significant extent.

The only area where there was some activity was in the commercial property sector. A large number of property transactions were undertaken in the boom periods during the 1970s and 1980s, and as financings became more sophisticated, some took on the character of project financings. When institutions eventually set up project finance groups aimed at UK business it was often the case that a large part of their activity was devoted to the property sector.

The first major infrastructure project financing to be concluded in the UK was the £135 million Dartford River Crossing facility which was arranged and lead-managed by Bank of America in 1986. This project was for a major bridge crossing the River Thames and was financed on a build, own, operate, transfer (BOOT) basis following a competition between groups of contractors supported by banks. A second major bridge project, the £530 million Second Severn Crossing, has also been won by a consortium supported by Bank of America. Each of these projects was financed on the basis of only nominal equity from the consortium members, with the coverage for senior lenders being enhanced by an institutional subordinated debt facility. The consortium members were responsible however for guaranteeing completion of the project.

Meanwhile the Channel Tunnel project was financed on a rather different basis. In this case there was real equity raised by public subscription, but a certain amount of completion risk was taken by project lenders. Unfortunately this structure meant that the success of the project could still be jeopardised by delays and cost overruns.

At the same time as UK project financing was making these modest beginnings, some of the commanding heights of the UK economy were being privatised by the Thatcher government. Many of these former state industries had significant requirements for new investment, and it was widely believed that this would lead to a significant expansion of project financing opportunities. In the event this has turned out to be only partly true.

Of the major utilities to be privatised, British Telecom and British Gas were both preserved as monolithic bodies with substantial balance sheet strength. In the case of British Telecom competition in the industry was limited to a duopoly with Mercury. British Gas faced no competition at all (except of course from other fuels) until the ability of others to supply gas through British Gas's pipelines eventually became a practical proposition.

The combination of massive financial strength and lack of competition led to these companies having little requirement for, or interest in, project financing. These factors are not, of course, present in all countries, and there have even been examples where state-owned monopoly companies undertook project financings, principally with a view to extending the range of financing opportunities available to the nation concerned.

It was the water and electricity industries which offered the best scope in the UK for project financing opportunities. The water industry had such large requirements for capital expenditure, however, that those responsible for its sale felt it necessary to invent a formula whereby the cost of these capital projects could be passed through to consumers. As a result of this system, known as the 'K factor' the cost of capital improvements in the water companies' core business sectors can be recovered directly by increases in water and sewage charges. There is thus a considerable incentive to the water companies to finance these projects on balance sheet. This situation may change in due course, either as a result of regulatory action or because the companies become more reluctant to increase charges for other reasons, but for the time being project finance opportunities in the water industry are likely to be essentially limited to non-core business areas.

The electricity industry has so far also failed to live up to expectations. While it was one of the stated aims of the government in putting forward the privatisation that competition should be increased, in practice only a handful of independent power projects have actually come to fruition so far.

The reasons for this are connected with the structure chosen for the industry. In the privatisation of the electricity industry in England and Wales, the function of electricity generation was separated from distribution and supply, the latter being divided between the National Grid Company and the twelve regional electricity companies (RECs). The existing non-nuclear generation business was split between two competing companies, National Power and PowerGen.

Unfortunately during the negotiation of these arrangements it was decided to retain the 'merit order' system. This was the system which the Central Electricity Generating Board had used to decide which of its power plants would run in any half hour period, by comparing price bids from each plant for each period. It was decided that the new system would have a pool into which all plants would bid to sell power, and the pool price would be set as the price below which sufficient bids had been received to meet the level of demand on the system.

This method was the most efficient way of deciding which plants to run when all plants were centrally owned; it still has advantages in allocating existing capacity. Unfortunately, however, it says nothing about which new plants should be built, and by whom. The deciding factor here will be the long-term costs of the plant. Because of the complete uncertainty over future pool prices, it has not yet been possible to finance new independent projects without firm offtake contracts with major power takers. There is surely an important lesson here for other countries wishing to encourage more competition in generation when privatising their electricity industries.

In the UK system, in practical terms the only major power offtakers available to contract with projects are the RECs, and it is at this point that the dice are really loaded against the new entrant. Firstly, the RECs do not absolutely need to sign up long term supply contracts at all; they can simply rely on buying their power requirements from the pool and can pass on the price fluctuation risks to their customers. Nevertheless they may decide to buy long-term supplies, either in order to compete in the industrial power sales sector or in order to make more money by beating the pool price over the life of the project.

If they do decide to contract for power, one choice would be to do so with National Power or PowerGen – large, established companies with much power generation experience and balance-sheet strength. Another would be to set up their own project – RECs are able to purchase up to 15% of their requirements from companies of which they are part owners, weighted by their percentage shareholding (eg 20% of a REC's requirement from a project company in which it owns a 10% stake would count 2% towards the 15%). This would have the additional benefit that the REC would gain profit from its shareholding as well as from the power contract.

Independent projects which are financed on a project finance basis are often regarded as risky by the RECs who after all would only enter into a power purchase contract as an insurance against pool supplies becoming scarcer and more expensive and would therefore be concerned about the risk of the project company foundering.

5 Financing of utility projects

Power

As discussed above power projects are often regarded as ideal subjects for project financing techniques. This is largely because the project revenues (deriving from power sales) and most of the costs (which consist overwhelmingly of fuel costs) can be secured by means of compatible long term indexed contracts.

The history of power projects in the UK is an interesting one. After nationalisation of the electricity industry in 1947, private generation was not permitted except for self-supply.

This changed with the Energy Act 1983 under which the industry was obliged to purchase surplus power from private generators at the 'avoided cost'. For bulk purchases into the grid the CEGB interpreted this as being the bulk supply tariff (the price at which they sold power to the area electricity boards), while the Boards published their own tariffs based on the BST for smaller scale sales into local networks. However since all of these tariffs were set by the industry annually, independent power projects were still inhibited by the absence of long-term contracts.

Despite these handicaps some progress was made, notably in the field of combined heat and power (CHP) projects. Following government-sponsored studies the cities of Belfast, Edinburgh and Leicester received support and formed consortia to investigate city-wide CHP projects. Other cities, notably Sheffield, Newcastle and several London boroughs also proceeded to investigate schemes.

In the event, Sheffield managed to instigate a district heating scheme using heat from a refuse incinerator, but the other schemes were either found to be uneconomic or ran into problems in selling electricity when privatisation changed the ground rules.

It is interesting to note that CHP has gained considerably wider acceptance in continental Europe, but in many cases this can be attributed to its organisation and financing on a municipal basis. There are also many examples of prices being adjusted to make CHP heat more attractive, or other sources of heat less attractive, to the consumer. In the UK, new CHP schemes have to compete for heat sales against relatively inexpensive indigenous natural gas, supplied through a well-established nationwide gas network.

Nevertheless, all the effort expended on CHP projects in the UK did result in some important achievements, notably the acceptance of gas burning, gas turbine combined-cycle power stations in the UK, the introduction of long term index-linked supply contracts by British Gas, and the inception of the independent gas supply market.

All of these developments are important in the context of today's independent power projects.

Another important new factor arising from electricity privatisation is the non-fossil purchasing obligation. Following pressure from the environmental lobby (including, incidentally, supporters of CHP) and in order to provide a method of continuing the subsidy of nuclear power, the government decided to oblige the RECs to purchase a proportion of their power from non-fossil (ie fuels other than coal, oil or gas) sources.

In order to provide these sources a levy is charged on fossil-sourced power and used to provide an uplift from the pool price to a fixed higher price for power from selected non-fossil projects.

In 1990, and again in 1991, a competition was held to select those projects which could provide power to meet the obligation at the lowest price. The selected projects will then receive a fixed price, indexed to RPI, for all the power they produce until the obligation terminates at the end of 1998.

Although these non-fossil contracts are fixed, so that it is not possible to pass through risks to the power offtaker as has been done in some of the conventional power projects, they do provide for a fixed price and do not contain excessive penalties for failure to supply, so that they do provide a good basis for project financings. However in subsequent years the decreasing term available for new projects as 1998 approaches will make projects more difficult to finance unless some way can be found to provide assured revenue after the end of the non-fossil contract.

Financing power projects

As discussed above, the financing of power projects presents relatively few problems of a specialised nature. Taking completion risk first, the adoption of proven technologies and widespread use of turnkey construction contracts has meant that completion risks in the industry are relatively easy to understand.

The main unique feature of power projects is the way in which long term revenue risk can be covered by matching power purchase agreements (PPAs) and fuel purchase contracts. In the UK as in many other countries, the conventional format for a PPA provides two revenue streams, a capacity charge and an energy charge. The former is related to the plant's contribution of capacity to the system and its payment may be linked to the plant's availability – the percentage of time elapsed during which the plant is actually able to provide power if called upon to do so.

Because this payment relates to the provision of the plant rather than directly to the amount of energy supplied, its function can be seen as to provide the repayment of the investment incurred in building the plant, and any other fixed costs.

The energy charge relates to the energy supplied, and its function can therefore be seen as to cover variable operating costs, which in the case of most power station projects are composed overwhelmingly of fuel costs.

In the new UK power market, PPA's take the form of 'contracts for differences' – that is to say a contract to pay the difference between the varying pool price and the contractually agreed price. The power producer is then able to bid into the pool a very low price – or even zero – to ensure the project is always able to run.

It is interesting to note that the pool price also contains both capacity and energy elements. The capacity element is calculated as the product of the value of lost load (VLL) – a notional cost of the loss of power supply to a user, adjusted from time to time by the Director General of Electricity Supply – and the loss of load probability (LOLP), a figure between zero and one calculated in each half hour on the basis of the amount of spare capacity in the system. Unfortunately the uncertainty inherent in this system has so far made it impossible for new entrants to finance plants on the basis of the pool capacity payments.

The RECs, who are the principal offtakers of power from projects, now have no formal obligation to supply their customers, so capacity has no intrinsic value to them. However the structure of the PPAs signed so far indicates that the concept is still of relevance in the construction of price indexation formulae.

The PPAs signed to date seem to fall into two main categories: very tight contracts with few risks passed through to the REC, normally with a minimum price and some form of profit sharing with the REC if pool prices are above the contract price level; and at the opposite extreme, contracts under which virtually all risks in the project are passed through to the REC. The latter, while theoretically more risky for the REC, should result in cheaper financing and a better return on equity since lower debt coverage will be required. It also lends itself to lease financings, as some of the additional risks which are unpalatable to guarantor banks may thus be passed to the REC.

The major type of fuel used in independent power projects to date has been gas, and this has led to some important developments in gas purchase contracts. There are some discrepancies between the gas producers' and power producers' views of the ideal gas contract.

Gas contracts have traditionally been on a field-depletion basis – that is, the buyer takes the whole contents of the field irrespective of the production profile, which may tail off over a long period of time.

The gas producer will seek a fast rate of production and a high level of take-or-pay commitment in order to guarantee the fastest possible return on his investment in developing the field. As most of the gas producers are oil companies, they also tend to be interested in indexation baskets with a high proportion of oil-related indices.

The electricity producers, on the other hand, are more interested in a supply contract, in which the supplier contracts to provide a certain volume of gas per year irrespective of the reserves or flow rate of a particular field. They would also prefer to have a low level of take-or-pay, to permit the maximum flexibility of plant operation and reduce financial risks in the event of downtime. Preferred indexation would be to electricity prices or some other closely related index (historically, electricity prices have been linked to UK coal prices and have moved at a rate comparable with general inflation (RPI)). Too large a proportion of oil in the index would not be acceptable to electricity offtakers because of the possibility of sharp price increases.

As mentioned above, power station projects are capable of being financed on the basis of very limited amounts of equity, and those projects which have been financed in the UK so far have only required between 5% and 20% of the cost to be financed by equity, with the remainder provided by senior debt in the form of either loan or lease.

Cogeneration and CHP projects

Cogeneration and combined heat and power (CHP) projects, that is power plants which sell heat as well as power, are financed similarly to other types of power project but there are important differences in operation and in revenue streams which can alter the risk profile.

There are two basic modes of operation for such plants, which can be characterised as heat-load following or electricity following. Heat-load following is the normal mode of operation for industrial cogeneration plant and in city-wide CHP schemes in continental Europe. In this mode, the plant operates in such a manner that at all times the amount of waste heat produced is equal to the heat demand from heat customers. This mode ensures that the maximum amount of usable energy is sold from the fuel consumed, and is thus often the most economically attractive mode.

Under some economic circumstances, however, principally if the market value of electricity is much higher than the value of heat, it may be more economically beneficial to operate at all times to produce the maximum amount of electricity, if necessary dumping surplus heat through a cooling system.

When evaluating any CHP or cogeneration project it is usually necessary to examine in detail the profile of heat demand and compare it with the available electricity price, in order to determine what effect the extraction of heat from the plant from time to time will have on electrical revenue.

Pipeline projects

Pipeline projects are another excellent example of a type of enterprise well suited to the requirements of project financing. These projects exist because of the need to move fluids from one location to another either because there is no viable alternative to using a pipeline (eg in the case of most gases) or because the alternatives are more risky or more costly (eg when transshipment is required to move bulk liquids for short to medium distances).

The owners of the materials to be shipped in general tend to be repeat users of the shipment service and to gain a considerable benefit from the existence of the pipeline. They are often the sponsors of the pipeline project. It is also the case that independent pipelines built as speculative ventures are relatively rare.

The usual approach to pipeline financing is therefore that the pipeline project company depends on one or more major customers who can be relied upon to make use of the capacity. In many cases these customers will sign put-or-pay throughput agreements which may be sufficient effectively to guarantee the cash flow of the project and so make the financing possible.

In other cases the sponsors may wish to retain an amount of uncommitted capacity in order to have some flexibility in their future marketing plans; however the sponsors themselves may have substantial additional quantities of material to be sold and moved eventually and may be willing to commit this to the project even if the final destination is not known at the time of signing.

Telecommunications projects

Telecommunications continues to be a rapidly growing field, but one which poses more problems for the project financier than those described above. The main reason for this is that although there are some telecoms projects, such as communications satellites, where capacity can be sold, initially at least, to a few major users, the majority of projects in the field have revenue streams which rely on consumers' spending decisions.

In addition, in most countries there is a relatively high degree of government involvement in the industry, either through ownership or through regulation. This situation is changing, however, at different speeds and in different ways from one country to another.

Cable television

Cable television projects are a typical example of projects which are capital intensive but which rely on individual customers for their revenue streams. In the UK there have been cable systems in some areas for many years, but the modern cable industry dates from the early 1980s when the Cable Authority was set up. This body issued new cable licences for a number of cities, but the conditions laid down for the operators had two main drawbacks: firstly, the cable network to be installed had to be the most modern technology, enabling the provision of a host of other services relying on data transmission as well as television channels. Cables had to be buried in the streets rather than being strung on poles. This meant that the capital cost of these systems was much greater than it would have been, for example in the US. Secondly, the duopoly in telephone services which had been put in place when British Telecom was privatised was retained. This meant that the cable licencees were unable to offer telephone services (which their systems would technically have been able to provide) unless they were able to negotiate access to the British Telecom or Mercury systems.

As a result, from a project-financing standpoint, it was necessary to finance capital-intensive utility systems on the basis of volatile entertainment revenues. The resulting difficulties in building systems and finding customers meant that the higher value services of the future (e g teleshopping) which had been hoped for became secondary priorities.

There are two major parameters which govern the growth of revenue to a cable television network, namely the build rate (i e the rate at which the network extends to pass the premises of additional potential customers) and the penetration rate (the percentage of premises passed which actually take the service).

In the UK it was widely assumed that the growth of cable systems' revenues would follow the pattern in the US, where penetration rates typically grew in more or less linear fashion to quite high levels (60%–70% in most cases). However, initially at least this proved not to be the case, as several of the new systems experienced a levelling off of penetration at about the 20% mark.

Difficulties such as those described above naturally lead to problems in raising finance for cable projects, and the structures normally adopted reflect this. It is normal for cable projects to be financed on the basis of a relatively large portion of equity capital (50% would not be unusual) and a virtually universal feature is the involvement of major companies, often of US origin, among the shareholders and providing at least implicit support.

Providers of senior debt for cable television projects have introduced structures designed to protect against their peculiar problems. The procedure most often adopted is to make the availability of debt drawdowns conditional on tests being passed. These tests would relate to the passing of milestones with regard to both network construction and market penetration. The effect is thus to ensure that before indebtedness is incurred the necessary cash flow to service it is assured.

The only significant area of doubt then remaining is the level of 'churn', that is subscribers ceasing to take the service and being replaced by new subscribers. However in most projects this level is low enough not to be a major factor.

The future of cable television as a source of projects remains uncertain. While the surviving cable companies are in some cases still expanding, the Cable Authority has for the time being ceased to issue further licences and yet more changes to the industry's regulations are planned. The government has recently announced that the provision of telephone services is to be liberalised, which could be very good news for the cable industry.

Cellular telephone systems

The financing of cellular telephone systems also depends heavily on the concepts of market growth and penetration, though in this case the basic economics can be expected to show more utility-like characteristics. In this market, however, the problems relate to the instability caused by rapidly changing technology.

The present generation of cellular phones use analogue electronic technology and operate at a frequency which permits reasonably large cells. However the available bandwidth at this frequency will certainly not be sufficient to accommodate the potential growth in system use. In addition, the standards presently in use differ between different countries so that mobile phones cannot be used abroad.

A number of improvements are being proposed. One is that the existing technology known as Telepoint – a lightweight portable phone which can be used within close range of transmitters sited at strategic locations might be used to relieve the pressure of numbers on the cellular networks. However Telepoint has been slow to take off for several reasons: its price advantage over cellular has not been as great as was anticipated, the base stations of the three operators are not compatible and there is the disadvantage of not being able to receive incoming calls.

Of more significance are proposals to change over the existing cellular networks to digital operation and at the same time adopt a common European standard. This development, which is scheduled to be operational in 1991, is in turn likely to be superseded by the advent of the Personal Communications Network (PCN), which will follow shortly thereafter.

PCN will involve higher frequencies than are now common, in order to accommodate a much larger number of subscribers, though this will naturally require smaller cell sizes. The objective will be to produce a cellular phone that is small enough and light enough to be carried everywhere, so that its number will relate to a person rather than a location. If this development is successful the PCN could in time largely replace conventional telephones.

The problems created for financiers by an industry so much in flux, are obvious. It is very difficult to consider project financing for new technological developments at any time, but here there are further risks relating to the development of the total market and the way customers will behave when additional generations of technology become available.

The conclusion must be, therefore, that for the present project finance funding for cellular telephone systems is likely to be very restricted until the new systems begin to develop proper markets of their own.

Waste disposal projects

In the UK, as in other countries, the waste disposal industry is another industry which is effectively being privatised, though in this case without the publicity accorded to other industries.

Waste disposal, which is at present run by local authorities, is conventionally divided into two activities, *collection* and *disposal*. The first stage in the privatisation process was to open up the collection activity to competitive tender. Where local authorities retained their own direct labour organizations these were made to compete with private contractors for contracts to provide the public waste collection service.

Of more interest from a financing standpoint are the waste disposal activities. The government decided in 1989 that these should be hived off into separate companies to be known as local authority waste disposal companies ('Lawdacs'), which could be joint ventures with the private sector. These would then bid for the disposal business on a competitive basis.

This decision, which has not yet been implemented, has caused a certain amount of confusion, but it seems clear that waste disposal companies do not necessarily have to be Lawdacs. There is therefore the possibility that new waste disposal projects can be set up in private companies which if necessary can contract with the Lawdacs.

One of the problems of waste disposal projects in the UK is that the local authority retains responsibility for the disposal of municipal waste. Therefore if it contracts with a project company which fails to perform under the contract, the local authority will not have succeeded in passing the responsibility elsewhere. Local authorities can therefore be expected to be extremely cautious about the arrangements they enter into.

Similar types of problem, and a general tightening of regulations, are occurring in most countries. It is particularly important to note that projects involving the transportation of waste materials across international boundaries for disposal in other countries are already banned in many countries and may soon be entirely eliminated by international agreement.

In landfill projects there is also the question of the long-term responsibility for what has been put into the ground. This, together with generally tightening regulations regarding landfill, means that a shift can be foreseen from the present situation where the majority of waste goes to landfill, to a much larger proportion of alternative disposal methods such as incineration.

Incineration projects can be regarded as highly suitable for project finance. They are capital-intensive, proven technology is available, and there are normally two or three sources of revenue to the project (waste tipping fees, heat and/or electricity sales). In the UK electricity can be sold into the non-fossil purchase obligation (see above) and so is a secure revenue stream, at least through 1998.

A difficulty with waste projects is often finding a secure source of supply. This is normally possible in municipal waste projects, but for other types of waste such as scrap tyres or biomass, operators in the industries concerned are often reluctant to tie themselves up with long-term contracts, though a limited number of projects have been successful to date. It remains to be seen whether increasing environmental pressure on alternative means of disposal will lead to changes in attitude.

6 Conclusion

In this chapter, a picture has been painted of the utility industries which should help to clarify why they contain, in theory, so much potential for the project financier and why, in practice, this potential often proves so difficult to realise.

In many countries the main limitation on opportunities for project financing arises as a result of government involvement in what are often seen as natural monopoly industries. This can be in the form of public ownership or of regulation.

The UK market, on which this chapter has concentrated, is an excellent example because of the opportunity it has provided to see the same industries under both public and private ownership. Because the regulatory systems put in place have had relatively little time in which to evolve, it is also easy to see both the motives behind the regulatory systems and the results that these systems have brought about in practice. It is clear that many lessons remain to be learned in this and other countries.

Michael Smith was born on 2nd November 1949. He was educated at Mirfield Grammar School before starting his career as a pre-university apprentice with

Rolls-Royce Ltd. After a year on the shop floor he took his place to read Engineering Science at St Catherine's College, Oxford. Following his first degree he went on to do research, gaining his doctorate in the field of gas turbines.

At this juncture Michael Smith made a career change out of both Engineering and the academic life and joined Lloyds Bank International as a graduate trainee. He was soon posted to the US where he spent three years, initially as a trainee in New York and subsequently as a member of a corporate banking team based in Chicago.

In 1978 he returned to London and began his involvement in project finance which has lasted ever since. He initially started on international projects, before transferring to the Oil Department. In 1985 he commenced work on general projects in the UK.

Michael Smith joined Bank of America at the end of 1989 and is in charge of its project finance activities in the UK and Europe.

9 Project finance in the developing markets of Central and Eastern Europe

Douglas Helfer, Cole Corette & Abrutyn

This chapter will address project financing in developing markets with particular emphasis on the countries of Central and Eastern Europe including what used to be the Soviet Union, where emerging democracies are considered by many to represent the world's largest untapped market. As these countries attempt to rebuild collapsing infrastructures and establish the foundation for a market economy, opportunities for Western business will undoubtedly grow. Government resources for restructuring in the region are already strained and private enterprise will be needed and welcomed. Project lending could become increasingly important in the region.

On the one hand, events in the region over the past few months have reassured Western lenders of the irreversible nature of the move away from totalitarian regimes and toward democracy and market economies. On the other hand, such change is still very much in flux and, ironically, conditions for investments are in many ways less certain now than a few years ago. New laws relating to business are often vague, untested and unreliable. Other basic questions like currency convertibility, profit repatriation, taxation matters, property and ownership questions, and import/export regulations are still evolving.

Moreover, grave uncertainty exists regarding the reliability of new political institutions. For example, it is not at all clear what the 'Soviet Union' will become and how, if at all, republic independence can be reconciled within some kind of economic or financial union or commonwealth political structure. One of the major unresolved concerns is how the debt burden of the former all-Union structure will be shared by the newly-independent states.

In spite of the uncertainty in the region, well conceived investment projects nevertheless offer the prospect of profitable operations. In situations of political turmoil, loans keyed to specific projects, rather than to a company or government for general purposes, can involve lower risk. In addition, as certain successful African and Latin American oil and gas projects have recently demonstrated, project lending can, to some extent, be more shielded from the general political climate than other types of financing.

Financial position of countries in the region

Although the hard-currency debt of the countries of Central and Eastern Europe had been increasing since the mid-1980s, up until 1990 the international financial community, especially private institutions, had maintained a positive attitude toward countries in the region. This may have reflected a general perception that leaders in the region had the ability to control their domestic economics and foreign exchange holdings.

However, by the beginning of 1990 a significant change in market attitude toward these countries emerged. The weakening of central control, resulting partly from the dismantling of central planning practices, contributed to a significant increase of external deficits. In spite of the advanced reform efforts in Poland and Hungary that resulted in improvements on current accounts in 1990, the borrowing requirements of virtually all countries in the region have increased dramatically. Rising debt and uncertainties associated with moves toward a market economy prompted the international financial community to change its views on the creditworthiness of countries in the region. Private institutions now seek to avoid new lending in most of the countries.

The downgrading of the region's credit rating has spread beyond the publicised capital markets, and banks increasingly will not accept new credits or renew maturing facilities. Traditional bank-to-bank and trade lines have been cancelled or not renewed and in some cases inter-bank deposits have been withdrawn. These efforts to reduce exposure by withdrawing credits have clearly aggravated the liquidity problems of the former USSR, Bulgaria and Hungary.

Most countries in the region have run into serious debt servicing problems, and a crisis comparable to that in Latin America in the 1980s now seems possible, a fact which no doubt alarms most lending institutions. The extent to which the countries of Central and Eastern Europe can get their credit ratings back in order will largely determine Western financial confidence in the region and, consequently, the availability of funds to finance projects.

Structuring a project in the present market

The market for Central and East European financing at present is extremely thin in terms of the number of financial institutions willing to participate and the exposure they are willing to accept on a particular project. Only those transactions that are well structured and secured are likely to succeed. The banks will look to other factors such as the importance and priority of the project to the country in which the investment will take place, its inherent logic and viability, the nature and market acceptability of guarantees offered, additional elements of security available, and the status of the project in relation to the state economic development programmes. Western banks have considerable difficulty assessing the viability of these projects; testing assumptions regarding availability and cost of local supplies, raw materials, utilities, etc; and establishing adequate security devices.

In part, this has been due to legal restrictions in some countries (particularly the USSR) affecting a lender's ability to obtain satisfactory security over assets located in the host country, and doubts about realising security or repossessing assets situated there. In the absence of clear legislation in this regard, there will continue to be uncertainties about how security interests in land and other assets (including contract rights) can be created and enforced under local laws. Consequently, lenders may be offered less security than they would expect in a typical project elsewhere – an added complicating factor for projects in the region.

Project finance lenders will need to evaluate the creditworthiness of host country guarantees and other commitments. In a typical resource processing project they will expect to see 'supply or pay' undertakings, and may want some linkage of supply prices to offtake prices. Some portion of supplier payments may also need to be subordinated to debt service depending on offtake pricing, with deferred payments (plus interest) paid from project cash flow when offtake prices exceed agreed levels.

Other important factors in such a project include the involvement of experienced contractors and efficient operators, quality production, and profitability. Lenders will typically expect to see foreign control over operations, either contractually or through ownership, with management or other fees at least partially subordinated to project debt service, and any deferred amounts repaid from cash flow. Assured transportation arrangements can be essential. Control over the labour force, including hiring and dismissal of labour, are important issues. These are particularly sensitive in projects which need to take account of mandatory provisions of local labour legislation.

A typical project may involve a fixed fee engineering and construction contract with a foreign firm having a strong international reputation and some prior experience in the country where the project is to be situated. The contract will cover engineering, procurement, construction and start-up. Typically, the contractor will be expected to provide some credit support for the project, including performance guarantees.

However, foreign contractors may have only limited ability to provide completion guarantees for projects, and in some cases the host party will undertake the construction and erection work, with the Western contractor supplying fairly standard equipment warranties.

Western lenders often prefer to have escrow and other bank accounts maintained outside the host county, and not under local control. In some cases, this has required special approval by local agencies (in the USSR, for example, from the State Bank of the USSR ('Gosbank')) and permission has sometimes been difficult to obtain. Failing such an arrangement, an onshore escrow account may be necessary.

A key factor in most projects is the presence of a substantial host country institutional commitment to provide some credit support – typically in the form of residual completion and performance commitments.

Some Central and East European borrowers have been unable to provide meaningful statistics and accounts, which complicates the lender's task in evaluating the feasibility of the project.

In general, project finance in the region demands an extraordinary commitment in terms of effort and perseverance, as compared with projects in other areas, and the political environment is increasingly uncertain in some countries in the region. It is not surprising, therefore, that few Western banks have an appetite for these projects, and that some banks prefer to work on a fee basis as financial advisers and syndicate leaders, rather than as major lenders.

Sources of financing

If outside finance is needed, this should be explored as early as possible. Few of the many projects in the region being proposed to Western companies will qualify for outside financing without additional guarantees. Finance involving limited recourse is likely to be available only for a very small number of projects in which there is a demonstrable source of hard currency earnings and adequate security.

Recent changes in banking legislation in several countries need to be examined for their possible impact on the rules and procedures for financing projects.

In the Soviet Union the Bank for Foreign Economic Affairs (BFEA) has in the past played a decisive role in hard currency financing. Its consent was needed for a Soviet entity (including Soviet joint ventures with Western investors) to borrow in hard currency, and the BFEA had used this authority to exercise strict control over borrowings. In January 1991 Gosbank took over this responsibility, and at the time of going to press it was unclear how this would be handled following the collapse of the USSR.

The BFEA was able to offer financial guarantees but in practice it was extremely reluctant to do so. Guarantees might be available from another Soviet bank, from a ministry or other agency sponsoring a Soviet party to the venture (local or republic), from other Soviet authorities, or from the Soviet party to the venture. However, the validity and enforceability of such guarantees need to be carefully scrutinised by prospective Western lenders who will want to be sure that they are in a position to call on any guarantees if need be, and that the guarantor is likely to have the necessary hard currency. Many of these entities will have had no track record in dealing with Western financial institutions, and their financial capacity to meet any hard currency commitments will be difficult to evaluate. In the past, Western banks could avoid commercial risk analysis, relying on the BFEA's track record as a sovereign borrower. Few projects will allow this type of approach in the future.

Western financial institutions are particularly sensitive to the risks associated with the reorganisation of Soviet entities and the effect this might have on contractual obligations of Soviet investors, borrowers or guarantors. In light of recent political change, the status of the former all-Union organisations (including banks) needs to be carefully examined. Also, it will be some time before the newly emerging republic institutions acquire a track record in international business.

Official export credit guarantee agencies

With deteriorated payment conditions in most countries in Central and Eastern Europe, the official Western government-supported export credit guarantee agencies play a critical role in the financing of exports to the region. Official export credit agency involvement can be an important element of a financial package by providing longer credit terms than are available commercially and at fixed competitive interest rates, thereby facilitating commercial lending. These credits and guarantees help minimise residual local risk exposure, free commercial lending for other issues, add credibility to the structuring of a financial package, and facilitate syndication.

Export credit agencies are increasingly apprehensive about extending credit to some countries in the region, particularly (at the time of going to press) in the former Soviet Union. As with private creditors, a process is at work in which these agencies are reviewing the region in order to monitor lending activity more carefully. In some cases, individual country risk ratings have been downgraded and availability of cover has been reduced or eliminated in practice (even though they may be officially 'open').

Although medium-term credits are not impossible, there is a striking trend towards shorter repayment periods, accompanied by much higher margins and commitment/loan management fees.

Export credit guarantee agencies are active in many Western countries and include the following.

ECGD of the UK

Most of the existing portfolio of the Export Credit Guarantee Department (ECGD) is apportioned to ten very large developing countries, including the USSR. Concerns about heavy dependence on the continued health of such vulnerable economies and several years of substantial losses has caused the ECGD to consider carefully the whole of its future operations. The ECGD's programmes in the USSR therefore, have recently undergone formal review. The share of ECGD's business accounted for by Central and Eastern Europe is small in comparison with most other European agencies.

Over the past few months, ECGD's attitude towards Poland has relaxed somewhat. Short-term credit coverage is available against a Bank Handlowy guarantee or letter of credit. Political risk coverage is available at 3.5% above base premium (about 0.35%), with the rate being charged on whole turnover rather than individual contract value.

Hermes

Hermes is the private insurance company that handles the German government's export credit guarantee scheme. In the past, Hermes was quite active; in the Soviet Union alone, its exposure is estimated at DM20bn. However, over the past three years the significant increase in demand for guarantees from Hermes has made it much more cautious, so that it is now more conservative than most other European rivals and more particular about the length of credit and the status of the buyer. In countries with clear payment problems, Hermes has introduced new restrictions. In Bulgaria, for example, Hermes no longer provides cover for any kind of credit.

In some countries in the region, Hermes has provided cover on a case-by-case basis and often demanded guarantees from agencies in the country hosting the project, for example in the Soviet Union from the BFEA and in Poland from Bank Handlowy.

OPIC

The Overseas Private Investment Corporation is a US government agency which provides loans, equity and political risk insurance for US investment in developing countries. OPIC assistance is available for new business investments and expansions in more than 100 developing countries and areas around the world, including most of the countries in Central and Eastern Europe.

US Export-Import Bank

The US Export-Import Bank (Exim) provides cover for US exports to most of the countries examined here. Although Exim is no longer barred from lending or providing loan guarantees to the USSR under the Jackson-Vanik restrictions (which linked US funds to liberalising Soviet emigration policy), the Stevenson Amendment to the Trade Act of 1974 continues to limit such credits or guarantees to an aggregate amount not in excess of $300m. Additionally, the Johnson Debt Default Act bars US financial institutions from lending to the USSR other than for export-related matters.

By late 1991 Exim had issued preliminary commitments for over $1.5bn in the USSR, all subject to approval by BFEA. Officially it was up to the Soviet government to select from among such applications, which projects to support. Of these, only a few small projects received preliminary approval, and with respect to some projects, the BFEA was seeking to raise the 85% covered by Exim by issuing Exim-backed bonds in he US capital markets and requiring US exporters to come up with the other 15%. How Exim will operate in the new Commonwealth of Independent States (CIS) was uncertain at the time of going to press.

COFACE

Coverage is provided to French exporters through Compagnie Francaise d'Assurance pour le Commerce Exterieur (COFACE). The organisation has traditionally been cautious toward Central and Eastern Europe, reflected in the modest share of its total commercial risk cover in the region. At least until recently, commercial coverage was available only for business in Poland and Hungary, but borrowers in other countries have been eligible for more extensive political cover.

According to COFACE officials, in order to obtain coverage, Polish and Hungarian borrowers must ensure that sufficient financial data on their economic health is available (i e company accounts for the past year), be able to prove access to hard currency, and COFACE must be familiarised with the company's position in the market.

In the USSR, COFACE was only considering export credits on a case-by-case basis with specific French government approval and support, typically based on a BFEA guarantee.

SACE

Sezione Speciale per L'Assicurazione del credito all 'Esportazione (SACE) is the official Italian credit guarantee agency and has one of the most progressive approaches in Europe to providing credit to Italian exporters, especially in the Soviet Union. According to informed observers, SACE even considered support on project financing activities without formal guarantees from BFEA. SACE is said to have accepted ministerial or other 'guarantees' in some cases.

Multi-lateral lending agencies

A number of other potential sources of hard currency financing may be available through various multinational organisations and financial institutions. The World Bank is rapidly expanding its presence in the region, especially in Poland, Hungary and the CSFR. The IMF recently announced the acceptance of the USSR as an associate member and full membership in the IMF, World Bank and IFC may not be far off. These organisations have already begun technical assistance programmes in the CIS.

The endorsement or partial funding of an area development bank, like the European Bank for Reconstruction & Development (EBRD), greatly assists in attracting commercial lenders to a project. The EBRD, which commenced operations in April 1991, was founded to foster the transition towards open market-oriented economies in its countries of operation which include: Bulgaria, the CSFR, Hungary, Poland, Romania, the USSR and Yugoslavia. The bank aims to provide advice, loans and equity investment, and debt guarantees designed to promote private and entrepreneurial initiative in the countries of Central and Eastern Europe.

The European Investment Bank (EIB) is an autonomous institution within the EC structure, established to finance capital investment projects that promote the balanced development of the EC. The bank finances viable public and private sector projects in infrastructure, industry, agro-industry, agriculture, energy, tourism and services of benefit to those sectors. The EIB has been authorised to lend up to ECU1bn for capital investment projects in Poland and Hungary and will most likely extend lending to Czechoslovakia, Bulgaria and Romania.

Other sources of finance

Governments may offer various types of direct and indirect assistance through governmental investment companies, grants, subsidised loans, tax concessions, subsidisation of costs of utilities, communications, transport, employee services such as schools, hospitals, and health services, and such local services as the building of roads, irrigation, sewers, water purification plants, and the supply of police protection.

Institutional lenders such as life insurance companies, investment management companies, venture capital providers, commercial finance companies, and local commercial and securities banks are among the wide range of additional sources of funding. There may be buyers willing to help finance a project so they can get the finished product or service they require. Similarly, sellers of by-products and raw materials may be prepared to consider financing for the chance to procure profitable contracts or enter new markets. Manufacturers, domestic vendors, and lessors of machinery are additional sources of finance.

Insurance

Insurance is often a key ingredient for project finance in the countries of Central and Eastern Europe. Western lenders may want to have a number of risks covered by insurance, like confiscation (including expropriation, nationalization, and denial of access); loss of profits/business interruption; contract frustration, repudiation and embargo; strikes, riots, and civil commotion; kidnap and ransom; certain war risks; and such contingency risks as failure to honour financial guarantees in the event of default on loans or supply commitments, revocation of export licences, or revocation of offshore currency repatriation arrangements.

To some extent these risks can be covered under certain government sponsored programmes, like the export credit guarantee agencies discussed above. Private sector coverage may also be available, although premiums for such coverage are escalating. Typically, insurance policy proceeds are assigned to lending banks to enhance credit support for the project. Special legal constraints may affect the borrower's right to insure certain risks with non-host country insurers.

When assessing risk in the region, one of the principal considerations for the insurer is the legal environment within which the project is to be established and operated. Underwriters will wish to see a clear and unambiguous legal structure in the host country. In addition, especially in the case of the newly-created CIS, a clear delineation of responsibilities for the procurement of operating permits and investment authorisations is vital, as is a stable and precise tax code. Underwriters also must be able to identify local currency regulations, to the extent these may affect the viability of a project.

There is also a strong desire to build a legal fence around the project against adverse future legislation.

Political and economic stability (fundamentally interrelated) are also clearly a major issue in assessing project risks. In some countries in the region, swift and effective action is needed to control the money supply and stem the tide of runaway inflation. An inflation rate of 300% per annum is generally considered by political risk underwriters to be alarming; yet inflation was approaching 1000% per annum in Russia at the time of going to press.

Insurers also consider the potential of a proposed project to benefit the host country. It is widely accepted that host country government interference at a later stage is diminished if the project creates new jobs for the local workforce, generates hard currency earnings for the host country, affords the transfer of technology to the host country, and if the project provides meaningful social economic benefits, like the provision of basic products, retail goods, distribution systems, communications, transportation and so on.

Although the issue of host country external debt has been discussed previously in this chapter, it is important to emphasize its bearing on finding insurance for a project. Many of the underwriters from whom insurance for a project would be sought are also underwriters for trade-related debt. The implications of this situation are twofold. While underwriters view expropriation and payment risks quite differently, they, like the banking community, set themselves country limits. Underwriters have a substantial accumulation of trade risk in the Soviet Union, for example, and are naturally concerned about the deterioration in payment delays. A clarification of the future operation of the banking system, and the creation of an orderly plan to deal with current foreign debt obligations can only enhance the attitude of underwriters towards accepting new risk. A solution to the question of responsibility for former all-Union debt, as well as real evidence of an improvement in payment delays will be vital.

Whatever the private insurance market capacity may be for a particular country, considering the amount of financing required in the region, it will not be sufficient to meet demand. This concern has led to increasing calls for the creation of a multi-government sponsored export credit and investment agency, to be set up under the auspices of the European Community or the Multi-Lateral Investment Guarantee Agency. A similar concept has been suggested in the US, centred in OPIC.

Examples of project finance in the region

Even in the USSR there are some examples of project finance.

In August 1989, Moscow Narodny Bank in London announced a novel limited recourse financial package for the 'Sherotel' joint-venture project at Moscow airport. Aeroflot, one of the Soviet parties, provided a limited guarantee, and ECU 42.3m in Belgian export credit was arranged by Generale Bank and insured by the Office National Ducroire, the country's export credit agency, on the same limited security basis as the total package, ie on a straight project risk basis.

An earlier project involved a FM 60m financing for a hotel in Tallinn, the Estonian capital. A Finnish travel agent with an equity involvement in the project ensured foreign exchange earnings by commitments to bring foreign tourists to the hotel. Loan guarantees in that project were provided by the City of Tallinn and the Republic Council of Ministers, and in part by the Finnish contractor, travel agent and hotel management company who, together, took 48.9% of the equity.

Project finance was recently arranged by Instituto Bancario San Paolo di Torino and Cofisov for a Soviet aluminium foil joint venture project involving FATA and Reynolds reflecting well-settled Western project finance techniques, including: syndicated financing of ECU 136m in two tranches, one with SACE cover; a deliver-or-pay undertaking from a recently-created Soviet association of aluminium producers, providing for deliveries of aluminium ingots in the event that the joint enterprise does not deliver foil; an undertaking by the joint venture to deliver foil; an undertaking by one of the parties, Reynolds, to make annual purchases of aluminium foil or ingots; an offshore escrow arrangement covering both the hard currency capital contributions of the Western parties in the joint venture and payments by Reynolds for the foil/ingots; and the necessary insurance coverage (provided by Ingosstrakh, the Soviet insurer).

Another recent example is the DM 410m project finance facility arranged by Moscow Narodny, Morgan Grenfell and Instituto Bancario San Paolo di Torino, for a Soviet joint venture to produce butyl and halobutyl rubbers at Tobolsk, in the Tyumen region. The Soviet participants in the venture are the Tobolsk Petrochemical Kombinat and Neftekhimbank (both formerly under the USSR Ministry of Chemical and Oil Refining Industry). The Western party is Pressindustria SpA (Italy).

An earlier industrial project finance deal, the ASETCO project, involved the UK contractor John Brown in a plan to modernise and expand two existing high-density polyethylene plants and add a capability for low-density polyethylene. An offshore joint venture was set up as part of the financial package, which included such traditional project finance techniques as an 'offtake' commitment by Union Carbide to purchase a portion of the product at a discount to world market prices, and 'supply-or-pay' feedstock commitments by the Soviet side.

Conclusion

In formulating a strategy to finance a project in Central and Eastern Europe, it is necessary to take into account the difficulties typically encountered in securing finance and to devise practical solutions. There are several features that make a project attractive to export credit agencies and foreign banks and increase the chances of obtaining financing support, including the following:

- *Export orientation*   projects or enterprises which require hard currency investments or imported technology or components should be able to service hard currency borrowings through hard currency export earnings.
- *Incremental investment*   the upgrading or refurbishment of existing plants through incremental investment which improves productivity or quality, or adds value using the existing workforce and infrastructure, may be viewed by the lenders as involving lower risk than a 'greenfields' venture.
- *Scale*   small scale investments with relatively low capital costs and financing requirements and a short payback period, may be more attractive to lenders.
- *Structure*   the proper evaluation, assessment, negotiation and structuring of projects in a period of change and uncertainty tends to require time, cost and effort.
- *Shared risks*   lenders will expect the investor to take real equity risks, putting their own resources on the line to ensure the success of the venture.
- *Investor commitment*   lenders will expect the investors to make a long-term commitment and not seek to maximise short-term profits – such a commitment must be clearly demonstrable, with the parties of the venture having compatible objectives and determination to make it succeed.

Many observers believe that the countries of Central and Eastern Europe represent a vast, untapped market. As they reform and move toward a market economy, opportunities for Western business grow significantly. Host country financial resources are minimal, and foreign debt and equity may be expected to play an increasingly important role. Project finance techniques may also become a significant factor.

As this chapter went to press, fundamental political and economic changes in many countries in the region (particularly the Soviet Union) were still unfolding. It is likely that the full impact of these events will remain unclear for some time. Until there is a clear picture of political stability and an indication of sound economic reform, Western business confidence in the area will remain shaky. Western investors will seek to minimise risk and chose the most secure of projects.

In other countries in the region recent economic and political reforms have done much to reassure Western financiers, but some of these, too, have debt service problems, in addition to relatively little recent experience with market economies and democratic political institutions. It is not surprising, therefore, that Western financial institutions remain cautious about major exposure in these countries.

Douglas Helfer received his MA in Contemporary Soviet Affairs from the School of Slavonic and East European Studies, University of London. For two years he worked as an assistant to the American Press Attache in the Embassy of the United States in Moscow. Presently Mr Helfer is Director of Research in the London office of Cole Corette & Abrutyn, an international law firm with offices in Washington, London, Moscow, St Petersburg and Warsaw.

10 Project finance – legal aspects

Roger McCormick, Freshfields

1 Introduction

A General trends

The financial markets, by their nature, are in a state of almost continuous change and development. The law relating to the transactions which feature in those markets is not. It is far from static but, at least in the industrialised world, it is relatively well-established. (In contrast, the law relating to the regulation of the markets seems to be incapable of standing still – however desirable this might be.) As a result, although there is always something new that can be said about project finance transactions, the legal commentator, if he is honest, will be hard pressed to identify legal developments that have significantly altered the picture from what existed 10 or 15 years ago. A general review and updating by reference to what is currently happening in the market will not, however, do any harm particularly in view of the apparent new generation of project financings inspired by the growing trend of privatising utilities and infrastructure facilities and the opening up to competition of industries which previously existed in command economies.

General trends affecting the legal structure of project finance transactions include:

(a) the gradual disappearance of 'alternative' means of borrowing; with the major exception of leasing, the exotic 'quasi-borrowing' techniques (production payment, forward purchase facilities etc) which were such a feature of the 1970s are now much less prominent. No doubt the accountancy profession's new (some might say overdue) attitude to 'substance over form' has something to do with this;

(b) the establishment of techniques such a 'build operate transfer' (or 'BOT') – a transaction structure particularly suitable for infrastructure projects;

(c) lenders' concerns over 'lender liability', particularly in the context of environmental laws;

(d) the continuing prominence of variations on the 'take or pay' theme – especially in the context of the financing of new industrial plant (including power stations);

(e) the fact that many of the new projects are located in countries where the 'legal infrastructure' is not only unfamiliar but very nearly non-existent.

B Definition of issues

It is of course typical for a lawyer to start with a list of definitions. The answer to the question 'what is project finance?' has, however, been dealt with in chapter 1. In any event most of us know what it is when we see it. Or do we? The question is by no means academic. It arises, for example, in the context of ordinary (ie non-project finance) transactions where borrowers might seek exceptions to, for example, negative pledge and/or cross-default provisions for 'project finance transactions'. The logic behind such exceptions is well-known. A project finance transaction can be regarded as 'non-recourse' (or, depending on the circumstances, 'limited recourse'). To that extent there is a case for regarding the assets which are the subject of any security as, in effect, being 'isolated' from other group assets and not properly available for the discharge of other group borrowings. Such assets would not exist without the project financing and (the argument runs) it is only proper that they should in a sense be 'dedicated' to it insofar as they provide security for it. Similarly the consequences of a default are 'isolated'. One might also expect project finance borrowings to be disregarded for the purposes of provisions involving debt-equity ratios and similar measures of corporate financial health.

If such exceptions are to be negotiated, it is clearly important that an appropriate legal definition of 'project finance borrowing' can be found. Since such transactions do not by their nature conform to any pre-established pattern it is not always easy to frame the definition in a way that both sides will find acceptable. The borrower will wish to anticipate a broad range of possible transactions to be entered into in the future but the lender will not wish the exception to be drafted in such a way that transactions which are not truly 'non-recourse' might be regarded as falling within it. As a result, the lender will certainly wish to exclude from the definition transactions which provide for recourse to other members of the group ie, beyond the (generally specially incorporated) subsidiary or other entity used for the project finance borrowing. The difficulty (as is explained below) is that most forms of project finance do involve, at least at some stage, some element of recourse to other members of the group. This is likely to be the case particularly during the period prior to completion of the project. It may also extend to certain kinds of provision which are in force after completion. For example, the borrower may wish to have access to funds which would otherwise be blocked (perhaps to cover, say, six months' anticipated debt service) on the basis that the replenishment of the blocked account is 'guaranteed' by the parent. In certain transactions the parent might be required to underwrite, say, the borrower's commitment to comply with all relevant laws and regulations, the conditions attaching to any licence or permit and the material provisions of the joint venture and other relevant project agreements.

Nobody would pretend to offer a legal definition which will be suitable for all purposes but, by way of illustration, the following wording based on a definition used in a recent Euromarket transaction is worth consideration.

'Project finance borrowing'
means any borrowing to finance a project:

(a) which is made by a single purpose company (whether or not a member of the group) whose principal assets and business are constituted by that project and whose liabilities in respect of the borrowing concerned are not directly or indirectly the subject of a guarantee, indemnity or any other form of assurance, undertaking or support from any member of the group except as expressly referred to in paragraph (b)(iii) below; or

(b) in respect of which the person or persons making such borrowing available to the relevant borrower (whether or not a member of the group) have no recourse whatsoever to any member of the group for the repayment of or payment of any sum relating to such borrowing other than:

   (i) recourse to the borrower for amounts limited to aggregate cash flow or net cash flow (other than historic cash flow or historic net cash flow) from such project; and/or

   (ii) recourse to the borrower for the purpose only of enabling amounts to be claimed in respect of that borrowing in an enforcement of any security interest given by the borrower over the assets comprised in the project (or given by any shareholder in the borrower over its shares in the borrower) to secure that borrowing or any recourse referred to in (iii) below, provided that (A) the extent of such recourse to the borrower is limited solely to the amount of any recoveries made on any such enforcement, and (B) such person or persons are not entitled, by virtue of any right or claim arising out of or in connection with such borrowing, to commence proceedings for the winding up or dissolution of the borrower or to appoint or procure the appointment of any receiver, trustee or similar person or official in respect of the borrower or any of its assets (save for the assets the subject of such security interest); and/or

   (iii) recourse to such borrower generally, or directly or indirectly to a member of the group under any form of completion guarantee, assurance or undertaking, which recourse is limited to a claim for damages (other than liquidated damages and damages required to be calculated in a specified way) for breach of any obligation (not being a payment obligation or any obligation to procure payment by another or an obligation to comply or to procure compliance by another with any financial ratios or other tests of financial condition) by the person against whom such recourse is available; or

(c) which the lender shall have agreed in writing to treat as a project finance borrowing.

Provided that where any borrowing is made to finance a project and that borrowing does not qualify as a 'project finance borrowing' pursuant to the above sub-paragraphs (a), (b) and (c) but would so qualify if there were not recourse to a member of the group under a form of guarantee, assurance or undertaking (a 'limited guarantee') which is either (i) limited as to the period during which it is in force (for example, during the period up to completion of the project) or (ii) limited as to the obligations of the borrower to which it applies, then, in any such case, the borrowing shall be regarded as a 'project finance borrowing' for the purposes of this definition to the extent that, and during such period that, the obligations of the borrower in respect of the borrowings concerned are not the subject of the limited guarantee.'

As can be seen, even an extensive provision such as that set out above leaves open the possibility of a consent by the lender for any specific transaction which has not actually been anticipated.

The above wording recognises that some degree of recourse to another member of the group is almost inevitable but deals with the difficulty by causing such recourse to disapply the definiiton *only to the extent that* the recourse exists. Thus a project finance borrowing that 'converted' to a non-recourse basis only on completion would only 'count' as a project finance borrowing once the conversion took effect.

2 Choice of structure: legal considerations

A Commercial influences

Perhaps the only general rule to be remembered when devising the appropriate contractual and security structure for a project financing is that there are no general rules. For the purpose of analysis it is helpful to distinguish what may broadly be regarded as 'commercial' influences from legal influences. Although the distinction is often blurred, the commercial influences will generally include:

(a) the extent to which recourse to the borrower group, as opposed to the project, is to be limited;

(b) credit appraisal of the borrower group and relevant assoiated companies. Even in the most attractive of projects, this will be relevant to the 'mix' of full recourse and non-recourse elements, the reliance placed on security and on both pre- and post-completion covenants and parent company support. They may be in the nature of 'comfort' or something more tangible;

(c) the nature of the project (for example, whether it is a natural resource project or an infrastructure project), the anticipated period to its completion, production profile (particularly relevant for natural resource projects) and subsequent life of the project. All of these are central to the determination of the key commercial factors in the transaction such as the size of the advance, the time when 'conversion' to a non-recourse basis can take place, 'cover' ratios and the final maturity of the financing;

(d) political risk (in which, for present purposes, is included not only the risk of nationalisation or expropriation but also the possibility of increases in taxation and royalties and the degree of state participation). It may not vary significantly according to the type of structure adopted, but can influence questions such as (i) the type of security taken (ii) the situation of any 'vehicle' companies and (iii) the reliance placed on any host government support which it is considered necessary to obtain;

(e) the extra cost over a conventional financing: the borrower group must balance the advantages of different types of project financing against the cost of higher margins and fees, greater set-up costs and the need for continuing administration; generally speaking, the more complex the structure (in particular a structure with substantial non-recourse elements) the more expensive and time-consuming it is both to establish and administer it;

(f) whether the finance is for an individual participant or for a group of participants: some structures can be adapted more easily to a financing involving a complete project and all the participants involved in it whereas others may be suitable only for the needs of an individual participant;

(g) whether the structure is to serve for one financing or for a series of financings (as in the case of, for example, pipeline financings or a major infrastructure project like the Channel Tunnel).

B Summary of types of structure

There are basically two ways for a commercial venture to raise non-equity money from 'outside sources'. These are:

(a) conventional 'full recourse' borrowing; and
(b) receipt of 'principal' sum as the price for the use or disposal (sale, lease or otherwise) of an asset.

The term 'project finance' is not normally used in the strict sense for method (a) even though the borrowing may be 'project-related', that is the funds are allocated for a specific 'project' purpose. Project financing often involves forms of financing other than a conventional borrowing (using, for example, method (b)) or at least severely qualifies method (a) by limiting the recourse of the lenders beyond the project itself. The simplest method, however, is to employ method (a) but to use a special purpose vehicle whose only assets comprise the project assets. If that vehicle (the 'SPV') goes into default, there is to be no recourse beyond it to other group entities. This is normally the natural result of using a limited company (or other limited liability entity) for the SPV. It will generally be necessary to structure the shareholding in the SPV in such a way as to avoid its borrowings being shown in the consolidated accounts of the parent company and its group. Various devices can be used to achieve this objective, depending on the accounting requirements that apply to the parent. It is not uncommon, for example, to arrange for all or part of the shareholding to be held by a charity.

(a) Throughputs and 'take or pay'

The throughput arrangement is commonly used in pipeline financings – indeed it is so commonly found in this context that arguably it may be regarded as the 'conventional' financing for pipeline projects. However, the technique is capable of adaptation to other forms of project which involve the payment of tolls or tariffs (or the payment for 'offtake' from, for example, a utility or manufacturing plant) and where the paying party or parties represent a realistic credit risk for the lending banks. In very simple terms, what happens, in the context of pipelines, is as follows:

(a) The lender or lenders advance money to a company controlled by the joint venturers which is usually concerned with the operation of, and will usually own, the pipeline. This company, which is commonly known as the pipeline company, will not have sufficient tangible assets to justify the credit on its own balance sheet.

(b) the pipeline company has a 'throughput agreement' with the joint venturers (sometimes known as the 'shippers') under which the shippers agree to use the pipeline, when it is built, for the transportation of petroleum.

(c) The shippers agree in the throughput agreement to pipe sufficent petroleum to produce, at the relevant tariff rates, the necessary funds in the hands of the pipeline company to discharge the latter's obligations to the creditors. Further, each shipper is required to advance to the pipeline company (for credit against future tariffs) its percentage of the relevant debt obligations. This obligation of the shipper is required to be performed even if insufficient petroleum is piped (for example, because the pipeline is not completed). It is subject to a form of 'hell or high water' clause. This clause ensures, as far as possible that the advance payments must be made in all circumstances notwithstanding events which otherwise might be considered to frustrate the contract or give rise to a claim by the shipper for non-performance.

(d) The rights of the pipeline company against the shippers are assigned to a common trustee to hold them for the benefit of creditors as security. In order to be admitted to the security 'club' constituted by those arrangements any particular credit has to qualify under the rules of the club (ie, meet the requirements of the Common Trust Deed) and be 'designated' for the specific purpose.

One of the effects of the trust arrangement is that the 'security' (ie, the right to claim against the shippers) is repeatable, enabling subsequent lenders to join in the security and rank pari passu with earlier creditors in respect of the rights against the shippers despite being later in time and without the need for deeds of priorities.

Thus the throughput arrangement gives the lenders, through the common trustee, a right to claim repayment from the shippers of amounts advanced to the pipeline company. It is essentially a form of 'take or pay' arrangement. It is particularly suitable for a financing where some degree of recourse is required to companies such as shippers or their equivalent (eg, long-term contract customers for product). It may be compared to a loan to a jointly-owned 'shell' company supported by unsecured 'quasi-guarantees' from its shareholders. It should be noted that it is in principle an unsecured arrangement – the shippers do not as a rule grant any security interest over their assets – and that the term 'quasi-guarantee' needs to be treated with caution. Although the throughput arrangement resembles a guarantee it is not (and should not be considered as equivalent to) a guarantee. Although every effort is made to close them, certain legal loopholes potentially exist which are not present in a straightforward guarantee; this is usually reflected in the terms on which the credit is given.

In any event, although the 'take or pay' approach may influence the basic structure, a full 'hell-or-high water' clause may not always be available. For example, the entity which commits to 'offtake' production may not always be prepared, as a commercial matter, to underwrite the financial obligations incurred for the project. An electricity utility might, for example, be prepared to make some form of 'capacity payment' (linked to financing costs) in the power purchase agreement but it cannot be assumed that there will be absolutely no exceptions to its obligation to make such payment. The same point will arise in similar contexts in many different kinds of project financing. A relatively recent project financing in Africa produced a lengthy clause which in effect defined force majeure risks which the sponsors were not prepared to accept. These covered the following:

- declared or undeclared war or hostilities, revolution, insurrection, riot or civil commotion
- the confiscation, seizure, nationalisation or other appropriation of property or assets of the borrower by the host government or any governing authority exercising effective control over the territory of the host country
- compliance by the borrower with any other action by the host government which has the force or effect of law
- action by the government of the country of the sponsor which effectively prevents sponsor and/or borrower or its affiliates from directly or indirectly continuing activities in the host country
- acts of God including fire, flood, earthquake or other natural disaster provided the same cannot be insured against.

The effect of these force majeure exclusions was 'softened' to some extent by provisions to the effect that they should not apply, for example, if the occurrence of the relevant contingency 'was provoked or substantially contributed to by any act or omission of . . .' the borrower or the sponsors. In effect, this was a contractual parallel to the difficult legal concept of 'self-induced frustration'. There were also provisions for taking all reasonable precautions, exercising due care, etc.

The concept of force majeure is imprecise in common law jurisdictions. It is not a term of art. The parties have to define what they mean. Once the concept is admitted, however, one finds it creeping into a number of different project finance documents. Not only may it form an exception to the commitment to pay for product, it can also qualify sponsor's obligations under, for example, completion guarantees. Considerable difficulties can arise where the force majeure event does not result in the project being cancelled but causes a delay in completion the duration of which is difficult to specify. As the parties negotiate who is bearing what risk in these circumstances and what action they can take if, for example, the delay continues for a very lengthy period, they are in effect 'drafting out' the concept of frustration. The English courts will not determine that a contract has been frustrated if the parties have clearly foreseen the event in question and have provided for what is to happen and what their position should be if it actually occurs. Not all systems operate in this way. In the Middle East, for example, it seems that there are certain events which could be regarded as having a sufficiently fundamental effect on the project as to release one or more parties from their commitments (for example, to pay lease rentals) even though the contract might provide otherwise. Extreme care needs to be taken if there is a risk that the local law could override the proper law of the contract in such circumstances. Needless to say, the problem would only be accentuated if it was necessary to obtain a judgment in a local court.

The throughput agreement is an exception to the general tendency for project financing to involve non-conventional techniques for the raising of finance (as opposed to securing the obligation to repay) since it does, of course, usually involve a conventional borrowing or bond issue even though this is supported by the 'quasi-guarantee' arrangement. Other forms of project financing rely more upon techniques which involve the disposal of an asset in order to raise money and of these one of the most popular – at least in the energy sector – is the forward purchase.

(b) Forward purchase (sale) agreement

In the typical case, a forward purchase financing (sometimes known as 'advance payment' financing) involves the provision of funds (by the lenders or a vehicle company funded by lenders) as the purchase price of (say) minerals yet to be delivered or produced. (The terms 'lenders' and 'borrowers' are used for convenience throughout – even if the structure does not involve a conventional borrowing.) When the minerals are produced the lenders have the right to take quantities in proportion to the retirement of the financing.

The relevant clause might read on the following lines:

> '. . . the quantity of [mineral] to be purchased shall be such that the cash proceeds from the resale thereof and available for the payment of [borrowing obligations incurred by lenders' vehicle company] will enable [vehicle company/purchaser] to make such payment . . .'

In order to enable the lender to turn the right to minerals into cash the minerals are usually re-sold to the project company or sold by the project company on behalf of the lenders (or their vehicle company). There is a full indemnity in respect of any liability which may arise by reason of title to the minerals being vested in the lenders (even if only momentarily). Sometimes an option for the project company to pay cash is included instead of the obligation to deliver minerals to the lender. This is to deal with small payments or when there is a delay in extracting minerals.

Express provision can be made dealing with the possibility of there being insufficient minerals available to discharge the financing. Thus the mineral company is required to make what are commonly called 'deficiency payments' which compensate the lenders for failure to deliver in an amount sufficient to discharge the financing. The requirement for such provision and the extent to which it is applicable will vary according to the degree to which the financing is considered to be full or non-recourse; or, put more simply, the extent to which the lenders are prepared to risk the anticipated level of production not being achieved.

(c) Production payment
The production payment technique, oversimplified, is the purchase by the lenders (for a principal sum) of certain rights of the borrower related to the project. It is regarded in the US as a conventional means of raising finance for oil and gas projects once they have reached or are about to reach the production phase. It can, however, be adapted to projects involving the recovery of other minerals such as, for example, coal and iron ore.

The 'production payment' is well-established in the US and, due to some extent to the influence of taxation cases, it has relatively clear rules of definition (unlike, say, the forward purchase). The rights acquired by the lenders are commonly described as the right to receive the oil (or other minerals) or its proceeds of sale, when extracted. It is sometimes structured as a promise to pay a given amount of money out of an agreed percentage of oil and gas as, if and when produced; or as a promise to deliver production until its value equals a certain sum. It can also be structured, at least in the US, as a grant or reservation of the title to a fraction of the oil and gas until the production causes the interest to realise a certain sum of money.

Thus, production payments may either entitle the holder to delivery in kind (sometimes called an 'in-kind payment') or to money derived from the sale of minerals (a 'proceeds payment'). Proceeds payments may be linked to particular contracts of sale (with independent third parties or affiliates of the company raising the finance), the rights whereunder are assigned to the banks providing the finance (or their vehicle company).

There appear to be three basic criteria for the production payment in the US; these are:

(a) the source of discharge must be restricted to production (the 'alternate source rule');
(b) its duration must be shorter than the reasonably estimated economic life of the project; and
(c) the lender should not be responsible for operating costs.

As a result, it does not have the same degree of flexibility as certain other structures. This accounts in part for its comparative lack of popularity in the UK and elsewhere. There are also certain legal difficulties (considered in more detail post). Proceeds payments, when linked to assigned long-term offtake agreements, fit more easily into established UK legal concepts. However, problems are encountered with the in-kind payment due chiefly to the fact that (if for example the mineral is located under the sea or on Crown property) the grantor of the in-kind payment may not have any interest in the mineral to grant until it is produced.

(d) Limited or non-recourse loans
Forward purchases and production payments adopt by and large the 'sale of an asset' approach in order to raise finance. Limited or non-recourse loans are, by

180 Projects under the new influences

contrast, generally structured as borrowings. They differ from conventional borrowings by virtue of the fact that the lender takes some risk in the project, the terms of repayment being linked to a greater or lesser extent to the success of the project rather than the borrower's assets and ability to repay in general. (They are sometimes made to a specially formed subsidiary whose assets are limited to the project (and as a result the recourse is so limited). This technique can, however, ultimately result in a parent company deliberately walking away from its subsidiary's liabilities if the non-recourse principle is to be preserved and as a result may be unsuitable for policy reasons). The basic structure may therefore be simply identified although there are many variations on the theme. In particular, the extent to which lenders can look beyond the project and as a result have recourse to the borrower is an issue which turns a great deal upon detailed negotiations after the initial structure is established.

(e) Other forms of alternative financing

There are many other forms of alternative financing which do not involve conventional borrowings and some of which may feature in project financings from time to time. These include leasings, hire purchase and conditional sales, bareboat charterparties, acceptance credit facilities and debt factoring. Leases, in particular, have been a feature in the recent re-emergence of project financing transactions in the UK. The privatisation of the power industry has resulted in a considerable number of new power station projects and many of the project assets have been financed on a lease basis.

C Legal influences

Any financing structure will have to take account of the underlying legal structure of the borrower's interests and will have to take account of external legal factors affecting both banks and customer. It is proposed to deal with these 'legal' influences by giving what is hoped to be a reasonably full list although no claim is made that what follows is exhaustive.

(a) Restrictions on conventional borrowing

Restrictions which affect a conventional borrowing, but which may not 'catch' a project financing of the type which is not legally classified as a borrowing (e g forward purchase agreement) may be found, typically, in:

(i) constitutional or corporate documents relating to the customer (e g articles of association, statutes and byelaws etc) where the power of the borrower or its directors to raise money by a borrowing and/or to give guarantees may be limted to, say, a given multiple of shareholders' funds;

(ii) loan agreements – especially unsecured loans where instead of taking security the lenders may be willing to rely on 'financial' covenants which require the borrower to keep to certain debt/equity ratios and other formulae; and

(iii) trust deeds for public debt issues where similar restrictions to those in (ii) may apply.

Such restrictions can sometimes be avoided by using one or a combination of the forms of financing just described. (However, restrictions which cover 'raising money' generally will usually apply.)

(b) Accounting treatment
This is more a commercial than a legal influence but it is often linked with the considerations just mentioned; a conventional form of financing may have a greater effect on the borrower's balance sheet than an alternative form of project financing. The borrower's credit rating can be affected as a result although here the real issue should be whether the financing is full or non-recourse rather than its impact on the balance sheet. Nevertheless although the accounting treatment differs from country to country, it appears that fewer and fewer alternative forms of financing escape the balance sheet altogether. Forward purchase arrangements for example often appear either in the notes or on the balance sheet itself (sometimes expressed as a deferred liability). However, where the accounting treatment follows the form rather than the substance, 'off balance sheet' considerations remain highly relevant. This seems likely to remain a material factor in relation to certain types of structure, notably throughputs (where the 'quasi-guarantee' commitment of the shipper company does not always appear as such on the balance sheet or in the notes).

(c) Negative pledges
The expression 'negative pledge' describes the type of covenant frequently found in bond issues and unsecured loan agreements where the borrower agrees that it will not create a security interest (e g a mortgage or a charge) over any of its assets without at least giving to the lender or lenders an equivalent security. The lender's objective is to ensure as far as possible that, if the borrower should become insolvent, the greater part of its assets would be available for distribution amongst its unsecured creditors and would not be swallowed up by the holders of floating charges or other securities. The negative pledge is often coupled with a 'pari passu' undertaking; the borrower agrees not only that it will not grant security to other creditors but that as far as possible it will not allow any other creditor to obtain priority over the credit given by those to whom the undertaking is given. This type of clause necessarily has to be subject to the rights of preferred creditors such as the taxman and certain classes of employees etc. It is important in jurisdictions where priority can be granted without necessarily creating a formal security over a given asset or class of asset (for example, in Spain where priority can be granted through the 'Escritura Publica' procedure). Negative pledges and pari passu clauses are familiar devices and it would be inappropriate to dwell upon the legal questions raised by them here except to point out that they may be relevant to the choice of structure for the following reasons:

(i) if the structure involves the creation of a security (e g over the project assets) it may be necessary to obtain the consent of creditors who already have the benefit of such undertakings – unless the undertakings contain agreed exceptions which cover project financing;

(ii) the negative pledge may or may not catch security given in particular types of project financing (depending for example on whether or not the negative pledge catches security given by a subsidiary or specially formed vehicle company);

(iii) any difficulty in obtaining a waiver or consent of earlier creditors may influence the timing and the giving of security in a project financing – for example, whether it should be given as soon as the money is raised or only upon 'conversion' to a non-recourse basis.

It is worth comparing the restrictions mentioned ante (ie those which catch conventional borrowing but not alternative forms of finance) and the negative pledge/pari passu restriction. It will be apparent that the choice of structure may be affected by a combination of these factors. For example, some forms of negative pledge may not apply to security given for a forward sale arrangement even though they may apply if the transaction is structured as a borrowing. However, the forms of restriction have become more and more sophisticated and, generally speaking, a modern clause is likely to anticipate most kinds of 'quasi-indebtedness' or 'raising money'. But, as bankers have insisted on more sophisticated and widely drawn clauses for this purpose, borrowers have tended to insist on appropriately worded exception clauses to the negative pledge so as to enable certain kinds of financing – typically project finance – to be raised on a secured basis without the need for consent.

(d) Cross-default clauses

Companies wishing to obtain project financing may have borrowed money already under agreements or bond issues containing cross-default clauses. The effect of these broadly is to give the lenders in those other financings the right to accelerate repayment if there should be a default in any financing entered into by the customer. A company proposing to raise project finance therefore needs to look not only at the effect which any acceleration of the project financing may have on a cross-default clause in another borrowing but also consider carefully the extent to which it is prepared to allow the principle of cross-default to be incorporated into the proposed project financing. The following points may have an effect on the structure adopted:

(i) The question will turn on the wording of the relevant clause and the relevant governing law. However, a borrower may find that a cross-default clause contained in other conventional arrangements could be triggered by a default of a vehicle company used in a project financing – even though the borrower does not have complete control over the activities of the vehicle company.

(ii) Joint ventures may raise finance as a group. A widely drawn cross-default clause may then have the effect that the default of one joint venturer results automatically in the default of the others (even where the first default is caused by the operation of another cross-default clause); this may be regarded as unacceptable in principle if the commitment of the joint venturers is intended to be several only.

(iii) A cross-default clause in other financings may or may not be triggered by acceleration of the project financing even though that acceleration is not technically a 'default' but the result of lenders exercising their right to bring forward repayment as a result of events affecting the project outside the borrower's control.

(iv) The cross-default clause proposed in the project financing itself may require acceleration of the project financing if the customer defaults in respect of a financing that has no connection whatsoever with the project; certain borrowers may question the principle underlying such a clause – particularly where the lenders of the project finance have taken security over all the project assets and under the terms of the financing do not have access to any other assets outside the project.

The outcome of negotiations on the above points may or may not require the borrower to obtain variations of its existing financing arrangements and can have an impact upon the use of vehicle companies and the like particularly in the context of group financings. Companies which are raising, or are likely to raise, project finance should consider carefully whether such financings should form an exception for the purposes of the cross-default clauses that are imposed on them in other financings.

(e) Restrictions in operating agreements, licence etc, and in sale agreements

In addition to the borrower's existing loan agreements and constitutional documents, restrictions may be found in the network of project agreements between the borrower, its co-venturers and the host government (and/or its state-owned resources company) that affect the kind of structure that may be used. Restrictions in sales contracts may also be relevant. The following should be considered:

(i)   restrictions on charging project assets;
(ii) pre-emption rights;
(iii) existing charges in favour of other co-venturers (to cover e g unpaid calls) and rights of forfeiture;
(iv) provisions on compulsory abandonment of the project;
(v)   provisions in sales contracts which prevent or limit assignment of rights to proceeds.

The commitments to the host government are usually covered separately. As far as other co-venturers are concerned, the necessary consents are normally forthcoming – at least from those with similar commercial interests – and indeed their requirement is often foreseen in the terms of the operating documents. Lenders, however, will usually have to accept that, save in the case of a group financing, their security over project assets will have to rank no better than pari passu with the operating securities that the co-venturers have already taken, or agreed to give, in their own favour.

Lenders will also be concerned, in any structure that involves security over sales proceeds (except, perhaps, purely floating security) that the security assignment of those proceeds is permitted by the relevant sales contracts. If, say, a long-term sales contract contained a prohibition on assignment it would be necessary to seek express consent from the buyer.

This particular topic is fairly well-covered ground and, with the exception perhaps of consents of buyers under sales contracts, does not normally have a material impact on the choice of structure. The general rule seems to be that if a consent of co-venturers or the government is required, it is likely to be required for any of the structures since one or both of the following tend to be common features:

(a) lenders will, at least in offshore projects, require some host government assurances since security of tenure is seldom granted to the borrower in terms which will be satisfactory in the context of the substantial amount of money required to be raised; and

(b) certain project rights granted by the government, or derived from project agreements, cannot be assigned or charged without consent – and lenders will normally require an assignment or charge in their favour in e g non-recourse loans, forward purchases or production payments.

(f) Restrictions and other factors directly affecting lenders
The borrower is not the only entity affected by restrictions which influence the structure of a financing. The lenders also may have to take into account considerations such as the following:

(i) restrictions on doing business other than lending: these may inhibit techniques such as the forward purchase or production payment;

(ii) restrictions on taking security: some jurisdictions limit the ability of foreign banks to take security over certain types of assets or to take certain formal types of security;

(iii) restrictions on doing business within a particular jurisdiction: various limitations may be applied to foreign banks and a combination of such limitations and those affecting the ability to take security can narrow the scope for some of the more imaginative forms of financing;

(iv) the risk associated with ownership of or other interests in the production – particularly liability to third parties for e g pollution damage, or to purchasers of production, can render some forms of structure unattractive.

With regard to the second type of restriction, where a significant proportion of the finance is in fact provided by local banks which are not affected by restrictions on taking security, it may be worth providing for security to be given at least to those banks and relying on a comprehensively-worded sharing clause so that at least part of the loan benefits from the security. However, any structure which places much reliance on the practical operation of a sharing clause may not currently be very popular in the light of experience in relation to defaults by Iran and Argentina.

In any event some of the above restrictions can be circumvented by the use of vehicle companies or trustee companies although great care needs to be taken that such devices cannot be 'seen through' for the purposes of the restriction or increase the risk of the transaction being regarded as a sham.

(g) Tax treatment
The borrower will wish to consider whether it can achieve lower costs through the use of tax advantages, such as capital allowances, and whether all or any

part of the payments are deductible for tax purposes. The former considerations are of course of central importance in tax-based leasing transactions and are a vast subject in themselves. Favourable tax treatment in the US played an important part in the development in popularity of the production payment technique and is now an influence on the legal structure chosen for private power station financings. Such considerations might also have a significant impact on the attraction of schemes such as the forward purchase. The treatment of the initial 'capital' receipt (which, in law, appears to be a trading receipt of the borrower) and the 'interest' element in any resales needs to be clearly established with the relevant revenue authorities concerned with income, capital or turnover taxes. Care also needs to be taken to ensure that the interest payable on a non-recourse transaction cannot be treated for tax purposes as a distribution on the grounds that it is a payment which (because of the non-recourse element) is dependent on the borrower's results.

All parties will also have to look at the effect of any withholding taxes, not only on any conventional interest payments but also on other payments from 'borrower' to 'lender' in alternative forms of financing. As with any international financing, the incidence of withholding tax may affect the use and location of vehicle companies or other entities in the structure.

Finally, stamp duties and similar documentary taxes can have an effect on structure – especially, where security is involved and in jurisdictions which, unlike the UK, charge high ad valorem duties on certain types of security documents.

3 Importing 'foreign' legal concepts

The adaptation of 'foreign' techniques frequently calls for consideration in project financing for the following reasons:

(a) it is inevitable that those involved in the provision of finance on an international basis will compare lending structures used in one jurisdiction with those to be used in another; and

(b) the use of security in project financing – which is rarely found in other forms of international lending – can give rise to the need to prepare a security 'package' which will compare favourably with similar packages on offer in other jurisdictions.

The development of project financing techniques owes a great deal to the ability of bankers, borrowers and lawyers (on both the 'importing' and 'exporting' side) to adapt ideas used in one part of the world to a legal system prevailing in another part of the world. Most of the structures have their origins in common law concepts but have now acquired, or are in the process of acquiring, an international usage. The export (or import) of such ideas is, however, subject to a number of constraints; for example:

(i) the laws of country A may have a quite different impact from those of country B in relation to certain elements in the structure; for example, the acquisition by a lender of any form of proprietary interest in a project or its production may carry with it responsibilities to customers or the general public in country A or elsewhere which cannot be avoided and which the lender finds unacceptable; the tax treatment may of course be different and impede the use of certain types of structure (although it is interesting to observe that this can also have its advantages, giving rise to the 'double dip' effect, where the same transaction is classified differently in countries A and B); a person with a limited interest in an asset (eg a long-term lessee) may be able to pass good title to the entire asset (without the lessor's consent) in country A, thus adversely affecting the lessor's security in country A, as opposed to country B where the law would not enable the lessee to pass freehold title under the 'nemo dat quod non habet' principle;

(ii) the rules relating to conflicts of laws may prevent a 'foreign' form of security, familiar enough in country A, being effectively executed over property situated in country B;

(iii) a borrower may not be able to execute any effective form of security interest over mineral rights if the law of country B does not accept that the borrower has any proprietary interest in such rights – even though this would not be the case if the project was situated in country A; alternatively, the legal position as to the borrower's title and associated rights and priorities may simply be too unclear – particularly, where the 'chain of title' goes back over many years or in the case of offshore rights;

(iv) in some countries it is the policy of the host government to require that the legal title to all or most of the assets used in certain kinds of projects be vested in the government, thus making it difficult or impossible for these to be charged in favour of lenders as security for advances.

Difficulties are more likely to be encountered where there is in effect a 'clash of style' between legal systems, as between civil code and common law systems. Whilst generalisations are dangerous most lawyers practising in this area would probably accept that the 'anglo-saxon' approach – which in project financing owes a great deal to financing techniques which border on legal 'fiction' (in the case of, for example, the more extreme take or pay contracts and forward purchases) – assumes a degree of flexibility in the law which is not always warranted in a codified civil system. This is not to say that the civil law systems cannot offer possible alternatives. It has for example been argued that the French delegation – comparable to a novation – is well suited to the 'take or pay' throughput structure. But project financing usually is secured financing, the nature of the security generally being a key element in the financing package, and it is when comparison is made between the security available in a common law jurisdiction with that available in a civil law jurisdiction that some difficult questions arise.

The role of security in project financing is described in more detail below but it is worth recalling in this context the point made earlier. In a large internationally-funded financing the lenders are bound to assess the security offered under the relevant local law at least in part by comparing it with what has been obtained in similar transactions elsewhere. The following legal questions will be relevant:

(a) Over which project assets can fixed security be taken?
(b) To the extent that fixed security is impossible or impracticable, can some form of 'floating' security be taken which will attach and 'fix' to the assets upon, say, acceleration of the loan?

(c) What is the order of priority on liquidation; would anyone rank ahead (eg preferred creditors) of the lenders' interest?

(d) Can the lenders be adversely affected by the creation of a second mortgage or charge?

(e) What remedies are available on enforcement? Can a receiver be appointed? Are there restrictions on the right of sale or foreclosure?

(f) What is the borrower's security of tenure and how good is the borrower's title to the project assets and production?

(g) What filing and other requirements are there associated with the security? Are there heavy documentary taxes that may have to be paid?

(h) Are there any formal requirements as to, say, notification to third parties which are difficult to comply with?

There are obviously many related questions. As an illustration of the kind of problem that can arise, consider the financing of an offshore project in a civil law jurisdiction. The forms of security available under civil law do not fit very easily into the format required for a normal security package in offshore project financing. The types of civil law security that might be considered in this area (in, say, a French law jurisdiction) include the nantissement du fonds de commerce, nantissement d'outillage et du materiel d'equipement, nantissement de creances, delegation and various forms of hypotheque. Whilst some of these securities bear a superficial resemblance to various common law types of mortgage, assignment and floating charge, a closer inspection shows that the remedies available to the lender wishing to enforce the security are much more limited. In particular there is no equivalent of the common law right to appoint a receiver and make that receiver the agent of the borrower.

A common lawyer looking at such a project might think at first that the security aspect can be covered in similar manner to, say, an 'anglo-Scottish' North Sea financing where the lenders' lawyers have traditionally hedged their bets and required both Scottish and English forms of security. Why not then take both civilian and common law forms of security elsewhere? By combining the two one might hope that reasonably satisfactory answers to the above questions could be obtained. To a degree this may be possible. But it will be appreciated that certain forms of security (in relation to, for example, real property) have to take the form required by local law and, under the local law, equivalent forms of security – and remedies – are not always available. The classic example is that very Anglo-Saxon creation, the floating charge. In project financing the floating charge is an extremely useful form of security since it can attach (on 'crystallisation') to assets which are not owned by the borrower at the time the advance is made (such as petroleum then 'in place' and future cash flows) and is often used to 'sweep up' other assets which cannot be caught by a first fixed security. It also carries with it the right to appoint a receiver whose powers of management, sale etc, are invariably widely drafted.

It will be appreciated that what we are most concerned with is the attitude of the local law to the floating charge: the fact that under English law a floating charge can attach to foreign assets will not necessarily help the lender trying to enforce its security before the local court.

There are exceptions but it is generally the case that a floating charge does not have extra-territorial effect in a civil law jurisdiction (unless special local legislation recognises the concept). Furthermore, a company incorporated under the laws of such a jurisdiction is likely to be unable to create such a security over assets situated there (although there are arguments to the effect that it should be able to create the security over assets elsewhere). Accordingly one of the tools of the legal trade, the floating charge, may not be available and the 'classic' forms of civil law security do not, as a general rule, effectively plug the gap by themselves.

Some civil law jurisdictions have adopted legislation which introduces all or part of the floating charge concept (and in some jurisdictions comparable local forms of security exist) but to date very few have done so. Civil lawyers dislike securities like the floating charge which give secured lenders a very considerable advantage over unsecured creditors in any insolvency (and even the common lawyers might concede that the floating charge tips the balance too far in favour of the lender). It will be interesting to see how the problem will be tackled in practice as more project financings become sought after by developing countries with civil law systems. It is perhaps arguable that the criticisms that may be levelled against the floating charge taken over all the borrower's assets are not fully applicable in the case of a floating charge taken only over project assets to support a non-recourse financing.

For the sake of completeness it should of course be noted that, even in jurisdictions where the floating charge is recognised, care should be taken to ensure that any local as well as other registration or procedural requirements are complied with.

4 Role of security

Virtually all commentators agree that the role of security in project financing is defensive and preventative. Most lenders do not consider that the prime purpose of the security is to give them the right to realise on the assets charged in the same manner as they would in a more conventional secured financing. One should not under-estimate the need to establish the security in such a way as to give the lenders the ultimate right, if the need should arise, to take over and run the project for the purpose of discharging the moneys advanced. If such a situation should ever arise, however, the chances of a group of banks running a project successfully where a commercial enterprise set up for that very purpose has failed must be fairly slim. The predominant view is that in most cases the purpose of taking the security is not so much for the positive rights that are conferred upon the lenders but to prevent any third party from acquiring such rights in priority to the lenders. It is obviously more effective than a negative pledge but it is the negative pledge concept which, nevertheless, appears to underly much of the thinking.

Emphasis on the negative role of security should, however, be qualified by recognising that it can play a more positive role in the following circumstances:

(a) where there are actual cash proceeds from production under contracts of a long-term nature which can be paid into a security account whilst maintaining the desired level of commercial flexibility for the borrower; and

(b) where there are specific tangible assets which can be attached and which have some intrinsic value on the open market when removed from the project site.

The former situation no doubt occurs more frequently than the latter. Comparison of the role of security to the negative pledge is borne out to some extent by the ability of borrowers with a high credit rating to negotiate a greater degree of flexibility over certain project assets such as production and proceeds than is the case with companies whose main assets consist of the project itself. Similarly, certain types of legal loophole in the security can sometimes be blocked for practical purposes by an appropriate unsecured undertaking from a creditworthy parent company. As mentioned at the beginning of this chapter, the credit appraisal of the customer remains relevant for a number of purposes and it can of course be highly relevant where questions such as cash collateral accounts and fixed charges over proceeds come up for negotiation.

The assets charged usually include the following:

(a) the licence or equivalent concession – at least insofar as it relates to the area of the project;
(b) the operating agreements or equivalent;
(c) the 'hardware' used in the project, eg rigs, platforms, pipelines and other facilities or their equivalent;
(d) sales contracts;
(e) insurances;
(f) production and proceeds of sale;
(g) any other miscellaneous contracts or rights which relate to the project or the hardware.

Some of the security may be fixed and some may be of a floating nature. As already indicated, this may depend to a great extent upon requirements of the law of the jurisdiction in which the project is situated but it is also a matter for negotiation insofar as a fixed security may limit the flexibility of the borrower. Lenders to UK projects will be keen to obtain fixed security wherever they can since this, unlike floating security, will, in the UK, rank ahead of preferential debts. According to the English case law and, in particular, following *Siebe Gorman v Barclays Bank* [1979] 2 Lloyds Rep 142 a charge will be a floating charge (even if expressed otherwise) if it:

(i) extends or is capable of extending to future assets of the debtor; and
(ii) leaves the debtor free to deal with the assets comprised in the charge in the ordinary course of business without first obtaining the consent of the holder of the charge.

Ironically what appears at first sight perhaps the most important part of the security package – generally agreed to be the licence or concession – is the one asset of the borrower over which security is not normally created effectively by the security instrument alone. This is because the host government which has granted the licence is normally able to revoke it in the very circumstances in which the lenders would wish to enforce their security and also in many other circumstances over which the lenders have little or no control, This, therefore, brings us onto the important 'quasi-security' which is placed under the heading of host government support.

5 Host government support

The degree of support obviously varies from country to country as does the degree of knowledge of the kind of assurance that may be obtained from host governments. Government assurances must clearly be framed by reference to the terms of the basic concession and the legal infra-structure affecting the project in the country in question. Generally speaking, assurances may be needed on the following matters:

(a) the host government (depending on the priority of the project) should confirm that it is aware of the financing and has no objection to it (or, better still, positively approves of it);
(b) the government should be asked to confirm that it has given the appropriate approvals and consent for the development and production to take place – at least for the period covered by the financing. It may be possible to obtain confirmation that the government will not call for changes to the development and production plans which would be detrimental to the lenders' interests without first consulting the lenders;
(c) in the event that the licence or concession is to be terminated, lenders would wish to know whether the government may grant a replacement concession on terms which effectively impose the burden of repayment upon the new licensees. If this is not possible the government may be prepared to give some other form of financial commitment in respect of outstanding indebtedness having regard to the current value of the lenders' interest in the project;
(d) the government should be asked to notify the lenders of any alleged breaches of the licence or concession and if possible give the lenders the opportunity to do something about it before the licence is terminated;
(e) if the lenders appoint a receiver or exercise similar rights under security held by them they would wish to know whether the government would recognise the receiver's rights and whether the government would co-operate to the extent of not immediately terminating the licence until the lenders have had a reasonable opportunity to recoup themselves from production;
(f) in some jurisdictions it may be appropriate to ask for assurances regarding tax, royalties, 'government take,' etc.

In many cases the support obtained from the host government gives more security in the positive sense than the somewhat negative formal security documentation. Obviously the reliance placed on these assurances assumes a certain assessment of political risk and will also depend to some extent upon the legal position in the jurisdiction where the project is situated.

6 Comfort letters

Comfort letters are frequently found in project financings either as the form of support given by the host government or by the parent company or sponsor of one of the equity participants. The wording of such documents can frequently be difficult to interpret – and indeed the reason for the document's existence is often that it represents a last ditch effort to overcome apparently irreconcilable negotiating positions.

Some recent cases on 'comfort letters' have, however, put the legal draftsman on due notice as to what the courts might do if confronted with the task of interpreting 'fudged' wording. In *Kleinwort Benson v Malaysia Mining Corporation Berhad* ([1989] 1 WLR 379) the Court of Appeal reversed a decision at first instance which effectively held that a statement which many practising lawyers would regard as a policy statement only did in fact have the effect of a legally binding undertaking which was similar in effect to (although not the same as) a guarantee. The Court of Appeal's decision should be contrasted with the recent Australian case of *Banque Brussels Lambert SA v Australian National Industries Limited* (1989) (5 October 1990, unreported) Commercial Division of the Supreme Court of New South Wales. In that case the court had to consider a comfort letter provided by Australian National Industries to Banque Brussels Lambert in relation to a US$5,000,000 eurocurrency facility granted to an associated company called Spedley. The letter stated that the defendants were aware of the facility and acknowledged that the terms and conditions had been accepted with their knowledge and consent. They also stated that 'it would not be our intention to reduce our shareholding in Spedley Holdings Ltd (the intermediate parent company in which the defendants held 45%) from the current level of 45% during the currency of this facility'. They undertook to give the plaintiffs 90 days' notice if they did decide to sell the shares, it being acknowledged that in this event the bank reserved the right to require repayment of the loan within 30 days. The crucial paragraph read as follows:

> 'We take this opportunity to confirm that it is our practice to ensure that our affiliate Spedley Securities Ltd will at all times be in a position to meet its financial obligations as they fall due. These financial obligations include repayment of all loans made by your bank under the arrangements mentioned in this letter.'

In fact the defendant sold its shares in Spedley Holdings without giving any notice and did not ensure that Spedley was in a position to meet its financial obligations to the plaintiff.

The court had to consider the Court of Appeal's judgment in the *Kleinwort Benson* case. A number of arguments were put forward by the plaintiff in an attempt to distinguish it, e g:

- the statement as to 'practice' regarding compliance with financial obligations was in itself a warranty and this warranty had been broken
- the requirement for giving 90 days' notice was a firm undertaking and the failure to comply with that contributed to the loss eventually suffered by the bank since 'the shares which were sold for some $14,000,000 would

have become unsaleable with the result that, as a matter of commercial reality, the defendant would have been obliged to pay the plaintiff'
- other arguments were raised on the basis of estoppel (a doctrine now becoming more fully developed in Australia) and section 52 of the Australian Trade Practices Act 1974 (which is concerned with misleading or deceptive conduct).

The court considered at length the negotiations that led up to the provision of the comfort letter and also reviewed recent commentaries on the practice of providing comfort letters generally. Whilst the court had no difficulty in finding that the letter was not intended as a guarantee, it did find that the letter was intended to result in a legally binding commitment since the promises contained in the letter 'had they been fulfilled, were calculated to put the plaintiff in a position to receive payment from Spedley'. The essential question, once it has been determined that the letter is capable of amounting to a legally binding commitment, is what exactly is the nature of that commitment and to what extent can the statements in the letter be said to be 'promissory in character' rather than merely reflecting a statement of intention or of policy. The Court of Appeal's decision in *Kleinwort Benson*, regarding the relevant paragraph in the comfort letter in that case, was that it was a statement of policy only and therefore not capable of being sued upon as a promise or undertaking. Rogers CJ in the *Banque Brusels Lambert* case impliedly criticised the Court of Appeal's approach as subjecting 'the letters to minute textual analysis'. He felt that 'courts will become irrelevant in the resolution of commercial disputes if they allow this approach to dominate their consideration of commercial documents'. Rogers CJ felt that the test under Australian law for determining whether a statement was promissory or only representational was different from the English test. He had no difficulty in regarding the 90 days' notice provision as a 'promissory statement' but recognised that the statement as to 'practice' proposed 'far more thorny' problems. The actual wording of this paragraph, it will be recalled, was:

'We take this opportunity to confirm that it is our practice to ensure that our affiliate . . . will at all times be in a position to meet its financial obligations as they fall due.'

Rogers CJ states:

'If the paragraph is read as follows: "it is our practice to ensure that Spedley is at all times in a position to repay all loans made to it by your bank", its promissory nature is much clearer. I see no relevant difference between that and saying that "we promise to ensure that" Spedley will at all times be in a position to repay the plaintiff.'

As a result, with one, or possibly two, bounds the court was able to construe the third paragraph as a contractually binding commitment and in effect elevated the paragraph from bring of 'mere' comfort to something on which the recipient could sue for damages.

If one looks at the *Kleinwort Benson* case and the *Banque Brussels Lambert* case together, one finds, in effect, three decisions (including Hirst J's decision at first instance in *Kleinwort Benson*) each of which reach rather different results on very similar wording. The court's decision can turn on, it is suggested, not only the methods and standards of interpretation which prevail in the relevant jurisdiction but also on the court's essentially subjective view of the moral behaviour of the parties in question. Those who accept 'fuzzy' wording in order to 'get on with' the transaction and hopefully bring it to a successful conclusion must appreciate that, at least as far as Commonwealth jurisdictions are concerned, there is now very considerable uncertainty as to how wording of a 'comfort' nature might be resolved before the courts. It may of course be argued that there always was such uncertainty but the apparent ability of the courts to convert 'policy' and 'practice' statements into legally binding undertakings is certainly striking. As the authorities stand at the moment, such statements can certainly not be given without risk unless they are accompanied by a clear additional statement to the effect that no legally binding commitment is given or intended.

Perhaps the most instructive point to emerge from these cases can be summarised by the extract of the judgment of Staughton J in *Chemco Leasing SpA v Rediffusion* (unreported) 19 July 1985, 11 December 1986, Court of Appeal (Civil Division), Transcript No 1115 of 1986, CA which was quoted by Hirst J in his judgment in *Kleinwort Benson*:

> 'When two businessmen wish to conclude a bargain but find that on some particular aspect of it they cannot agree, I believe that it is not uncommon for them to adopt language of deliberate equivocation, so that the contract may be signed and their main objective achieved. No doubt they console themselves with the thought that all will go well, and that the terms in question will never come into operation or encounter scrutiny; but if all does not go well, it will be for the courts or arbitrators to decide what those terms mean. In such cases it is more than somewhat artificial for a judge to go through the process, prescribed by law, of ascertaining the common intention of the parties from the terms of the documents and the surrounding circumstances; the common intention was in reality that the terms should mean what the judge or arbitrator should decide that they mean, subject always to the views of any higher tribunal. Those considerations are, as it seems to me, particularly likely to apply to a letter of comfort, which is a subsidiary part of the business transaction and one upon which the parties, ex hypothesi, are likely to find difficulty in reaching agreement.'

7 Re-characterisation

When the parties deliberately 'fudge' an issue in order to conclude their negotiations, they have little grounds for complaint if a court arrives at an interpretation of what they have agreed which is at odds with what one or more of them felt to be their real intentions. More serious is the risk that although precise and clear legal language has been used the court takes it upon itself to re-characterise completely the nature of the transaction that they have concluded. This is always likely to be a risk in project financings which use contractual techniques other than the relatively straightforward concept of lending and borrowing. Such techniques are more likely to be found in situations where the borrower or another party needs to avoid the adverse consequences that a straightforward loan or similar arrangement would have in

194 Projects under the new influences

relation, for example, to its borrowing limits, negative pledges, its balance sheet or its tax position. In this sort of situation we tend to find transactions involving the forward purchase of product, production payments etc, used as a substitute for conventional loans. Provided these are structured properly there is no reason to suppose that they will not work but a recent English case gives a graphic illustration of what the courts can do if they feel that the arrangement for some reason acts unfairly vis-à-vis third parties.

In the case of *Welsh Development Agency v The Export Finance Company Ltd* [1990] BCC 393[1] the court had to consider an export financing arrangement whereby the exporter sold goods (floppy disks) to a finance house on terms under which the exporter then acted as the finance house's agent to resell those goods to overseas buyers. The intended effect of the arrangement was that the debts owed by the overseas buyers were payable to the finance house and that the title in the goods sold (until vested in the overseas buyers) was vested in the finance house under the contract of sale. Not surprisingly, when the exporter became insolvent, its creditors, not knowing about this arrangement, sought to challenge it on the basis that in substance it amounted to a loan on a security which had not been properly registered. The creditor objecting to the arrangement was the Welsh Development Agency which in fact had taken a charge over the assets of the exporter which was sufficiently all-embracing to cover debts owed to the exporter by any person; it was clearly in the WDA's interest to seek to show that the debts owed by the overseas buyers were in substance owed to the exporter rather than the finance house.

The court clearly took a strong dislike to the arrangement with the finance house which, it noted, was intended to have an 'off balance sheet' effect and would 'involve correlative disadvantages to all other creditors of [the exporter] who would deal with [the exporter] in ignorance of the special rights enjoyed by [the finance house].' On several occasions it was noted that the arrangements were artificial or indeed 'highly artificial'.

The ratio decidendi of the decision (which did in fact re-characterise the arrangement as a loan on an unregistered security) was somewhat narrow and technical. The court noted that the finance house's offer to buy the goods from the exporter did not cover goods which did not comply with certain warranties including a warranty as to merchantable quality. Since, in relation to any given parcel of floppy disks to be exported, it was not possible to know at the time of contract whether or not they had some latent defect, it was not possible to know whether there would be a breach of the warranty. Therefore, it was reasoned, there could not have been any valid offer by the finance house to buy the goods and therefore no authority for the exporter to sell them on behalf of the finance house. This ratio decidendi is, perhaps, open to question in itself but it is the alternative ratio decidendi which will prove to be of wider interest. The court accepted that there was no question of the arrangement amounting to a 'sham' (all parties accepted that the documents in question represented the true agreement between the relevant parties). Nevertheless, the court, relying to a significant extent on the case of *George Inglefield Ltd* ([1933] Ch1) considered that, despite the adoption of the language of sale, the substance of the matter was a loan on a security. It is difficult to extract from the judgment any one particular factor which was conclusive in persuading the court to come to this decision. The following, however, were clearly important:

1 See note to p 199, below.

- the finance charge levied by the finance house represented a floating rate of interest rather than a fixed rate
- the transaction was considered to be 'highly artificial' – the finance house had no need for the floppy disks it was buying and it was not in the business of trading in floppy disks: 'the manifest purpose of the document was to clothe the advance of money in the legal form of a sale of goods and that was the only purpose of the sale'
- the sole subject matter of the sales was the goods rather than the book debts from the overseas buyers
- the definition of the price did not tally with the total amount of money to which the finance house was actually entitled (at first sight a drafting point but clearly influential to the court's decision)
- there were provisions under which, on termination of the arrangement, the exporter became liable to pay the finance house amounts owed by the overseas buyers ('a strange requirement')
- there was also a provision to the effect that once all sums due from the exporter to the finance house had been paid, all the interest and benefits that the finance house had in the floppy disks or the debts from overseas buyers would be relinquished in favour of the exporter. The court regarded this as a 'clear right of redemption' and as such a significant 'badge' of lending rather than sale.

Many of these factors can be found in certain kinds of project financings and the *Welsh Development Agency* case is perhaps a timely reminder that transactions which are designed to avoid limits, registration requirements or similar matters risk being upset if they are too artificial and if the factors described above, particularly anything equating to a right of redemption, are present. The statement of the Vice-Chancellor in the *Welsh Development Agency* case sounds a note of warning:

'I observe that the master agreement is very far from being a layman's document prepared by businessmen for ordinary business purposes. It is a most skilfully drawn lawyer's document, manifestly designed by its exact legal provisions to cast in the mould of agency and sale an agreement which, in commercial terms, is a financing agreement equally capable of being expressed as one by way of secured loan.'

Pressed by counsel for the exporter to look beyond a narrow construction of the contract in relation to the warranty point described above, the Vice-Chancellor observed that 'those who live by the sword may also die by the sword'.

Such words may send a chill down the spine of those of us who have been involved in some of the more inventive and innovative financing structures. Nevertheless, it is to be hoped that the traps set by decisions such as the *Welsh Development Agency* decision can be avoided, particularly if financings which are structured on the basis of advance payments for products do not involve the vendor having anything which could be equated to a right of redemption. It is suggested that the mere fact that a scheme could involve the borrower repurchasing product would not in itself amount to a right of redemption unless the repurchase was in some way linked with the whole or partial discharge of all the financing. Options or similar claims in favour of the vendor or 'quasi-borrower' in such circumstances would have to be studied extremely carefully.

Insofar as the purchaser or 'quasi-lenders' regard the product as conferring any valuable security interest they would have to consider whether it might be appropriate to register some form of security to take effect if the form of the agreement was re-characterised at a subsequent date.

8 Recurrent elements in negotiations

The matters covered under this heading may not be easily categorised as 'legal' or 'commercial' issues. Invariably the two overlap. For example, one of the key issues in any project financing involving limited recourse financing – and the remarks which follow are almost exclusively limited to such financings – will be the criteria which determine when the project has come 'on-stream' which in turn usually affects the amount of limited recourse borrowings that can be made or left outstanding (notwithstanding that some degree of completion risk may be taken by the lenders). The determination of the criteria may be a commercial issue; but it will be 'legal' issue for a borrower to ensure that the wording of any such condition is phrased as objectively as possible, and that; on the occurrence of certain specified events, the borrower should be entitled to borrow on a limited recourse basis without the matter being subject to the discretion of the lending banks. Many negotiating points revolve around the conflict between the lenders' desire for discretion and the borrower's desire for an objective test in relation to the vital issues that affect the availability of limited recourse finance.

A Independent expert or engineer

An independent expert or engineer will almost invariably be involved in determining the level of limited recourse financing which a project can support. What is his position to be? Is he to be appointed by the borrower or the banks? To whom is he to be accountable? Will it be possible for the named engineer to be replaced, and if so, how often? What are the mechanisms to be for challenging an engineer's report or evaluation?

The mechanism for challenging the engineer's report, and the circumstances in which the lenders and the borrower are bound by it, are of vital importance. And additional complications arise in this area. Is there to be a 'de minimis' provision whereby the engineer's report can only be rejected if the lenders' or the borrower's view of the project differs from the engineer's by a certain margin? Is the borrower to have the right to pay out dissenting lenders? How many lenders have to disagree with the engineer before the report is rejected? Lenders understandably seek to avoid situations where they have reduced control over their obligations to make advances, particularly on project financing and so each lender will want to have the right to reject the engineer's evaluation. Whatever mechanism is involved, the final determination of the level of the limited recourse element is likely to take some time. Should, therefore, the borrower be able to take some advances on a limited recourse basis in the interim, with the final amount being determined when the engineer's report is agreed or it is no longer possible to challenge it?

B Change in produiction profile and determining factors

Another important issue is the frequency with which either lenders or the borrower may require an engineer's report to be drawn up, to take account of the changing nature of the production profile. In any minerals or hydrocarbons project, the production profile is likely to shift frequently, and therefore the parameters for the engineer's calculation need to be carefully determined in advance.

These parameters will include the formulae for determining the cash flow of the project, which will themselves determine the repayment liabilities of the borrower. Since the level of limited recourse financing will be determined on the basis of the projected cash flow from the project, they will also determine the amount of limited recourse borrowing that may remain outstanding at any one time. The borrower will want the criteria here to be as objective as possible, while the lenders will wish the engineer, in addition to considering a fixed formula, to be able to take into account in determining the production profile such factors as he may consider appropriate. So consideration will need to be given in the calculation of the potential cash flow from the project to the treatment of taxation, interest costs, royalties, running costs, the market price of production and any governmental restrictions on production.

C Application of cash flow/acceleration

Consideration of the projected cash flows affects the amount of limited recourse borrowings at any one time. The lenders will usually provide that a coverage factor must be maintained, and that the proportion of the proceeds of any period of operations which must be used in repaying the loan must be such that the coverage factor is maintained by reference to the latest production profile. It follows that, whilst the project is going well, it would be possible for less than all the proceeds to be paid to the lenders. But what happens if the course of the project changes? Are the lenders to have recourse to all the proceeds of prior operating periods? And what about the proceeds of the current operating period? We have already touched on this topic when looking at the role of security. From the lenders' point of view, direct secured access to proceeds may be a vital issue of security; from the borrower's point of view, too much security results in too little flexibility. Some financings provide that the cash flow from the project is to be paid into a blocked bank account. Only when the amount of any repayment due at the end of an operating period has been determined is the amount in the account which exceeds the repayment requirement released to the borrower; alternatively no cash flows are released to the borrower until final repayment of all the limited recourse indebtedness, or only so much as will leave a certain amount in the account which will be available to the lenders in the event that the project goes adrift.

Allied to these considerations is the question of when the lenders are to be entitled to apply all the cash flow from the project in reducing the limited recourse indebtedness. The situations in which all the cash flow must be applied in repayment of the loan will include those where the coverage factor is no longer maintained, due, perhaps, to a fall in the market price of the project product, or a hiccup in production. The question then arises of whether it will ever be possible for the borrower to 'get back on course', if the project subsequently picks up, and for the borrower to revert to the position where cash flow is only applied in repayment of the borrowings to the extent necessary to maintain coverage.

D Loss of limited recourse treatment

A key conceptual question on any limited recourse financing concerns the circumstances in which the limted recourse nature of the borrower's liability is to fall away, and the lenders have recourse to all the borrower's assets. Such a consequence might result from a breach of covenant or representation, and it is therefore on those areas that the attention of the parties – particularly the borrower – must be focused. Breach of a covenant gives rise to an action on the covenant itself, which, in the absence of express words, would not be caught by the limitation on the liability of the borrower to repay the loan. The extent of the damage suffered by the lenders in such a case might not necessarily be identical to the outstanding amount of the loan, but in certain circumstances it could be. Some loan agreements do, in fact, provide that in the event of certain breaches of covenant or representation, the limited recourse character of the loan will fall away.

Generally the type of breach of covenant or representation which gives rise to this consequence is a deliberate breach on the part of the borrower, and, in particular, the borrower not using its best efforts to ensure that the project is successful, by, for example, committing a breach of the operating or joint venture agreement which governs the running of the project. Difficult questions arise in this area in relation to the obligations of the borrower to take up the participations of joint venturers who drop out or default on their obligations, and, in particular, the question of when the borrower is to be entitled to abandon the project in the event of catastrophe or in the event of the project no longer proving economic.

E Parent company support

The borrower's ability to raise finance may, if it is a small company or a vehicle for the project, depend on the willingness of the parent to stand behind the borrower. What sort of undertaking, short of a guarantee, should be obtained from the parent? Ideally, from the lender's point of view, an undertaking that the parent will provide sufficient finance to the subsidiary to enable it to carry out its obligations under the financing agreements. The borrowing group, though, may only wish to give the most limited form of 'comfort' letter (see above), including, possibly, an undertaking to maintain ownership of the subsidiary, and perhaps a form of comfort to the effect that group subsidiaries have always been supported in the past. What proves acceptable to lenders varies from case to case and is obviously influenced by the creditworthiness of the borrower and the borrowing group as well as the view taken of the project as a whole.

In addition to the above points, the negotiating parties will of course devote a great deal of attention to the more 'standard' areas, such as the terms of the events of default, covenants, representations and warranties, etc, but such negotiations are not in substance radically different from negotiations on the same clauses in other forms of financing although the scope of the clauses is much wider and of course specific covenants concerning the project will be required. The borrower may also look for undertakings from the lenders as to such matters as confidentiality which would not normally be found save in the context of a project or similar financing where the lenders are given access to a great deal of confidential and price-sensitive information.

Roger McCormick has been a partner of Freshfields since 1981. He has worked in the City of London since 1973 (with Freshfields since 1976) and had a spell in Freshfields' Paris office between 1988 and 1990. He now leads the firm's International Project Finance Group.

Roger is Chairman of the Banking Law Sub-Committee of the City of London Law Society. He has also been a member of the International Bar Association since 1982 and is a Vice-Chairman of Committee E (Banking Law) of the Section of Business Law. He has also had a number of articles published including: 'Legal Issues in Project Finance', (1983) 1 *JERL* p 21; 'Legal Aspects of Pipeline Project Financing', *International Financial Law Review Jan '86*; 'Financial Services Act 1986', *International Financial Law Review Jan '87*.

He was educated at Manchester Grammar School and Wadham College, Oxford.

Note
On 19 November 1991, the Court of Appeal handed down its judgment in the *Welsh Development Agency* case (unreported). The Court of Appeal declined to support the views expressed in the first instance decision (discussed in this section) relating to the re-characterisation of transactions. The Court of Appeal reiterated the traditional English law approach to ascertaining the substance of a transaction, namely that:

(1) a judge should confine himself to interpreting the language of agreements and not look to external (eg policy, commercial or economic) factors; and
(2) parties to a contract should be free (except in a narrow range of circumstances, eg shams or landlord and tenant law) to enter into agreements providing for the division of risks and benefits as they choose.

Persons involved in the structuring of complex financing transactions may derive comfort from the Court of Appeal's decision. However, because of trends in non-legal areas, especially in the accountancy field, no one can afford to be complacent and assume that a given transaction will not be the subject of a claim based on a re-characterisation argument.

11 A borrower's view of project lending

Tony Lighterness, The RTZ Corporation plc

The earlier chapters in this book have shown that the term 'project finance' now encompasses a wider spectrum of funding concepts than was previously the case. Whereas project finance was originally a financing associated with a physical mining, industrial or infrastructure project it is now a term used for virtually any financing where the debt is serviced from and secured by a series of cash flows at the first level and the assets generating those cash flows as secondary security.

As the concept has expanded so, as a corollary, has the range of borrowers. But perhaps it should first be said that the term 'borrower' is itself in the sense a misnomer. One of the prime motives in opting for project finance by the sponsors of a project is that they wish to remove themselves from the normal obligations of borrowers. A significant part of the financial negotiations relates to this very point. The so-called borrower undertakes the negotiation of debt funding in many cases when the project is still in a conceptual stage and does not have a mature and financially competent team to undertake this task itelf. But in the negotiations the so-called borrowers spend considerable time and effort either to establish that they themselves have no obligations with regard to the debt, hence the term non-recourse, or alternatively, they define very clearly the areas and circumstances in which they may have residual obligations in what then becomes limited recourse debt. The true borrower is the project company or other vehicle.

Even so, the sponsor of a project is often referred to as the borrower because of his dominant role in structuring, arranging and negotiating the loan elements of the financing package and because lenders look to him in areas of project support and, particularly, any guarantees. So we will continue to use the term in this sense.

The borrowers that opt for project finance range, somewhat surprisingly, from the very strong to the very weak. In many cases it is this particular strength or weakness which is the reason for choosing the project finance route.

A major multi-national corporation (MNC) which borrows in the international bank credit and capital markets at a corporate level will jealously guard its rating, for example, to maintain competitive pricing in the US commercial paper or MTN market. A US debt rating will also affect its ability to issue and its cost of funds in Euro-markets and other bond markets such as the Japanese yen or Swiss franc as the basis of access to funds via currency swaps. Undue exposure to new projects might very well influence the rating agencies in down-grading the MNC, so increasing its cost of debt world-wide. The MNC will therefore favourably regard non-recourse or very limited recourse project finance as a means of expanding its business without unduly jeopardising its shareholders' wealth, balance sheet and credit rating.

At the other end of the spectrum there are borrowers who are obliged to go the project finance route simply because they themselves are totally uncreditworthy. A classic example in the early 1990s is that of the Eastern European governments. The countries of Eastern Europe desperately need to build their infrastructure in the form of transport systems and power generation, as well as their industry base if their sudden conversion to a free market economy is going to enable them to compete with not only the US and Europe but the highly efficient and low-cost producers of the Far East. However, several of these countries are bankrupt with debt far above the levels at which banks would consider lending. A comment in the Financial Times on 1 March 1990 summed up the situation:

> 'Western commercial banks, while applauding economic and political reform in Eastern Europe, are privately expressing reluctance to extend new loans to the region for any purpose except specific project finance.'

Where lenders can see potential projects in Eastern Europe or LDCs in the form of toll roads or bridges, mines based on good grade ore bodies, or industries to service an undoubted market they will be prepared to lend on a project-finance basis, but they most certainly will not lend to either governments or corporations (such as exist) without the security of a dedicated cash flow and access to the assets in the case of default.

Between the very strong and very weak borrowers who embark on project finance for opposite reasons there is a whole range of other sponsors of projects who may choose this financing structure. One example would be a small exploration or mining company which discovers a world class ore body but is itself unable to raise the hundreds of millions and possibly billions of dollars to exploit the ore body. Companies in this situation may be able to develop the mine without bringing in partners if the ore body is exceptional and the risks very few. This would not be on their own balance sheets but by classic project finance. However, the more common route would be to seek out a partner well-known for not only technical expertise and with a track record of success in that particular industry, but also with a high reputation among the world's leading commercial banks.

In 1962 two small companies merged to form what is now The RTZ Corporation, the world's largest mining group. RTZ's exploration efforts were particularly successful in the 1960s and the fledgling group initiated five would-class mines, all but one of which (Bougainville, due to political problems) are still major contributors to its profits. However at that time it would have been imprudent for RTZ to take on to its balance sheet the full entrepreneurial risk of these five mines. Failure of one or two could very well have destroyed the company. It was at that time that RTZ developed sophisticated project financing techniques which are regarded by Harvard Business School[1] as one of the main reasons for its success. Now a £5 billion company, RTZ continues to use project finance to minimise the exposure to any one project and to enable it to undertake several projects at a time for a given risk exposure.

1 Harvard Business School 9–389–093 revised 1/90.

The term 'borrower' in the sense of arranger also has to be understood in the context of several institutions jointly bringing in a new project. The case of a small company having discovered a major ore body and bringing in a partner has been cited. However, variations on the theme are numerous. Quite often major corporations will develop projects in partnership. An example is the Escondida copper mine in Chile, which has been developed by BHP of Australia, RTZ and Mitsubishi Corporation. The interests of BHP and RTZ as miners are very different from those of Mitsubishi as takers of copper concentrates and suppliers of capital goods, but the interests of all three parties were essential to a successful project financing.

Often the host governments will require participation in a natural resource or industrial project and will nominate a government agency to hold its stake. The only real means of financing a project where major highly-rated corporations, small unrated partners and a government agency of a debt-laden LDC can put together a financial package is by relating the finance primarily to the project. It is very seldom possible to lay off all the risk to lenders and the residual obligations of the MNC, small partners and government agencies will be uneven, unequal and the subject of considerable negotiations.

In summary, there is no archetypal project finance 'borrower' but MNCs' developing natural resource projects in the third world continue to be major players and this chapter will approach the subject largely from that viewpoint, with variations as appropriate.

Project finance vs corporate debt

The financing of a project is part of the progressive development of that project. A number of aspects of the project have to be undertaken in parallel. There are governmental, provincial and local authority approvals; technical testwork and designs; commercial research and, later, negotiation of sales contracts. In the multi-faceted conceptual stage of the project the financing can itself only be conceptual. But as technical and commercial factors are firmed up, so the financing must be in place, ready for commitment. The moment of project release requires term sales contracts to be signed, contracts to be let for the construction and development of the project, and at this stage the financing package must be in place. It is absolutely essential at this point that all aspects of the project are capable of becoming fully effective simultaneously.

Early in the conceptual stage the borrower has to answer the question: 'Why project finance?'

In the case of an MNC, corporate debt is preferable by far in all areas but one. It is easier to negotiate on the basis of an established balance sheet, with little or no direct security; covenants are standard and fairly toothless; pricing is undoubtedly cheaper; and the whole range of bank credit and securities markets is available with the added range provided by swaps, both currency and interest rate. Financing for the project can be encompassed in the corporate's full range of facilities and maturities. In many cases, the only ground on which project finance should be considered at all is exceptional risk.

Project finance – a form of risk management

Project finance is quintessentially an exercise by the borrower in risk management. The risks have to be identified by the borrower, then quantified, allocated and managed at the conceptual and negotiating stages and right through the life of the project, or at least the term of the debt. Borrowers or sponsors usually assume the first and the last risks with lenders coming in between, as we shall see.

The first risk capital to be put into a prospect is the money spent in identifying and evaluating the prospect to see whether it is indeed a project. Often this can take several years and costs tens of millions of dollars. In the case of an infrastructure project such as a railway or toll road it may involve studying a range of schemes, testing public reaction, estimating the cost of acquiring land, lobbying local and provincial authorities and central governments – often to find that the project is simply not feasible for economic or non-economic reasons. This represents the 'bravest of the brave' high-risk capital which is properly subscribed by equity shareholders. But it is also during this phase that the sponsors will attempt to draw up in concept a possible financing package to see whether it is possible to lay off sufficient risk for them to be prepared to undertake the project.

Mining companies are continually engaged in primary exploration to find new ore bodies and secondary exploration to prove up the volume of reserves at a sufficient grade to establish a viable operation. This phase will also include laboratory and pilot plant test work to see whether, for example, impurities can be removed and a saleable product produced, which is essential for a viable project. It is during this phase that the borrower will review possible sources of project finance and attempt to construct in concept a package which will lay off sufficient risk to lenders and other third parties so that the investment by the borrower as an equity shareholder, and possibly the residual risk under limited recourse finance, can be contained at an acceptable level.

The borrower is aware that the elimination or reduction of risk at an early stage will improve the possibility of attracting lenders and keep the pricing within acceptable limits. On occasions considerable time and money has to be spent to have any hope at all of attracting providers of credit and absorbers of risk.

Project risk can generally be analysed under four headings: technical, commercial, political and environmental.

Technical risk

On the assumption that the project is part of the normal business of the sponsor/would-be borrower, it is important to evaluate the technical risk at an early stage.

Technical risks to be identified by the borrower fall broadly into two categories.

Firstly, there are those arising from the geological, geophysical, climatic and similar factors of the project site. Project financiers of double-story bridges between San Francisco and Oakland will look harder and longer at the earthquake factor after the disaster of 1988. Over 90% of the deaths from the quake took place on the bridge. Flash-floods can be equally devastating. An open-cast mine can be badly set back by mud-slides and destruction of pit-walls as was the case with OK Tedi in Papua New Guinea. These risks will be critically exposed by lenders such as the World Bank and commercial banks if the borrower does not identify and mitigate them first.

The second area of technical risk to be addressed by a borrower is that associated with the process and operation of the project itself.

Quite often a mining group will go to an expert firm of construction engineers and commission a feasibility study to confirm the existence of sufficient mineable reserves, the capital cost of plant and equipment and operating costs to establish a viable operation. This can then be presented to lenders who will look to the reputation not only of the sponsoring company but to the construction engineers in their view of the technical risk. One area where technical risk is different from the other risks associated with the project is that the lenders will probably require the sponsor to take technical risk in the pre-completion period. That is, they will require an undertaking by the sponsors to construct a project to produce a given quantity of a defined saleable product to generate the cash flow which is the lenders' prime security. An example would be that a mining company would be required to construct a plant which would produce at 90% of capacity for a period of 90 days as a completion test so releasing the sponsors from guarantees. They would also be required to warrant that the product, for example copper concentrates, would be sufficiently free from impurities as to be saleable in world markets even in a period of over-supply. A further exposure of the borrower to technical risk is that if there is an area in what is often a very complex metallurgical process where the design has been inadequate or a difficulty has not been identified, and further capital expenditure is required it is often the obligation of the sponsor to provide this capital. Overrun finance is sometimes available but usually carries a penal interest rate.

Commercial risk

Commercial risk, unlike technical risk, is an area where borrowers take the view that the lenders can form some opinion as to the evaluation of risk. Many have separate commercial departments which have econometric models forecasting probable commodity prices.

Where the product price is related to world markets, as in the case of oil or minerals, there will inevitably be robust discussion between the sponsor and lenders as to what product price should be used. It is very difficult to convince banks to accept a price which is higher than the current market price for a project which is due to come on stream five years hence. However, this is often the best time to mount a project in that it is better to commission the mine in a low price cycle and bring it into production at the high price cycle than vice versa. However, banks are very strongly influenced by the price on the day. In 1987 the author was involved in negotiating project finance for the £1 billion Escondida copper project in Chile, attempting to convince banks that his company was bringing in this project on a long-term copper price of 85c per lb (1988 terms). In June of that year the price was 62c and the negotiations were difficult. The whole climate changed by December when the price had doubled to 124c. The borrower therefore needs to take a view not only of his own assumption for a long-term project, but that which may be assumed by lenders

– with downside sensitivities. It is on this basis that he will run his financial model and test the balance sheet and cover ratios which he may expect banks to impose.

Where a project is marginal the borrower may consider a sharing or hedging of commercial risk. The borrower can either guarantee a floor price, usually adjusted to a form which ensures that it does not only operate in short troughs, or he can directly or indirectly sell forward part of the production to service debt. Gold loans are a classic example of this form of risk diminution and commercial risk sharing. The borrower will review the whole range of these mechanisms as they might well affect the ultimate debt/equity ratio which is acceptable to lenders and therefore determines the risk to the sponsor.

Political risk

Political risk is probably the most common reason for natural resource companies engaging in project finance. Industrial companies such as the manufacturers of motor cars or video recorders can choose where they build and assemble their products. They will obviously avoid politically sensitive areas or if they do not it is because the costs are so low that they are prepared to accept the political risk on that particular risk/reward formula. But an ore body has to be mined where it is or not at all. Natural resource companies do not have the luxury of choosing the countries in which they operate. If an ore body is situated in a politically sensitive area then political risk becomes a predominant factor in deciding whether or not to develop an otherwise viable ore body.

In this situation it is often a question of whether sufficient finance is available at all under these circumstances. In some cases it is not. Where sufficient parties can be identified as potential lenders an allocation of risk becomes a sensitive and delicate negotiation, especially as the host government does not perceive political risk in the same light as the rest of the world.

Environmental risk

Projects which were developed in the 1960s and 1970s probably did not consider environmental risk to the extent that sponsors do today. Corporations have become much more responsible and it is debatable to what extent they are influenced by pressure groups or responsibility in areas in which businesses are developed. In any case the overriding factor is often newly-introduced legislation which will impose strict controls on pollution, disruption of the landscape and the endangering of fauna and flora, and almost invariably will require rehabilitation at the conclusion of mining activities. Provision needs to be made for this added area of risk. In the case of one major mining operation significant pollution is taking place because of the discharge of tailings into the river and the host government knows that the capital expenditure required to prevent this would cause mining operations to cease. The Government needs the revenue in the form of taxes and there is therefore no pressure on the company to incur this expenditure which would be absolutely essential for a new mining venture. Failure to identify environmental risks could mean heavy increased costs either in the development or operating stages of a mine, adversely affecting the economics, the lenders' security and the equity investor's return.

The risk to the balance sheet of an MNC imposed by the equity portion alone of a billion dollar project is substantial – and the greater the risk the higher the equity component will be. A mining development in Nova Scotia was project-financed on a 80/20 debt/equity ratio because of the low perception of the risk. 60/40 is more common but the sponsor may have to accept 50/50 on a riskier project, unless some other form of support is given.

It follows that project finance not only removes 50% and more of the risk from the borrower but that the borrower is able to develop more projects than would otherwise be the case for a given risk exposure relative to balance sheet size.

It should perhaps be stated that reference to balance sheets and risk is purely in the economic sense. The accounting profession is reviewing the purpose and meaning of a balance sheet – and well it might. In the context of project finance an MNC has been known to have 53% of a national holding group, which in itself had in excess of 50% of an operating subsidiary incorporated for the purpose of developing a mining project on a non-recourse basis. But consolidation rules do not provide for non-recourse covenants and 100% of the debt was consolidated on to the MNC's balance sheet. The balance sheet figure was totally unrepresentative of the legal, equity, or economic risk.

The project holding structure

The holding structure of the project sponsor is an important factor in the conceptual stage of the financing, and this will often be strongly influenced and, on occasions, determined by tax considerations.

An MNC will be concerned with money-in and money-out at source, so the financial model, IRR, NPV and all other considerations in the economic evaluation will include the whole range of corporate and withholding taxes. Indeed, sub-models will often be constructed to compare the economics of different holding structures.

The simplest structure from the lenders' and legal draughtsman's point of view is normally a specially incorporated company in the country of the project. This company will hold the grants, leases or other rights which form the basis of the project and all plant and equipment will be owned by it. Commercial contracts will be concluded in its name and the security package will be fairly straightforward (if a security package can ever be straightforward). The local operating company structure will almost certainly be preferred by the host government, too, as it becomes a corporate citizen with appointed officers with whom the government can deal. But if, for example, the country of domicile of one or more of the sponsors does not have a double taxation treaty (DTA) with the host government, then double full corporate tax could make the project uneconomic.

This problem has been circumvented by channelling the investment through an investment company in a third country which has DTAs with both the other countries, but this is the exception rather than the rule. New projects are often in third world countries which have not developed a full range of DTAs.

The branch structure then becomes an option with the MNC operating in the host country directly as a branch but this gives rise to considerable problems, especially if there are other partners. The problems of partial ownership of assets, rights to differing proportions of the product, and realisation of security become immense. There are often the added problems of multilateral agencies and import/export credit agencies not being permitted to lend to first world countries – and a branch is part of the first-world MNC.

The question of access to project finance provided by these agencies also becomes an issue for the borrower. Joint financing, in which the joint venture is treated as closely as possible as a corporation and all assets are owned by it, is one route. But separate financing is another possible route, especially if one partner, by reason of its domicile, has access to funds not available to the others. A US corporation can access Opic, Australians EFIC, British ECGD.

The partners then agree who will have access to which assets for export credits, for example, and who may approach which agencies. The security package, nevertheless becomes very complicated and issues such as lenders' rights of management on default by one party (as the project itself is not an entity) stretch lawyers' abilities to the full.

Joint venture operations have been developed, but they take much longer, are more complicated and will be avoided by the borrower if possible.

Appointment of financial adviser

The borrower will also decide early in the conceptual stage whether or not he needs a financial adviser. Financial advisers are usually selected from certain international commercial banks specialising in project finance, or US investment and UK merchant banks which have proven expertise in this area.

In the case of a first world project where the borrower has a project team in his finance department this may not be necessary, especially if he is able to retain an experienced project lawyer.

Good project advisers charge substantial fees, with monthly retainers or minimum charges, not inconsiderable expenses in the form of first class airfares with hotel bills to match, with no restraint on the number of people who travel and how many times they travel. Added to this, a seven-figure success fee is often payable on first draw-down of the project debt.

They are, however, very useful if they have had recent experience with the host government. They will not only be aware of local laws and regulations but also what other borrowers have been able to achieve in Foreign Investment Agreements (FIA) or similar contracts between investors and the state. They will also know of attitudes towards what appear to be attractive financing options. For example, at a time when Brazil had an emotional block on debt/equity swaps, Chile encouraged their use in certain circumstances.

One problem the borrower has to resolve is whether he wishes his financial adviser to be explicitly excluded from the bank syndicate, to be permitted to compete for the lead bank role, or to be required to lead the bank syndicate. There are different scenarios which may influence the decision in any one of these directions.

The obvious first choice is to exclude the financial adviser from the lending role and to have separate banks as advisers and lead lenders. The adviser can be independent in all respects and can even sharpen up the lending bank and its syndicate. But the other side of the coin is that the leading international commercial banks which a reputable borrower would wish to be part of his project syndicate may not be happy with this structure – for the very reason that the adviser can be somewhat unrealistic in what may be achievable, not having 'to put his money where his mouth is'.

The concern that the financial adviser should also be required to be the lead bank in the provision of credit is twofold: firstly there is the obvious advisory vs adversarial conflict in that the adviser will be required to produce a package and indicate a price appropriate to the product. He will then sit across the table and negotiate the price with his client. This advisory vs adversarial situation is, of course, not unique. UK merchant banks advise clients on rights issues, with appropriate discounts, and then negotiate the underwriting fees with those clients. The second cause for concern is that the adviser may take too conservative a view of the security package in that it is a product which he will later be required to syndicate. This can largely be overcome by permitting the financial adviser to compete for the lead bank role in competition with others, but with some preferred status.

This leaves the situation where the adviser will be a commercial bank which will actually be required to lead the bank syndicate. Where the sources of finance are scarce, and the debt package is to consist of multilateral and exim agency credits, supplemented by bank credits to reach the required total amount of debt, it is important for the borrower to require the adviser to commit to underwrite a given sum. This will ensure that the advice is realistic and that the proposed bank contribution does not evaporate as project release approaches. Indications of available bank credit should be given by the adviser/lead bank as the package is developed, but full appointment as financial adviser is often dependent on the lead bank giving the strongest indication short of a legal commitment not only of the bank credit which it considers will be available, but of the actual amount it will itself contribute and underwrite, subject of course to there being no significant adverse change in the project or world conditions.

It has been the writer's experience on several occasions that the financial adviser has been invaluable in the contribution made by the individuals undertaking part of complex negotiations in several parts of the world at the same time. For example, simultaneous negotiations may well take place with several import and export agencies, multilateral agencies, banking groups and host government agencies with inter-related implications for the security package. Financial advisers may be expensive but if they assist materially in arranging a strong and successful financing which stands the test of the first years of a project's life, the money is well spent.

The range of lenders

In all negotiations for the provision of credit the relative strength or weakness of borrower and lender determines the tone of the negotiations and the shape of the final product. This is so in the case of project finance, but of course the strength of the project itself is an all-important factor in the equation. This will strongly influence the extent to which the borrower will be able to lay off risk and isolate itself from obligations.

A strong, first world project mounted by an MNC with a successful track record will see a queue of the world's top banks vying for the advisory and/or lead bank role. The borrower can be selective, dictate a favourable debt/equity ratio, insist on minimal covenants and virtually non-recourse lending at a favourable price.

The same borrower attempting to develop the same project in a debt-ridden LDC will receive only apologies from those same banks. Provisioning in terms of their central bank matrix has a ratcheting effect on ability to lend and earn returns on assets, so they stay away from projects in LDCs.

If the banks, whose business it is to supply credit for a commercial return, are not prepared to lend, the borrower is in the position of having to see whether there are sufficient other parties who will lend on acceptable terms for the project to be worthwhile. Again, the first and last elements of risk are with the borrower and it is the quantum and conditions of the middle-risk debt element which is the deciding factor.

At this stage it is necessary to review all prospective lenders and other agencies such as insurers who have an interest in the project being developed.

The multilateral agencies such as the World Bank and its private sector sister, The International Finance Corporation, which were formed to provide funds which might not be available in commercial credit markets, are obvious candidates. The World Bank is limited in its scope but often an infrastructure element can be assigned to it. In joint venture separate financing, for example, the World Bank might fund a power station, or harbour, or dam which can be related to the host government agency's obligations. This reduces the size of the private sector project. The IFC can come in as a small equity partner and lender. The latter role is particularly useful in that it can open the door for commercial bank participation. If the IFC is the borrower of record and banks contribute by buying subparticipations they are not always required to provide against the loan. This is because the IFC, as part of the World Bank, is virtually exempt from rescheduling.

Other interested parties are import and export agencies. It is essential for countries such as Germany and Japan to secure the supply of energy and raw materials, and import finance is made available against long-term contracts for the supply of these commodities. Export agencies likewise provide credit to ensure that their finished goods, in this case in the form of mining plant and equipment, are in a favoured situation in the market.

A case in point was the financing of the Escondida copper project in Chile. The sponsors, BHP-Utah (the US subsidiary of The Big Australian), RTZ, and Mitsubishi were of undoubted strength and reputation. The project financial model was so strong that no reasonable downside sensitivity made an impact – yet the commercial banks could not lend to Chile. In the event, US$680m debt was raised from import and export agencies and the IFC. The negotiations took 30 months – equal to the lead-time of the project itself – but finally the project was funded. The borrowers had stated very clearly that they were not prepared to develop the $1.14 billion project at that stage other than on a 60/40 debt/equity ratio.

Borrowers need to identify parties with an interest in the project being developed to raise the debt, but often innovative thinking is required to persuade them to lend. In the case of Escondida, Japan Exim was targeted as a major lender. But its charter requires it to supplement bank lending. The question was: how do we persuade the Japanese banks to lend? After numerous proposals a formula was found:

- Japanese banks sold Chilean debt to the sponsors;
- The sponsors converted the debt to equity by government-approved (for this deal only) debt-equity swap;
- The Japanese put the proceeds of the sale of debt back in as a loan, plus an equal amount of new money, protected by an FIA.

Commerical negotiations are often conducted in parallel with financial ones as project finance is essentially cash flow lending and the first level of security is the proceeds of sales contracts. The wise borrower will ensure that he does not commit himself too early in the provision of debt and so permit himself to be held to ransom on commercial terms.

The weakness and strengths of the parties will determine whether actual cession of the sales proceeds is required. Probably the most common structure is for the proceeds to flow through an offshore trust account usually in dollars with a New York bank. In this case the interests of borrowers and lenders in keeping proceeds in a hard currency offshore are identical. Borrowers and lenders will negotiate together in an approach to the host government for the creation of a trust to receive the proceeds with a clearly determined order of priority as to application of funds. The borrower will require the first call on funds to cover operating costs and will agree with lenders the period to be funded. One month is the minimum but he will probably try for three months. Approved capital expenditure up to a given amount will be included in this formula. The lenders will require a sinking fund, buffer, or other form of ensuring that the build-up of funds to the date of each debt service is well covered. Remittance of funds to pay taxes will follow, with dividends ranking last. Clearly the borrower has an interest in ensuring that the buffer for debt service is not too generous as this effectively represents a lock-up of a block of distributable funds from the beginning of the project until the loans are paid off.

The negotiating stage

As the prospect progresses towards becoming a viable project it is necessary for the borrower to move from general discussions with lenders to firm negotiations for the provision of project finance.

Where the borrower has the luxury of a range of sources of finance there are some options which are preferable to others. But even when this is not the case, borrowers should resist the almost inevitable attempt by lenders to gain a psychological advantage by implying that they are doing the borrower a favour in lending to the project. They are not. Everyone across the table has an interest in lending to the project otherwise he would not be there. There is no altruism in project finance and the borrower must never allow himelf to be in the position of having to agree to unreasonable demands. Exim agencies are securing preferential positions for their nationals; officials of multilaterals are fulfilling the purposes for which their institutions were formed. Commercial banks have to lend to make profits; and the borrower should be aware that they will only do so after careful appraisal of risks and rewards. The cost of not establishing from the outset that the borrower and lenders are negotiating as equals can be enormous in concessions right through the negotiations.

If major international commercial banks are prepared to lend in the 1990s it probably means that the project is in a low-political-risk area. And as either all or none are usually prepared to lend the borrower is in a competitively advantageous situation when they are willing to lend. The leading banks are experienced, competent, professional and a clean deal can be negotiated at a competitive price reasonably quickly. The cost is, of course, commercial and will be above agency funding.

Import finance ranks higher than export finance on the borrower's agenda as it is usually 100% utilised and is cheaper. Firm commercial contracts for the supply of product usually need to be signed with national processing companies as security anyway and the finance becomes available throughout the development period as required.

By contrast export finance is linked to specific items of plant and equipment and can only be drawn down as and when they are purchased. The borrower may set up lines in different countries, expressly to put suppliers in a competitive position. For example, massive 150 ton haul trucks are supplied by American, Canadian and Japanese manufacturers. The technical management will have preferences, often based on previous experience and as they are required to perform to a given percentage utilisation in order to provide sufficient ore to the mill, this preference cannot be discounted. Furthermore, the competitive situation of the suppliers can change dramatically during the procurement and development period, simply on a movement in exchange rates. This occurred in the writer's experience on the yen's long overdue appreciation against the dollar in 1987. The Japanese supplier moved quickly from first to last choice on price alone. It is therefore useful to have several export credit lines open – but it follows that if three lines are set up for pit equipment, two will probably not be used. This gives export credit agencies an understandably jaundiced view of borrowers requirements, which is reflected in negotiations.

Multilateral agencies such as the World Bank and IFC can provide a make-or-break contribution. But they are often hide-bound by their charters, stifled by bureaucracy and painfully slow. Staff changes with different philosophies during negotiations further delay matters and other lenders are often exasperated in negotiating a common security package because of the preferred status required by the multilaterals. Even so, they can and do provide finance when it is not available from commercial sources and provide invaluable comfort to commercial banks and export–import agencies.

Finally, the borrower will consider the insurance agencies. MIGA is performing well in its early life and has a required three-month turn-around from application to response. The sums insured are limited but useful. Other insurance agencies such as the UK's ECGD combine with commercial banks to perform the function of their counterparts such as EDC in Canada to make funds available. In the case of the Porgera financing in Papua New Guinea the borrowers arranged and paid for agency insurance of commercial bank debt. Other borrowers would resist an approach by commercial banks to cover them in this way, but may well have to accede.

The borrower will review all these, and other options to see whether the funds they provide add up to an acceptable level of debt to match the equity it is prepared to contribute.

The security package

The security package has been dealt with in greater detail in earlier chapters but factors on which the borrower will focus strongly are as follows.

The debt/equity ratio
This is the basic determinant of the risk-sharing ratio between borrower and lender and all else will be viewed against this ratio.

Where the borrower has contributed considerable high-risk capital in the early years of a project he will seek to have this included in the total project cost to which the d/e ratio will apply. The two ends of the negotiating spectrum are for the lenders to contribute all the funds after signature until they have 'caught up' and a scaled contribution so the agreed project d/e is only reached on the final draw-down.

The completion test
This is important because it is the point of release of the borrower's guarantee. Negotiations will centre around the percentage of rated capacity to be maintained for a given period and possibly product purity. The borrower will avoid operating cost tests as unit costs will be unrepresentative in the early days on the learning and efficiency curves.

Suspension and termination
These are all-important. The circumstances and period in which the borrower as project developer can suspend activities in the event of, for example, civil unrest, and the lender can suspend the right of drawdown will be the subject of intense negotiation. Clausing on termination and the right to walk away will also be hard fought. The problem is that it is virtually impossible to foresee what will happen.

Security
If an offshore trust arrangement is incorporated this covers most of the convertibility and transferability risks in the first-line security of cash flow.

Much time and effort is spent over hypothecation of leases and grants but these are of little value to lenders if the borrower–sponsor defaults.

The rights of the lenders to take over management will be sought but the borrower will seek to restrict these to extreme situations.

Default
The borrower will seek to secure a generous time period to remedy default, especially as this can arise from a failure in communications in the third world. The lenders, conversely, will wish to act quickly in case it is not merely a technicality.

Cross-default
This arises mainly in the case of joint ventures.

When the joint venturers are mature and reputable corporations it is usually possible to avoid onerous cross-default clausing. Lenders will understandably wish to cover the position where one partner fails, but so will the other partners.

Where a major MNC is in partnership with a smaller, more vulnerable partner it should ensure that default by its weaker partner does not trigger the cross-default clause on the joint venture debt. This aspect is not always given the attention it deserves.

Financial ratios

The borrower will try to ensure that default is not triggered by a breach of ratios due to a weakness in the market for his product which may be of relatively short duration, whereas long-term prospects for the project are good. Provision should be made for temporary breaches of ratios in these short troughs. This could be achieved by a formula taking account, for example, of immediately past and future years.

Excess cash sharing

This inevitably leads to both lenders and borrowers taking extreme positions and is usually one of the last negotiating points to be resolved.

The term of the debt and its servicing profile is established reasonably quickly. The shareholder/borrowers' rights to dividends are harder won. But the sharing of super profits is most difficult. Lenders have an emotional block on seeing equity shareholders taking more out of a project than they do, but the shareholders maintain that this happens only when commencement of production coincides with a high price cycle. In any case, the borrower–sponsors maintain that banks provide the relatively low risk/low reward capital and the spread reflects, inter alia, the servicing profile and maturity of the loan. Early repayment is 'something for nothing'. The borrowers are the 'high risk, high reward' contributors of capital and they are entitled to these returns. Furthermore, when profits are lower then anticipated, borrowers then suffer the full reduction in the cash flow.

The borrower may also further require providers of import finance to maintain the loan for the full term of the sales contracts – say eight to ten years, regardless of the level of super profits. This precludes early repayment, a provision which may upset other lenders in the security package which usually provides for pro-rata early repayment to all lenders, and that prepayments are applied to the last maturities.

The excess cash-sharing problem is sometimes resolved by lenders having the right to empower the project to claw-back super dividends in the event that debt servicing is endangered or financial ratios threatened. The claw-back is usually restricted to one to three years.

The way forward

The project has been formally approved; contracts for construction and development have been signed; suspensive conditions in sales contracts have been fulfilled; the signing ceremony for the financing has taken place with all parties present in a plush New York hotel. The project is launched.

But much can happen between project release and completion. Technical, commercial and, especially, political factors can change. The experienced borrower will have made some provision for this in the loan documentation – if only on a 'sympathetically considered' or 'best efforts' basis.

Rossing Uranium Ltd went through the above stage and commenced development of the world's largest uranium mine in August 1973. The 2,500 ton-a-year production was to add 20% to the oversupplied world market. At US$6.50 per lb it was not easy to finance as it was only marginally economic. However, the sponsors believed the market would be undersupplied by 1976/77 when the mine was due to be commissioned.

Then came the Middle-East War and first major oil crisis in October of 1973. By early 1974 the uranium price had trebled to $18 lb and was to reach $40 lb in two years. Power utilities pressed Rossing for increased tonnage.

It was not difficult technically to mirror the whole processing plant from crushers through to final product recovery and so double up to 5,000 tons per annum. But once all available security had been demanded and given in the form of mortgages over mining grants, notarial bonds over pit equipment and cessions of the sales proceeds of contracts (*not* assignment of the contracts themselves), any approach for further debt would normally have been regarded as 'dilution of our security' by lenders. However, Dresdner, the lead bank were impressed by the economics and did provide further debt. The balance came about almost by chance. The 1973 war had also produced unprecedented hyper-inflation and one power utility was alarmed at the price it might have to pay for reloads for its reactors three, four and five years out. It therefore offered to pay for the material in full in 1974 at the going price with no escalation. Rossing saw this as a source of funds it required immediately, free of interest. It so happened that it would be in an effective tax holiday situation in the first three years of its operating life, which meant that the proportion of tonnage which would normally generate cash to pay taxes in those years could be sold forward without damage to the cash flow or endangering cover ratios. The proposition was put to other consumers, several of whom took the offer up enthusiastically. The expansion was therefore comfortably financed almost entirely by advance sales of part of the production in the tax holiday period.

Other changes are not as happy a this one. Borrowers can allow for 5% or 10% sensitivities which become irrelevant when they are badly hit by political upheaval.

This leads to what is probably the final area of risk to be considered by the borrowers. What if something goes wrong? What legal and moral obligations do I have? To what extent will my reputation in the markets be damaged if the project cannot service its debt and I walk away?

Political risk can largely be laid off with the agencies which are formed expressly to take it – but it should be clearly defined in relation to abandonment of a project. The borderline between, for example, industrial action and civil unrest, can be very blurred.

Commercial risk is usually reasonably foreseeable and manageable and total project failure due to this cause in the debt servicing period is unusual. Lenders can assess this risk and should bear or share it. The bearing or sharing will, of course, be reflected in pricing. Again, clear definition will be critical.

Technical risk is vitally important. As a minimum, the technical exposure during the development period as to both equity and debt remains 100% with the borrower. Technical problems at Tenke Fungurume in Zaire, Selebi Pikwe in Botswana and OK Tedi in Papua New Guinea are but three examples of major world mining projects which have embarrassed borrowers and lenders alike and have delayed returns to shareholders, in some cases permanently. Elimination of all foreseeable exposure to project failure in this area is of highest priority.

In the final analysis, the view of RTZ, probably the world's most experienced developer of mining projects, is that it will do everything it considers reasonable to ensure the survival of a project and to protect the interest of lenders. But it does end at 'everything it considers reasonable'. Come the crunch RTZ will walk away from a project and lenders should understand that they should not rely on reputation or anything else which is not in the documentation in the event of project failure. The risks lenders undertake is reflected in the spread and RTZ advises lenders very clearly at the outset of negotiations that it does not pay for something which is no more than Scotch mist.

Furthermore, RTZ takes the view that it could be sued by its shareholders if it effectively made an ex gratia payment to lenders when it had no legal obligation to do so.

A case in point is the East Kemptville tin project in Canada developed by Rio Algom, a 52% subsidiary of RTZ. The project seemed to be the safest of the safe as to political, technical and commercial risk. But on the collape of the International Tin Council price mechanism the tin price fell to 30% of its previous level. The project became uneconomic and was ultimately closed with financial loss to the shareholders and the banks.

It may be of interest that those same major international banks have made the point to RTZ that they fully accept what happened and that they would wish to be considered by RTZ as project finance banks in the future. That, perhaps, says it all as far as the borrower's view of project lending is concerned.

To summarise: project lending is a fundamental and important source of finance for the development of major capital projects, especially in politically sensitive and economically difficult areas of the world.

It is of benefit to project sponsors in identifying and, at a price, laying off extraordinary risks, while it provides lenders with a dedicated cash flow for the service of debt which is isolated from the national creditworthiness or otherwise of the country in which the project is being developed.

There is no doubt that without this financing technique many major infrastructure and natural resource projects which are presently contributing to the well-being of the first and third world economies would not have been developed.

Tony Lighterness FCIS, FCT is Deputy Finance Director and Group Treasurer of The RTZ Corporation plc, the world's leading mining company.

He started his career with Shell in London, then spent three years in Rhodesian government service. He joined RTZ in South Africa in 1963 becoming Finance and Commercial Director in 1974 before moving to RTZ's London Head Office in 1982.

Tony Lighterness gained considerable practical experience of project finance in the development of four of the world's great mines: Palabora in South Africa; Rossing Uranium in Namibia; Neves Corvo in Portugal and the Escondida copper mine in Chile.

Index

Advance payment financing, 178
Aircraft and other mobile assets –
   aircraft asset, suitability for asset financier, 84–89
      comparison with other assets, 85
      criteria, necessary, 84–85
      meeting the criteria, 85–89
         identification, 85
         recoverability of finance, 86–87
         registration of interest, 85–86
         resale potential, 87
         resale value, 87–89
            actual, 87–88
            prospective future, 88–89
   commercial aviation market, the, 81–84
      business development since 1970, 82–83
         growth trends, 82–83
      general development, 81
      growth prospects, 83–84
         aircraft fleet growth, 83–84
         traffic volume growth, 83
         warning, 84
   examples, aircraft finance, 93–99
      balance sheet enhancement, 96–97
      credit enhancement, 93–96
         corporate, 93–95
         country credit risk, 95–96
      'financial structuring' reasons, other, 97–99
      financing going wrong, 99
   finance, key issues/principles, 89–93
      current/prospective value, 90
      generally, 89
      security, tangible, other available, 90–91
         deposits, security, 90–91
         export credit agency guarantee, 90
         guarantees, other, 91
         manufacturer's deficiency guarantee, 90
         repossession insurance, 91
         undertakings, other, 91
      transaction structure, 91–92
      value of asset, preserving/ensuring, 92–93
   introduction, 80–81
   summary and conclusions, 99–100

Approach, traditional, to project lending –
   introduction, 3
      corporate or country lending with project element, 5–6
      definition, 3–4
      pure project lending, 4–5
      qualified or partial lending, 5
   lenders' attitudes to risks –
      market, 11–12
      operating, 11
      pre-completion
   new influences, 20
   protections available to lenders –
      equity, 12–13
      market risk, 14–16
      operating, 14
      pre-completion, 13–14
   risks in –
      market, 8–9
      operating, 7–8
      pre-completion, 6–7
   why borrowers choose, 16–17
      special features, 17–20
         governments, 19–20
         insurance, 17–18
         security and documentation, 18–19

Balloon payments (shipping), meaning, 48–49
Banks, roles of, 9–10, 18, 21–22, 26, 30–31, 58, 107, 147–149
Borrowers' choice, 16–17
Borrowers' view of project lending –
   financial adviser, appointment of, 207–208
   introduction, 200–202
   negotiating stage, the, 210–211
   project finance, a form of risk management, 203–206
      commerical risk, 204–205
      environmental risk, 205–206
      political risk, 205
      technical risk, 203–204
   project finance vs corporate debt, 202
   project holding structure, 206–207
   range of lenders, 208–210

218 Index

Borrowers' view of project lending – *contd*
  security package, the, 212–213
    completion test, the, 212
    cross-default, 212–213
    debt/equity ratio, 212
    default, 212
    excess cash sharing, 213
    financial ratios, 213
    security, 212
    suspension and termination, 212
  way forward, the, 213–215
British Gas, 150
British Telecom, 150

Cable television, 155–156
Cash flow available for debt service, 45
Cases referred to in the text –
  Banque Brussels Lambert SA v Australian National Industries Limited (1989), 191
  Chemco Leasing SpA v Rediffusion. Staughton J. quoted, 193
  George Inglefield Ltd (1933), 194
  Kleinwort Benson v Malaysia Mining Corporation Berhad (1989), 191
  Welsh Development Agency v The Export Finance Company Ltd., 194
Cellular telephone systems, 156–157
Central and Eastern European markets, 160–170
Channel Tunnel, 6, 7, 9, 25–26, 27, 138, 149
COFACE, 165
Commercial aviation market, 81–89
Contributors, notes on –
  T.H. Donaldson, 20
  Chris Elliott, 145
  Douglas Helfer, 170
  Ian Hosier, 100
  T. Lighterness, 215
  Roger McCormick, 199
  Dr Keith Palmer, 79
  Dr Michael R. Smith, 158–159
  Brian H. Weight, 31
  Peter J. Whitney, 118
  Taco Th van der Mast, 64
Covenants, financial (shipping), 52–53
Credit analysis (ship finance), 44–47
Credit enhancement (aircraft), 93–99
Credit structuring (shipping), 48–49
Cross-border leasing, 112–113
Cyclical supply pattern, 9

Debt reclassification, 113
Developed countries, 28–29, 74–76
Developing markets of Central and Eastern Europe –
  conclusion, 169–170
  export credit guarantee agencies, official, 163–165
    COFACE, 165
    ECGD of the United Kingdom, 164
    Hermes, 164
    OPIC, 164

Developing markets of Central and Eastern Europe – *contd*
  export credit guarantee agencies, official – *contd*
    SACE, 165
    US Export/Import Bank, 165
  financial position of countries in the region, 160–161
  introduction, 160
  multi-lateral lending agencies, 166
  other sources of finance, 166
  project finance in the region, examples, 168–169
  sources of finance, 162–163, 166
  structuring in the present market, 161–162
Double taxation agreements, 114–117

FCGD of the United Kingom, 164
Energy Act 1983, The, 151
Environmental factors, 10–11
Equity, meaning, 12–13
Export credit guarantee agencies, 163–165

Financial adviser, appointment of, 207–208
Financial vehicle, structuring, 76–77, 174–185
Financier's interest, registering, 85–86
Force majeure exclusions, 177
'Foreign' legal concepts, importing, 185–188

Gold market, the, 75–76
Governments, influence of, 19–20, 24–28, 137–138

Hermes, 164

'Import finance', 73–74
Influences, new, 20, 21–31
Infrastructure finance, characteristics, 142–143
Insurance, 17–18, 58–59, 166–168
International Finance Corporation, The, 71, 209
Iraq/Kuwait conflict, effect on aircraft financing, 84, 89

Jurisdiction of incorporation (shipping), 57
Jurisdiction of registration (shipping), 55–57

Kuwait/Iraq conflict, effect on aircraft financing, 84, 89

Latin American economies, 23
'Lawdacs', 157
Leasing, defined, 101
Leasing and tax-based project finance –
  leasing, 101–102
    contract hire, 103
    direct benefit, 105
    finance leasing, 102
    operating leasing, 103
    purchase options, 104–105
    rental, hiring, plant hire, 103

Leasing and tax-based project finance – *contd*
  leasing – *contd*
    sales-aid leasing, 103
    taxation benefit, 103–4
    third-party risk, 105
  power project, 106–113
    appendix (1977 *text* of OECD agreement), 119–134
    benefit, 108
    cross-border leasing, 112–113
    lease risk, 108–109
    loan profile, 106
    mining, 117
    non-UK, 110
    off balance sheet, 111–112
    participators, 107
    plant, 110
    property, 111
    quasi-equity, 117–118
    re-classification, 113
    special areas, 110–111
    tax concessions, other, 114–117
    taxation, 109–110
    withholding tax, 114–117
Legal aspects and considerations, 171–199
Legal aspects of project finance –
  choice of structure, 174–185
    commercial influences, 174–175
    types, summary of, 175–180
      alternative financing, other forms, 180
      forward purchase (sale) agreement, 178–179
      limited or non-recourse loans, 179–180
      production payment, 179
      throughputs and 'take or pay', 176–178
  comfort letters, 191–193
  importing 'foreign' legal concepts, 185–188
  host government support, 190
  introduction, 171–174
    definition issues, 172–174
    general trends, 171–172
  legal influences, 180–185
    accounting treatment, 181
    cross-default clauses, 182–183
    negative pledges, 181–182
    restrictions and other factors affecting lenders, 184
    restrictions in operating agreements etc., 183–184
    restrictions on conventional borrowing, 180–181
    tax treatment, 184–185
  re-characterisation, 193–196
  recurrent elements in negotiations, 196–199
    application of cash flow/acceleration, 197–198
    change in production profile and determining factors, 197
    independent expert or engineer, 196
    loss of limited recourse treatment, 198
    parent company support, 198–199
  role of security, 188–190

Legal influences on project finance, 180–185
Lenders and risks, 9–12, 55
Lenders, range of, 208–210
Lesser developed countries, 22–23

Mega-projects, 30–31
Mining, extracting and processing –
  developed countries, project finance in, 74–76
    completion risk, 74–75
    price risk, 75–76
  finance vehicle structuring, 76–77
  introduction, 65–66
  new approaches, 78–79
  processing industries, 78
  risk, country or political, 66–74
    political risks, sharing, 70–72
    who will share political risk, 72–74
  sponsor rights, 67
    economic stabilisation, 69–70
    foreign exchange, 68
    non-discrimination, 68
    termination of, 68–69

National Power, 150–151
Negotiating stage, the, 212–213
Negotiations, recurrent elements in, 196–199
New influences in project lending –
  emergence of, 24–31
    capital market capacity and banks' response, 30–31
    developed countries and new world order, 28–29
    financiers' involvement, increased scope for, 30–31
    governmental deregulation and privatisation, 24–28
    mega projects, 30–31
    new places for opportunity, 28–29
    opportunity, new types of, 24–28
    historical perspective, 21–24
    project financing today, 31
New opportunities for project lending, 28–29
New world order, 28–29

OECD model agreement, 119–134
'Off balance sheet' financing, advantages of, 111–112
Oil Pollution Act 1990, The, 40, 43
OPIC, 164

Pipeline projects, 154–155
Political risks, 70–72, 72–74
Pollution as a risk, 59–60
PowerGen, 150–151
Power projects, 152–154
Pre-selling, 15–16
Profits, 30–31
Project finance as form of risk management, 203–206
Project finance vs corporate debt, 202

220 Index

Project holding structure, 206–207
Project lending –
   corporate or country, with project element, 5–6
   defined, 3–4
   pure, 4–5
   qualified or partial, 5
Projects under the new influences –
   See: TRANSPORTATION INFRASTRUCTURE
           UTILITY INDUSTRIES
           DEVELOPING MARKETS OF CENTRAL AND EASTERN EUROPE
Protections available, 12–16

Risks, 6–9, 9–12, 49–50, 55–57, 59–60, 66–74, 70–72, 74–76, 99, 101, 105, 108–109, 139–142, 202–206

SACE, 165
Security and documentation, 18–19
Security package, the, 76–78, 91–92, 212–213
Security structure (shipping), 50–52
Ship finance –
   banks, roles of, 58
      hedging strategies, 58
      syndication vs 'club deals', 58
   conclusion, 63–64
   covenants, 52–55
      financial, 52–53
      information, 54
      minimum value clause, 53
      minimum working capital and liquidity, 54
      negative pledges and prohibition on dividends, 54
      obligatory interest rate hedging, 54–55
   credit analysis, 44–47
      asset quality and cash flow, 47
      cash-flow lending vs asset-based finance, 44–45
      cash-flow modelling, 45
         cost side of a shipping project, 46–47
         income side of a shipping project, 46
      cash-flow projections, 45
   credit structuring, 48–49
      balloon payments, 48–49
      repayment, 48
      term of loan, 48
   history, 36–37
   industry characteristics, 37
   insurance, 58–59
   introduction, 35–36
   lender liability, 55
   newbuilding financing, 49–50
      completion risk, 50
      contractual risks, 50
      pre-delivery risk, 49
      refund guarantees, 50
   newly emerging risks, 59–60
      concentration risks, 60
      pollution, 59–60

Ship finance – *contd*
   risks, country of flag and corporate residence, 55–57
      jurisdiction of incorporation, 57
      jurisdiction of registration, 55–57
      flag, choice of, operational considerations, 56–57
      lender as mortgagee, 56
      single ship-owning companies, 57
   security structure, 50–52
      assignment of earnings, 51
      assignment of insurances, 52
      guarantees, 52
      mortgages, 50–51
      pledge of shares, 52
   summary, 36
   types of finance, 41–44
      acquisition of second-hand tonnage, 41–42
      leasing, 43
      newbuildings, 42
      subsidised, 43–44
   types of shipping, 37–39
      cruise, 39
      liner, 38
      special purpose, 38–39
      troop, 38
   vessel employment, types of, 39–41
      bareboat charter, 40
      contract of affreightment, 41
      hell-or-high water charters, 41
      time charter, 40
      voyage charter, 39–40
   work-outs, 60–63
      documentation, 61
      foreclosure, 63
      foreclosure alternatives, 62–63
      managing the work-out
Shipping types, 37–39
Short Brothers: **US sales finance facility,** 98–99

'Take or pay', 14–15
Taxation benefit, leasing and, 103–104
Tax-based project finance, 101–118
Telecommunications, 155
Transportation infrastructure –
   characteristics, 142–143
   experience to date, 138
   government policy, 137–138
   introduction, 137
   lessons to be learned, 144–145
   risk profile, 139–142
      operating, 141–142
      pre-completion, 139–141
   role of sponsor, 143–144

Utility industries –
   cable TV, 155–156
   cellular telephone systems, 156–157
   co-generation and CHP projects, 154
   conclusion, 158
   ideal areas for project finance, 146–147

Utility industries – *contd*
  introduction, 146
  pipeline projects, 154–155
  power, 151–152
  power projects financing, 152–154
  sources of finance, 147–149
  telecommunications, 155
  UK, finance in,
  utility projects, financing of, 151–159
  waste disposal, 157–158
UK Enterprise zones, 111
UK infrastructure, 26

US Export-Import Bank, 165
US Overseas Private Investment Guarantee Corporation, The, 72
US, Project lending in, 24
Vessel employment (shipping), 39–41

Waste disposal, 157–158
Western Europe infrastructure, 27
Work-outs, 60–63
World Bank, The, 209
World Bank Multinational Guarantee Association, The, (MIGA), 72